NINJAK

THE SIEGE OF KING'S CASTLE

MATT KINDT | DIEGO BERNARD | ULISES ARREOLA

CONTENTS

Collection Cover Art: Lewis LaRosa
with Brian Reber

Assistant Editors: Danny Khazem (#15-17) and
Lauren Hitzhausen (#17)
Associate Editor: Tom Brennan (#14)
Editor: Kyle Andrukiewicz (#15-17)
Editor-in-Chief: Warren Simons

VALIANT.

Ninjak®: The Siege of King's Castle. Published by Valiant
Entertainment LLC. Office of Publication: 350 Seventh Avenue, New
York, NY 10001. Compilation copyright © 2016 Valiant Entertainment
LLC. All rights reserved. Contains materials originally published
in single magazine form as Ninjak #14-17. Copyright © 2016
Valiant Entertainment LLC. All rights reserved. All characters, their
distinctive likeness and related indicia featured in this publication
are trademarks of Valiant Entertainment LLC. The stories,
characters, and incidents featured in this publication are entirely
fictional. Valiant Entertainment does not read or accept unsolicited
submissions of ideas, stories, or artwork. Printed in the U.S.A. First
Printing. ISBN: 9781682151617.

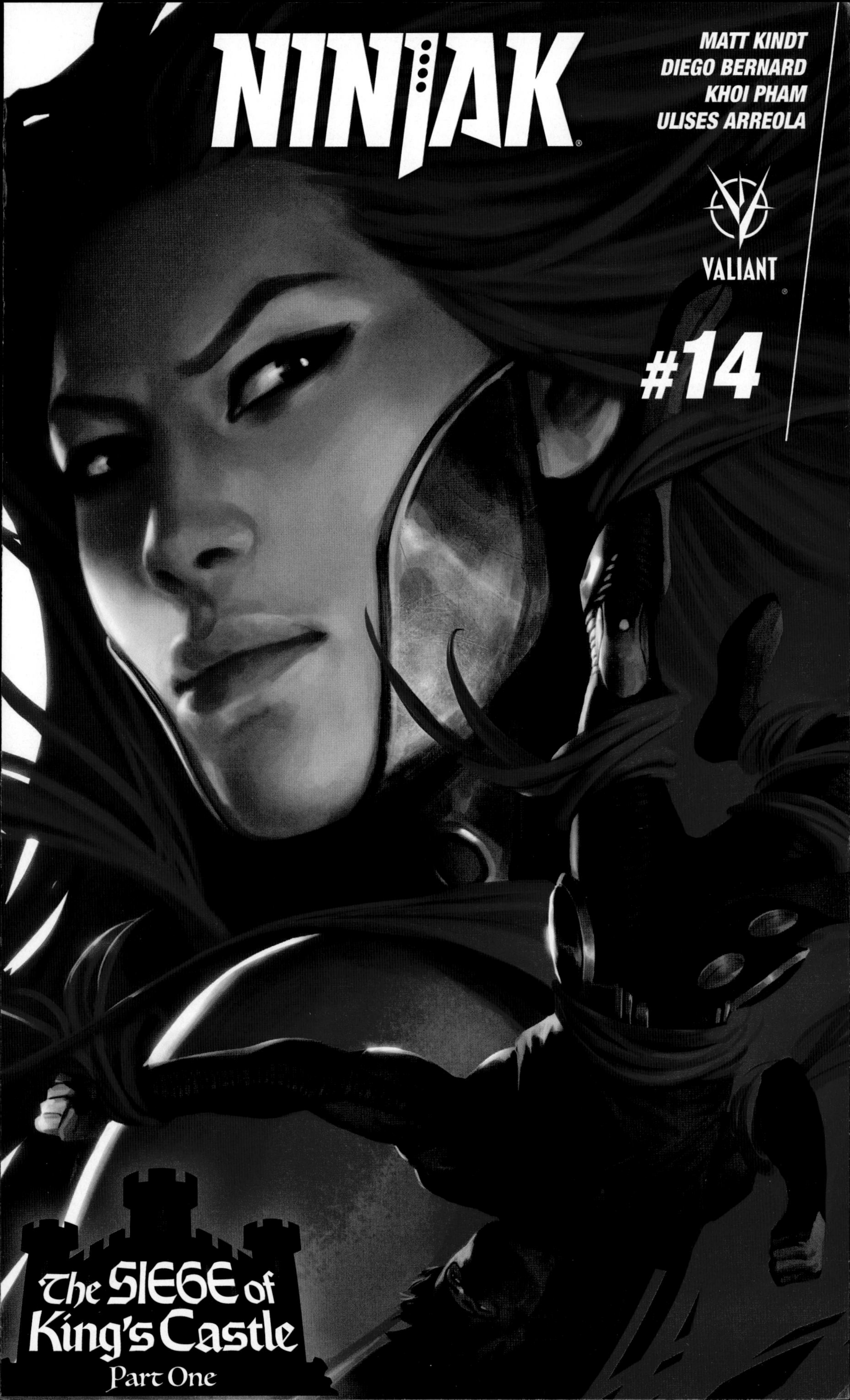
NINJAK
MATT KINDT
DIEGO BERNARD
KHOI PHAM
ULISES ARREOLA
VALIANT
#14
The SIEGE of
King's Castle
Part One

His name is Ninjak, spy and mercenary for hire. He is also Colin King, wealthy son of privilege. He works for the highest bidder, though his conscience often aligns him with the good guys. He is an expert in combat and espionage. He is as ruthless as he is charming. He is...

NINJAK

When the otherworldly creature Ember destroyed a famous British museum — which hid an MI-6 safe house — and kidnapped Ninjak's enemy Fakir, Colin King was called into action to pursue the creature and recover the fugitive.

He was teamed with the enigmatic Punk Mambo, a mystic with an attitude, who traced the fugitive to the Deadside, an alternate dimension ruled by the dead. Mambo was selected, in part, due to her previous mission to the Deadside, which ended in the disappearance of her military escorts.

Ninjak and Mambo returned to the Deadside and rescued her team, besting Ember and capturing his master, Magpie, who was reveeealed to be Shadowman. They returned to Earth with him as a prisoner.

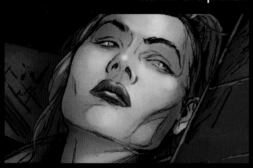

The SIEGE of King's Castle

Colin was debriefed and headed home to relax. But someone's following him...someone with vengeance on their mind.

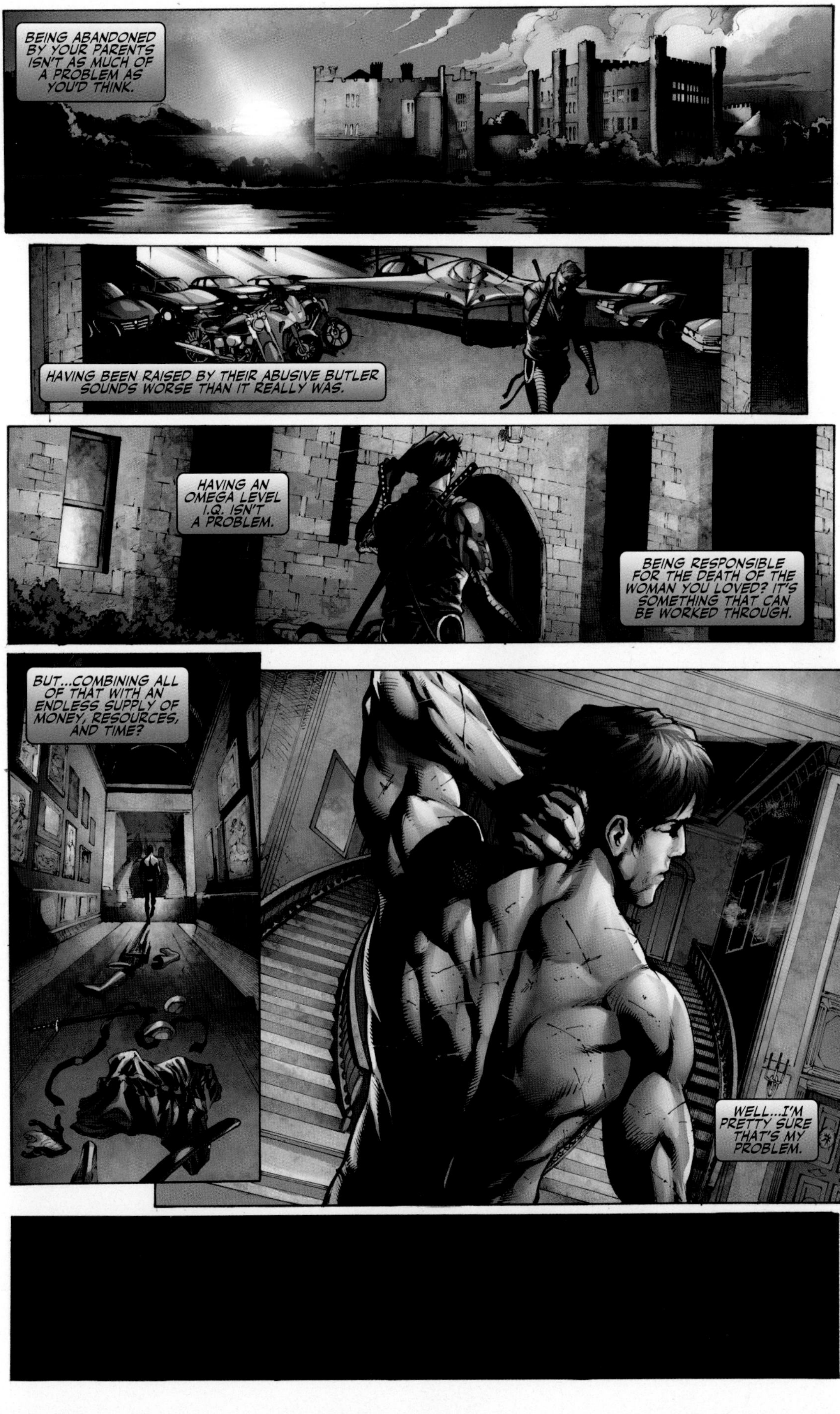
BEING ABANDONED BY YOUR PARENTS ISN'T AS MUCH OF A PROBLEM AS YOU'D THINK.
HAVING BEEN RAISED BY THEIR ABUSIVE BUTLER SOUNDS WORSE THAN IT REALLY WAS.
HAVING AN OMEGA LEVEL I.Q. ISN'T A PROBLEM.
BEING RESPONSIBLE FOR THE DEATH OF THE WOMAN YOU LOVED? IT'S SOMETHING THAT CAN BE WORKED THROUGH.
BUT...COMBINING ALL OF THAT WITH AN ENDLESS SUPPLY OF MONEY, RESOURCES, AND TIME?
WELL...I'M PRETTY SURE THAT'S MY PROBLEM.

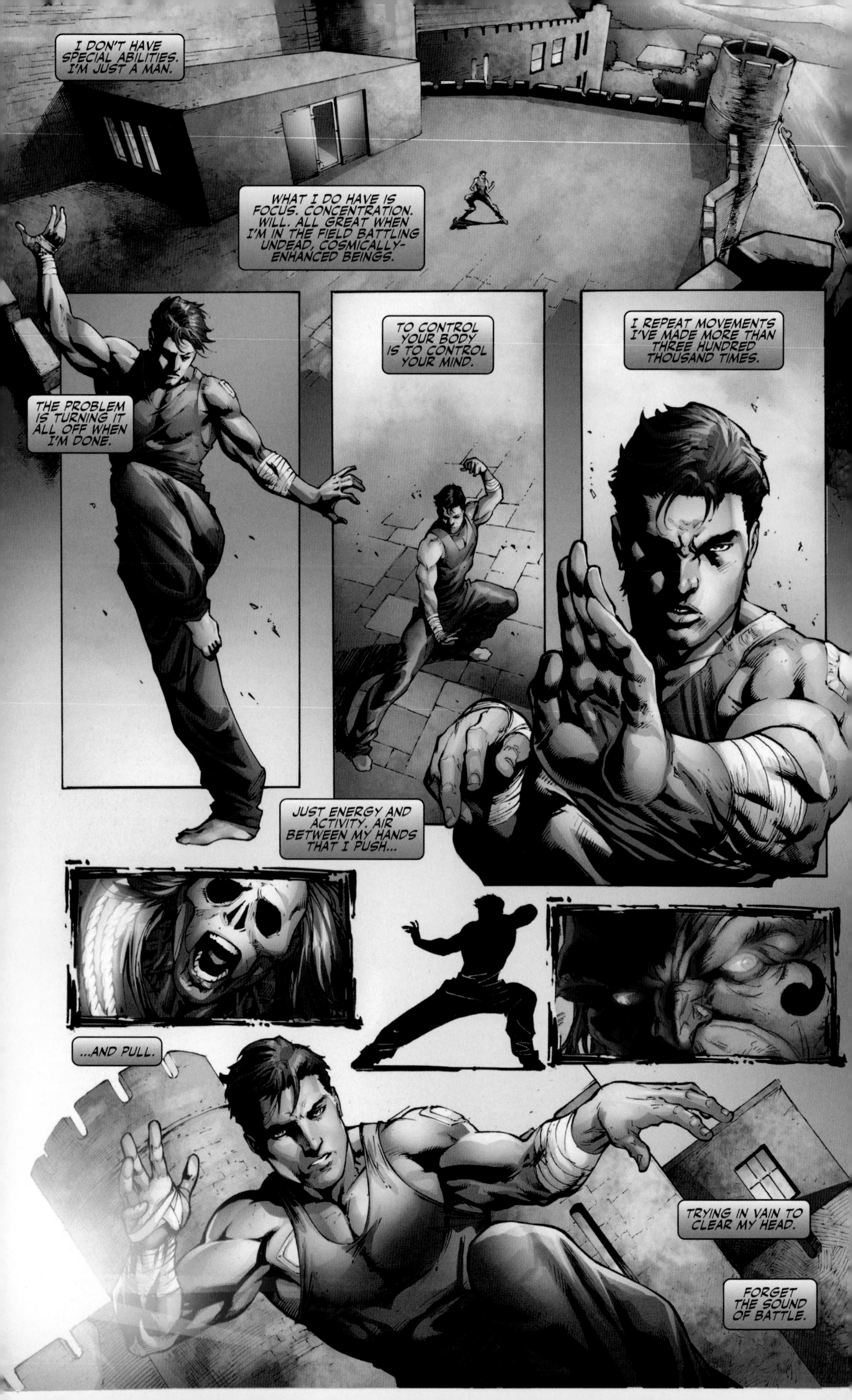
I DON'T HAVE SPECIAL ABILITIES. I'M JUST A MAN.
WHAT I DO HAVE IS FOCUS. CONCENTRATION. WILL. ALL GREAT WHEN I'M IN THE FIELD BATTLING UNDEAD, COSMICALLY-ENHANCED BEINGS.
THE PROBLEM IS TURNING IT ALL OFF WHEN I'M DONE.
TO CONTROL YOUR BODY IS TO CONTROL YOUR MIND.
I REPEAT MOVEMENTS I'VE MADE MORE THAN THREE HUNDRED THOUSAND TIMES.
JUST ENERGY AND ACTIVITY. AIR BETWEEN MY HANDS THAT I PUSH...
...AND PULL.
TRYING IN VAIN TO CLEAR MY HEAD.
FORGET THE SOUND OF BATTLE.

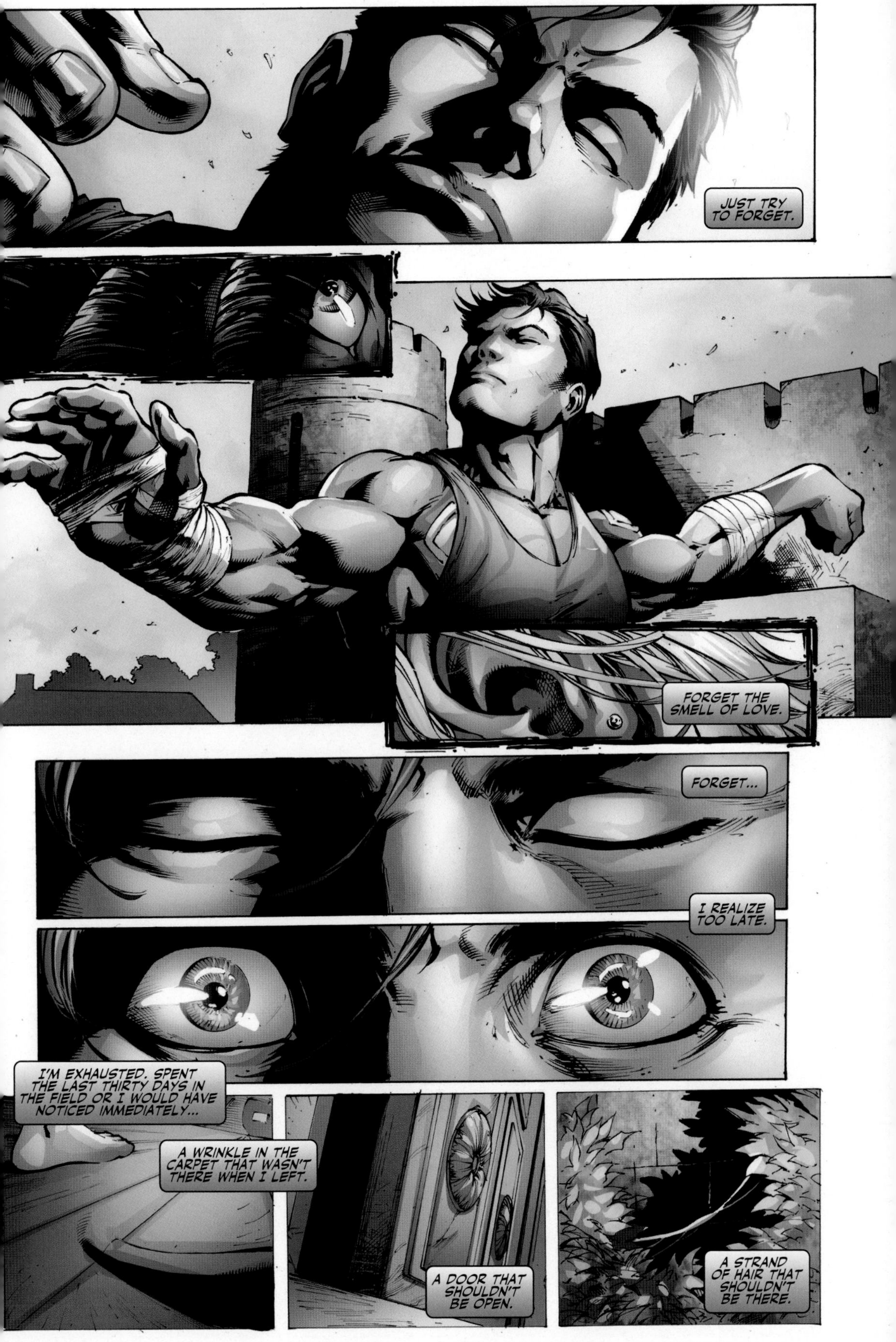
JUST TRY TO FORGET.
FORGET THE SMELL OF LOVE.
FORGET...
I REALIZE TOO LATE.
I'M EXHAUSTED. SPENT THE LAST THIRTY DAYS IN THE FIELD OR I WOULD HAVE NOTICED IMMEDIATELY...
A WRINKLE IN THE CARPET THAT WASN'T THERE WHEN I LEFT.
A DOOR THAT SHOULDN'T BE OPEN.
A STRAND OF HAIR THAT SHOULDN'T BE THERE.

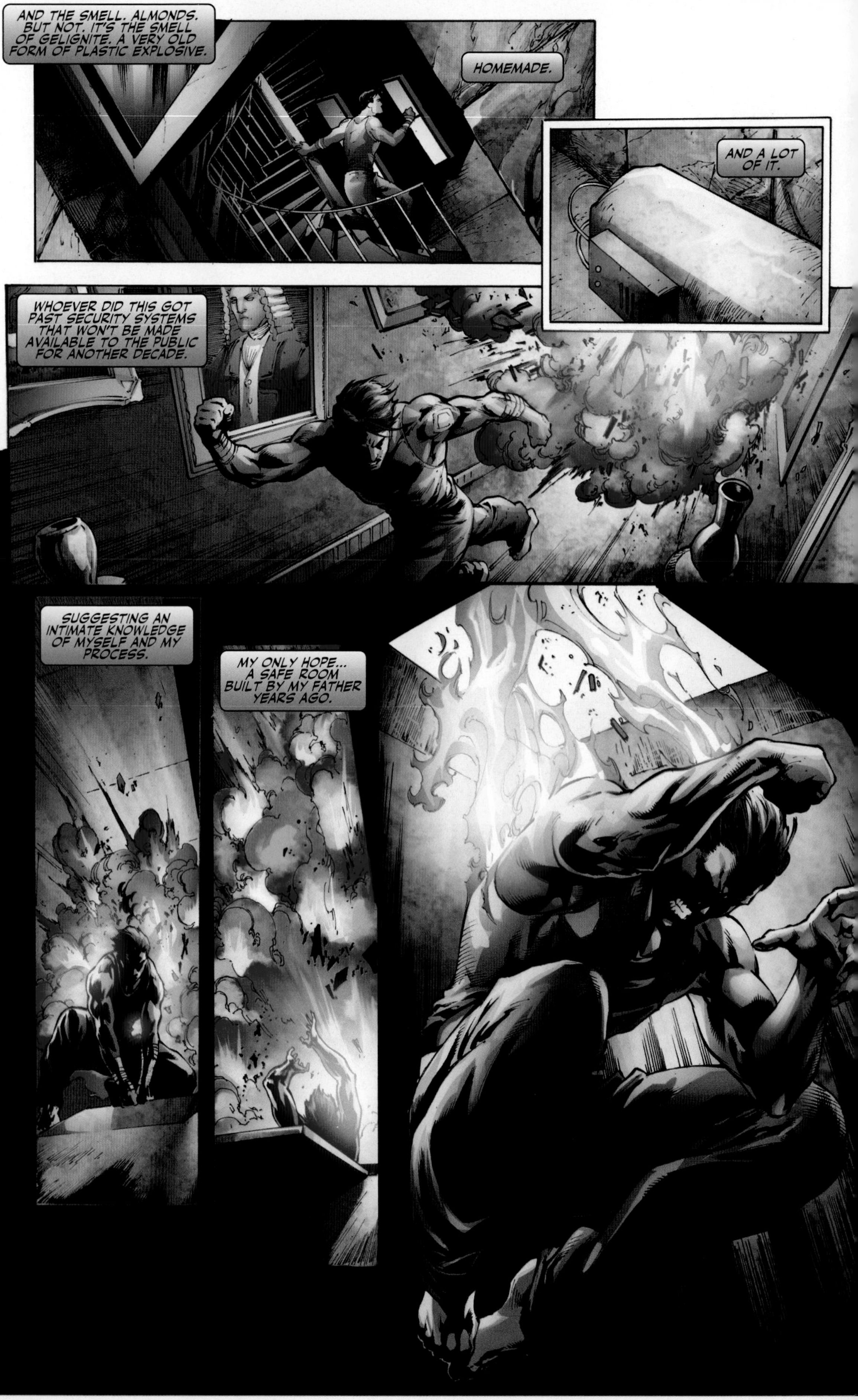
AND THE SMELL. ALMONDS. BUT NOT. IT'S THE SMELL OF GELIGNITE. A VERY OLD FORM OF PLASTIC EXPLOSIVE.
HOMEMADE.
AND A LOT OF IT.
WHOEVER DID THIS GOT PAST SECURITY SYSTEMS THAT WON'T BE MADE AVAILABLE TO THE PUBLIC FOR ANOTHER DECADE.
SUGGESTING AN INTIMATE KNOWLEDGE OF MYSELF AND MY PROCESS.
MY ONLY HOPE... A SAFE ROOM BUILT BY MY FATHER YEARS AGO.

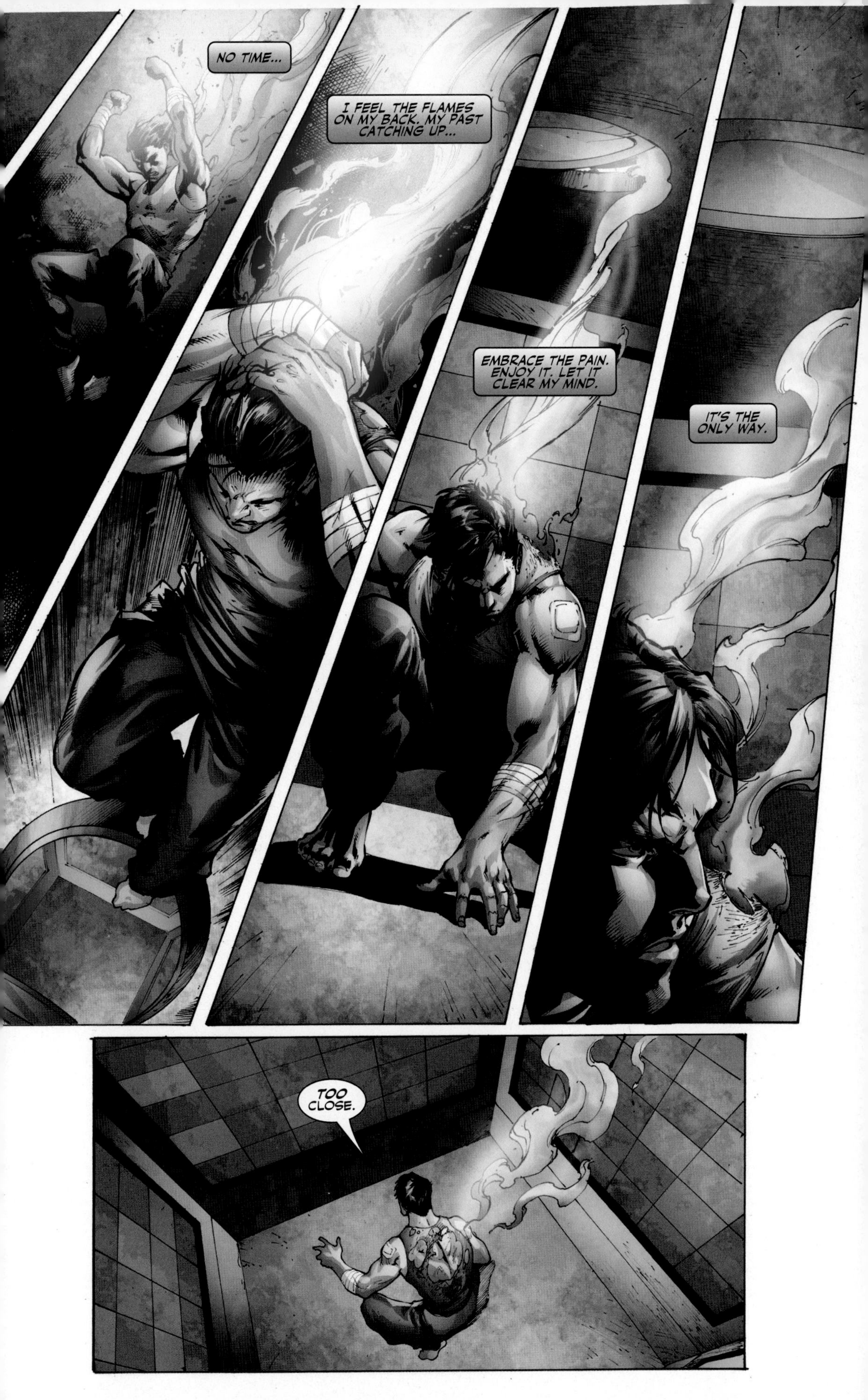
NO TIME...
I FEEL THE FLAMES ON MY BACK. MY PAST CATCHING UP...
EMBRACE THE PAIN. ENJOY IT. LET IT CLEAR MY MIND.
IT'S THE ONLY WAY.
TOO CLOSE.

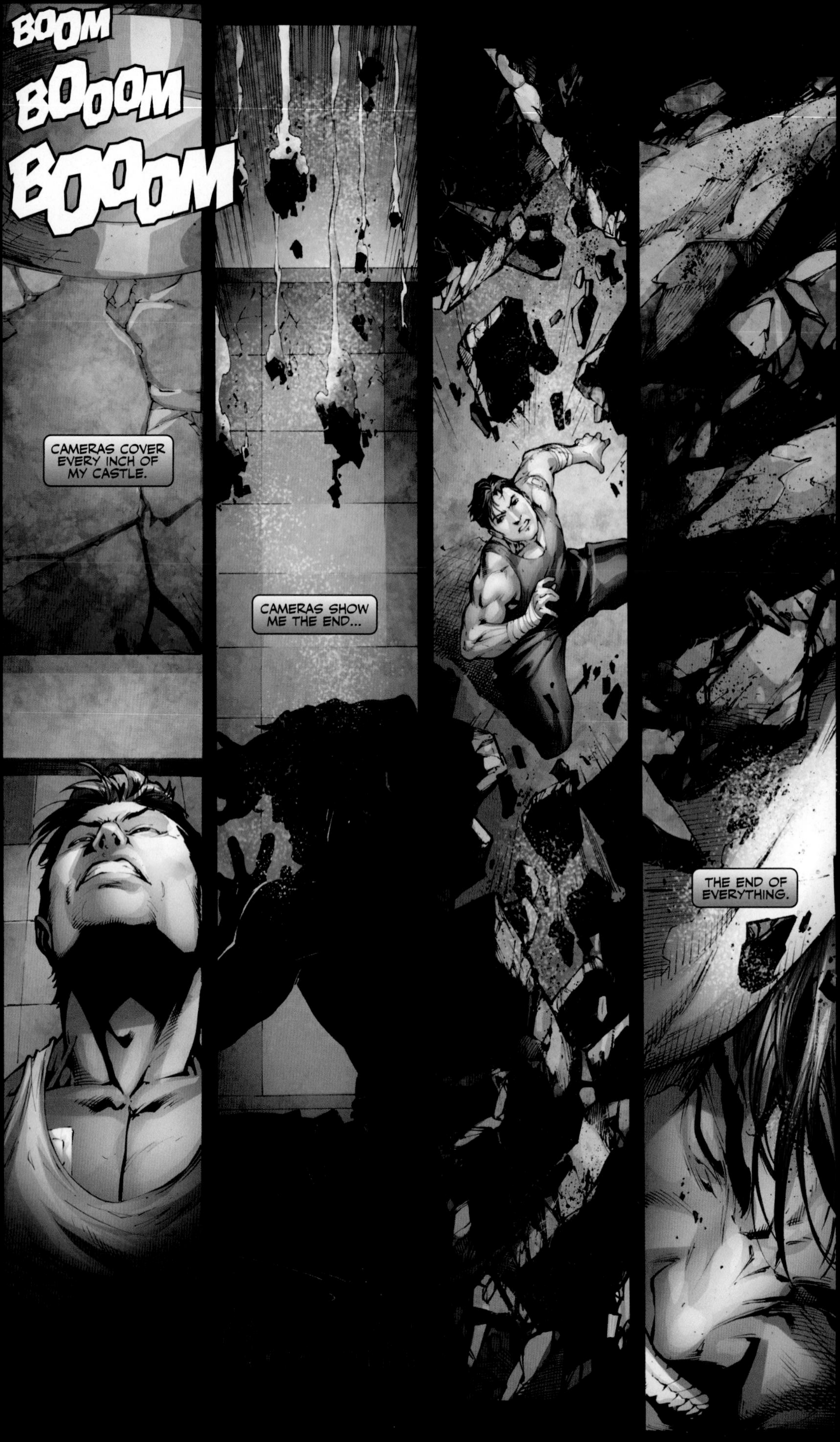
BOOM
BOOOM
BOOOM
CAMERAS COVER EVERY INCH OF MY CASTLE.
CAMERAS SHOW ME THE END...
THE END OF EVERYTHING.

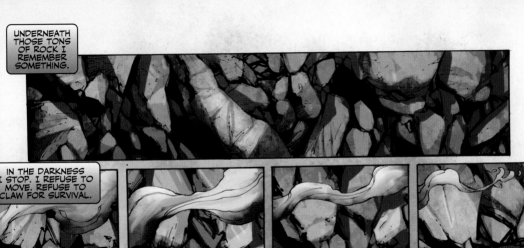

UNDERNEATH THOSE TONS OF ROCK I REMEMBER SOMETHING.

IN THE DARKNESS I STOP. I REFUSE TO MOVE. REFUSE TO CLAW FOR SURVIVAL.

INSTEAD, I LET THE QUIET...THE NOTHINGNESS, WASH OVER ME.

AND I REALIZE ONE OF MY EARLIEST LESSONS.

INFORMATION IS NOT ENLIGHTENMENT.

TRUTH IS ENLIGHTENMENT.

AND THE FIRST OF THE FOUR GREAT TRUTHS...

...THE ONE THING THAT WE ALL SHARE, FROM BIRTH TO DEATH...

...THE ONE THING THAT BINDS US ALL TOGETHER...

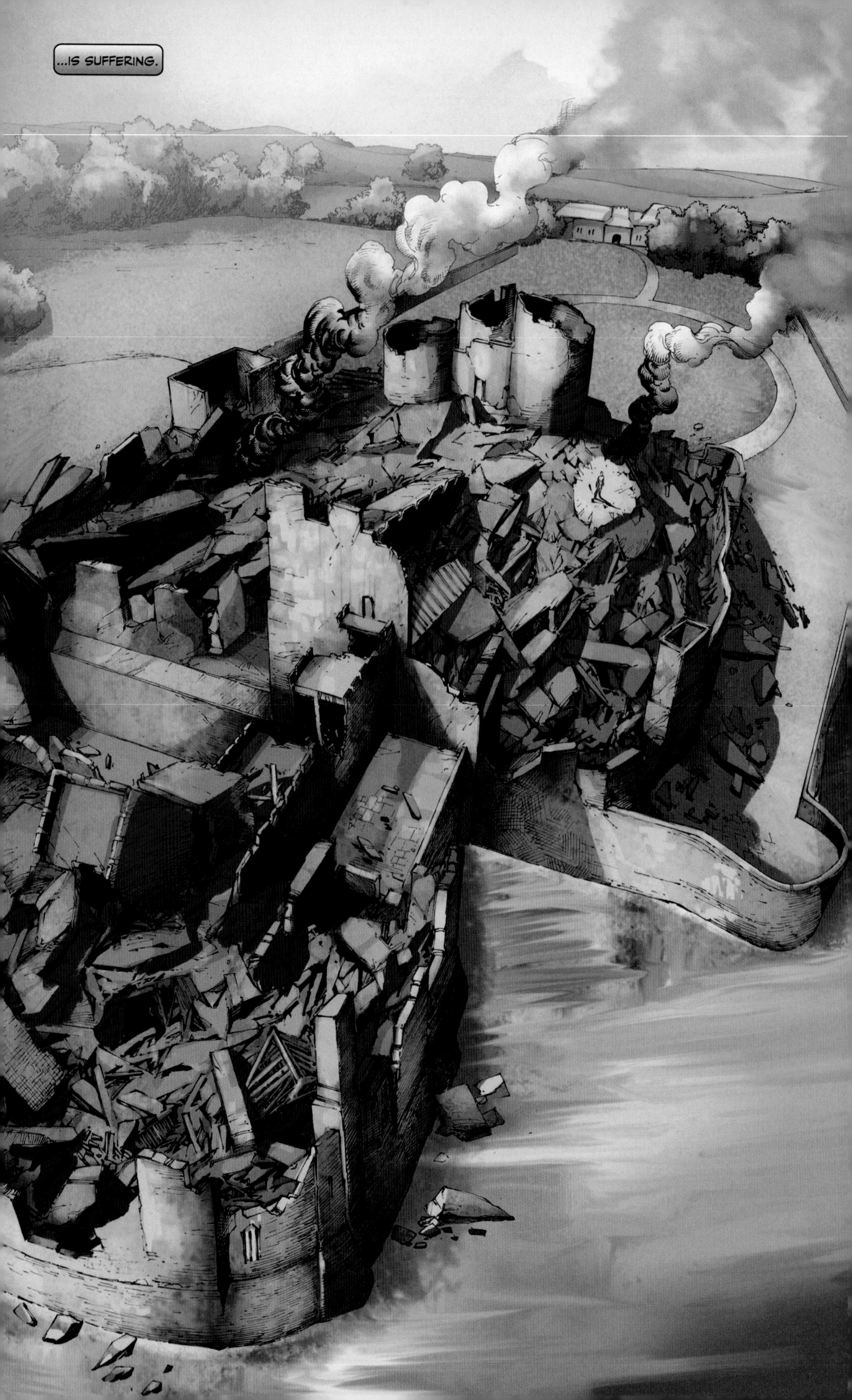
...IS SUFFERING.

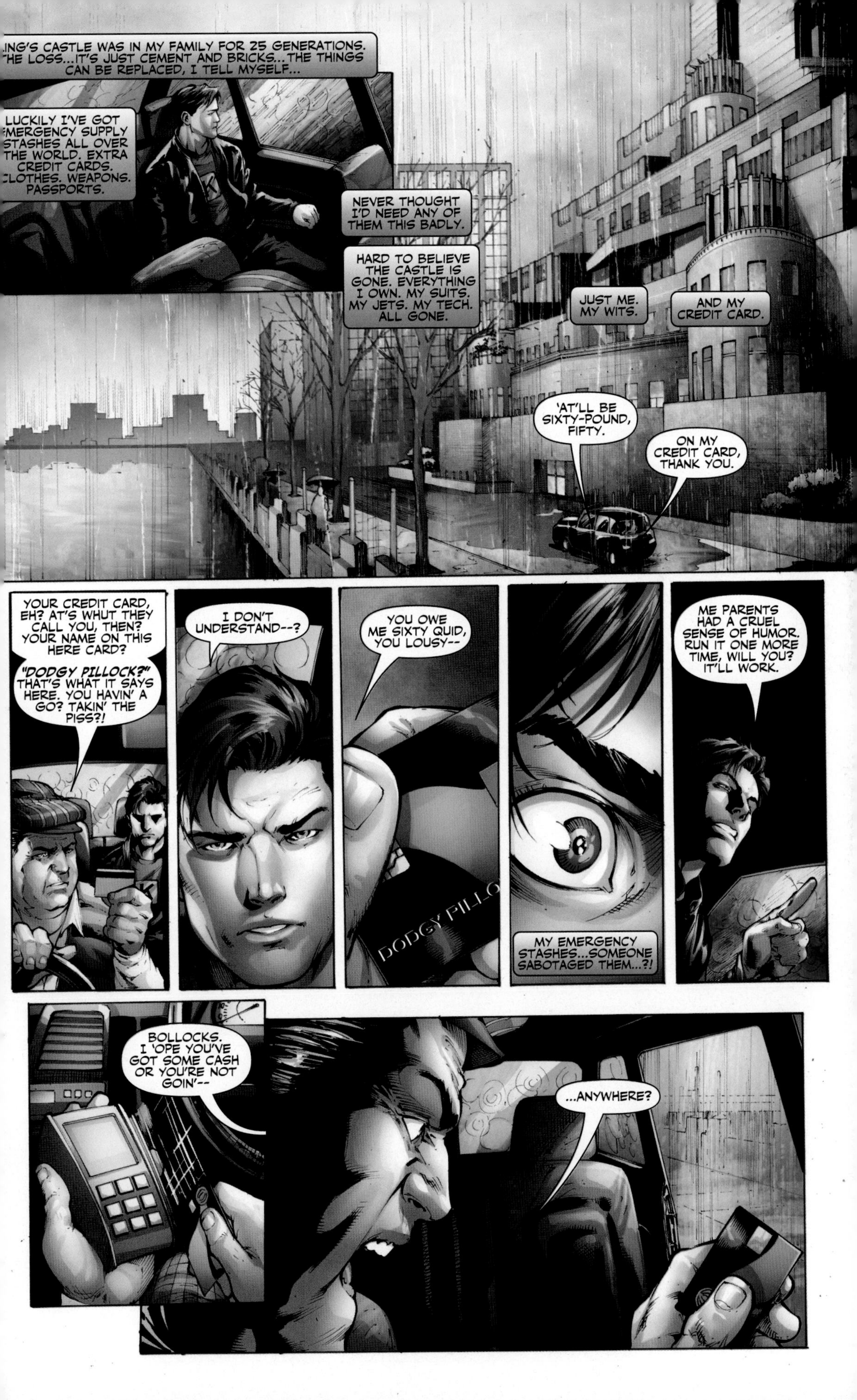
ING'S CASTLE WAS IN MY FAMILY FOR 25 GENERATIONS. HE LOSS...IT'S JUST CEMENT AND BRICKS...THE THINGS CAN BE REPLACED, I TELL MYSELF...
LUCKILY I'VE GOT MERGENCY SUPPLY STASHES ALL OVER THE WORLD. EXTRA CREDIT CARDS. LOTHES. WEAPONS. PASSPORTS.
NEVER THOUGHT I'D NEED ANY OF THEM THIS BADLY.
HARD TO BELIEVE THE CASTLE IS GONE. EVERYTHING I OWN. MY SUITS. MY JETS. MY TECH. ALL GONE.
JUST ME. MY WITS.
AND MY CREDIT CARD.
'AT'LL BE SIXTY-POUND, FIFTY.
ON MY CREDIT CARD, THANK YOU.
YOUR CREDIT CARD, EH? AT'S WHUT THEY CALL YOU, THEN? YOUR NAME ON THIS HERE CARD?
"DODGY PILLOCK?" THAT'S WHAT IT SAYS HERE. YOU HAVIN' A GO? TAKIN' THE PISS?!
I DON'T UNDERSTAND--?
YOU OWE ME SIXTY QUID, YOU LOUSY--
DODGY PILLO
MY EMERGENCY STASHES...SOMEONE SABOTAGED THEM...?!
ME PARENTS HAD A CRUEL SENSE OF HUMOR. RUN IT ONE MORE TIME, WILL YOU? IT'LL WORK.
BOLLOCKS. I 'OPE YOU'VE GOT SOME CASH OR YOU'RE NOT GOIN'--
...ANYWHERE?

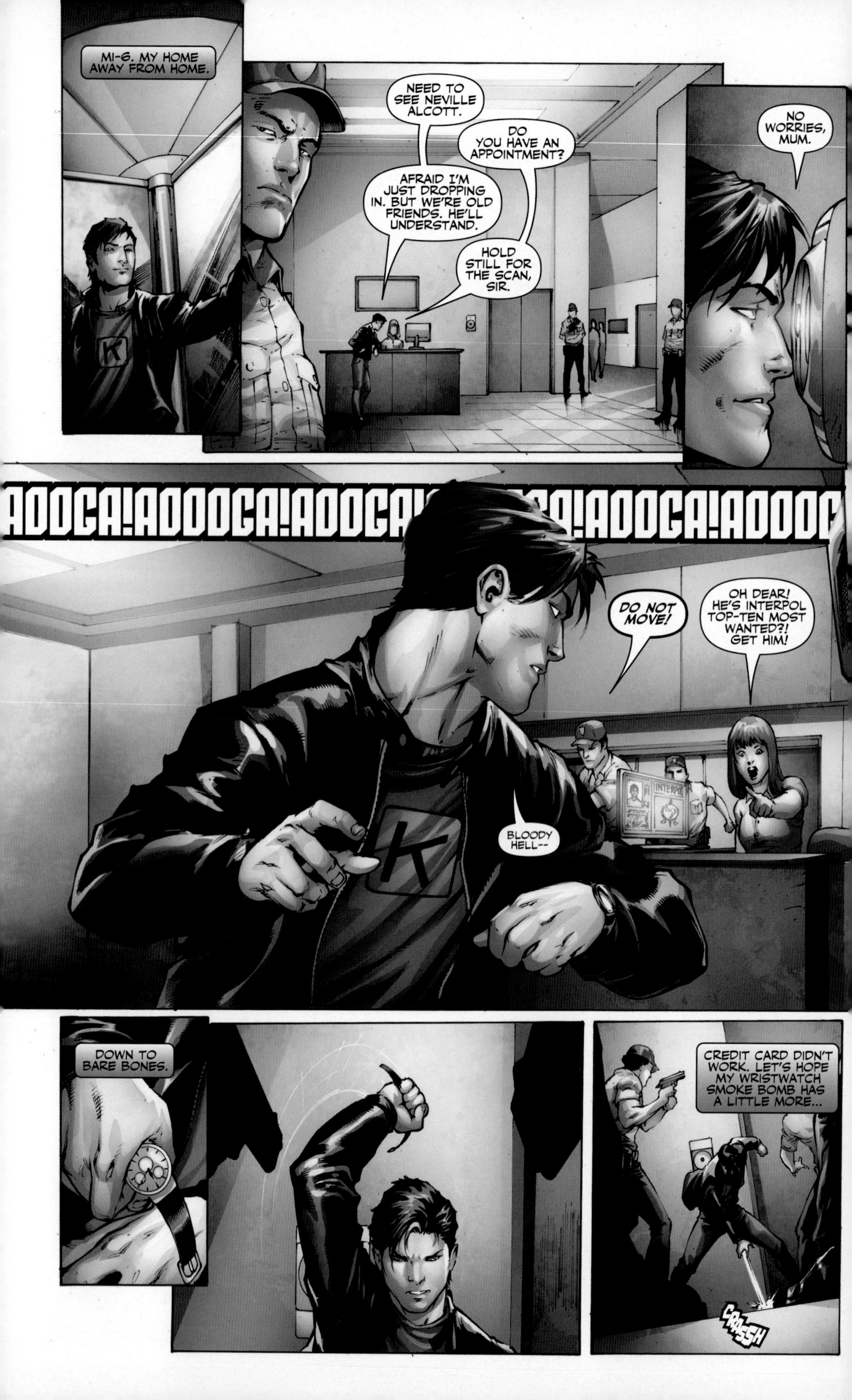
MI-6. MY HOME AWAY FROM HOME.
NEED TO SEE NEVILLE ALCOTT.
DO YOU HAVE AN APPOINTMENT?
AFRAID I'M JUST DROPPING IN. BUT WE'RE OLD FRIENDS. HE'LL UNDERSTAND.
HOLD STILL FOR THE SCAN, SIR.
NO WORRIES, MUM.
AOOGA! AOOOGA! AOOGA!
AOOGA! AOOOO
DO NOT MOVE!
OH DEAR! HE'S INTERPOL TOP-TEN MOST WANTED?! GET HIM!
INTERPOL
BLOODY HELL--
DOWN TO BARE BONES.
CREDIT CARD DIDN'T WORK. LET'S HOPE MY WRISTWATCH SMOKE BOMB HAS A LITTLE MORE...
CRASSH

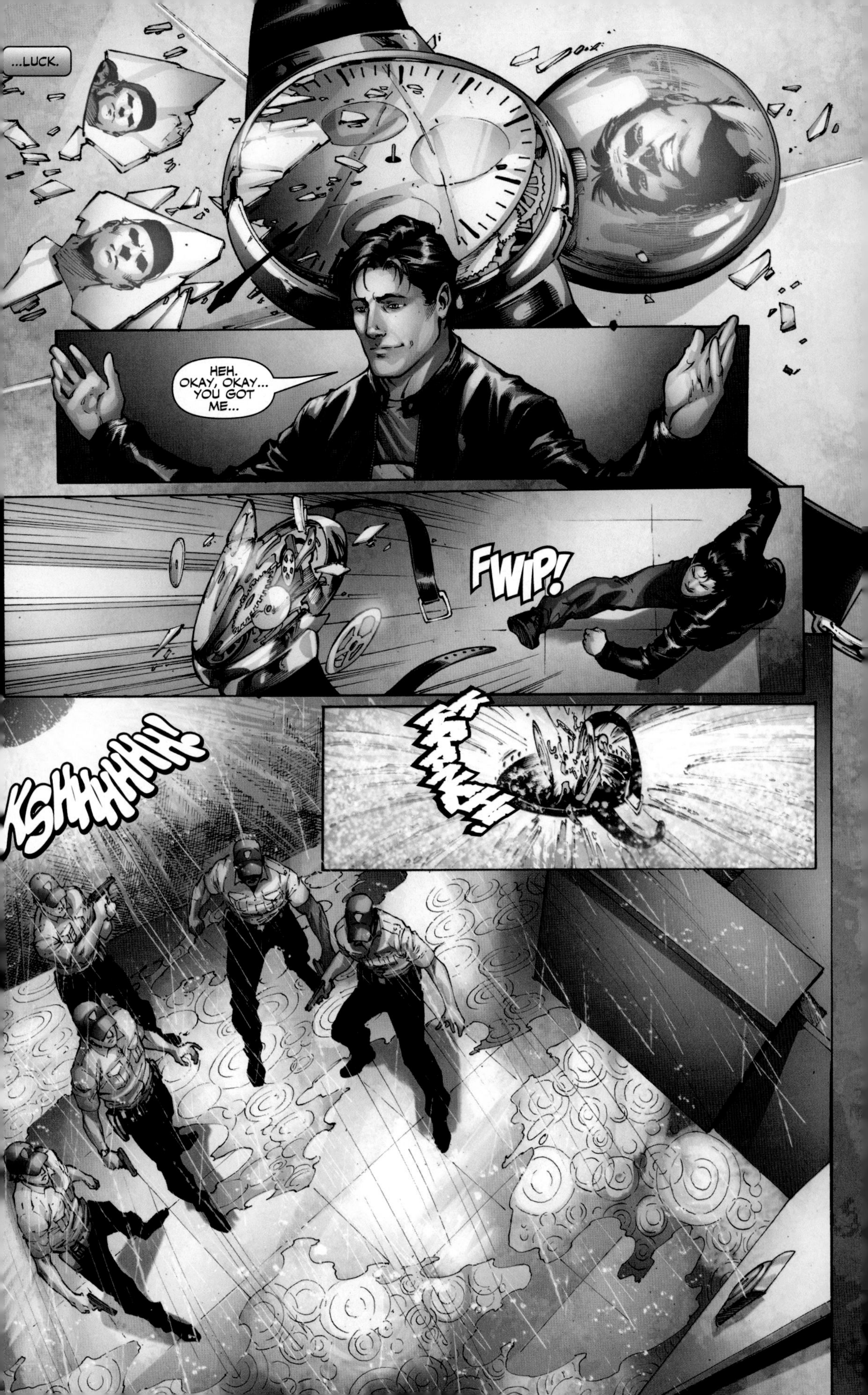

...LUCK.
HEH. OKAY, OKAY... YOU GOT ME...
FWIP!
KSHHHHH!
KRANCH!

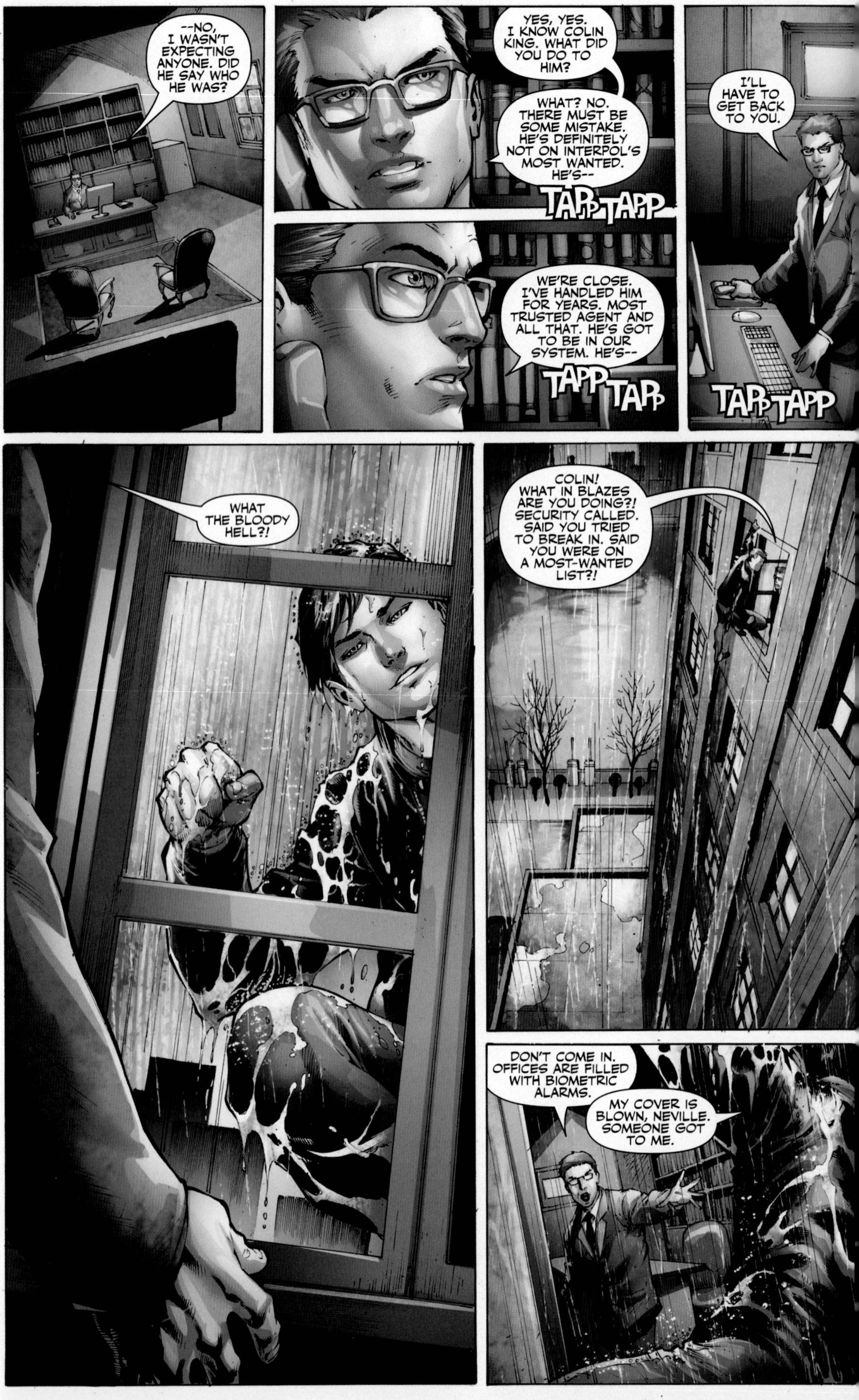
--NO, I WASN'T EXPECTING ANYONE. DID HE SAY WHO HE WAS?
YES, YES. I KNOW COLIN KING. WHAT DID YOU DO TO HIM?
WHAT? NO. THERE MUST BE SOME MISTAKE. HE'S DEFINITELY NOT ON INTERPOL'S MOST WANTED. HE'S--
TAPP TAPP
WE'RE CLOSE. I'VE HANDLED HIM FOR YEARS. MOST TRUSTED AGENT AND ALL THAT. HE'S GOT TO BE IN OUR SYSTEM. HE'S--
TAPP TAPP
I'LL HAVE TO GET BACK TO YOU.
TAPP TAPP
WHAT THE BLOODY HELL?!
COLIN! WHAT IN BLAZES ARE YOU DOING?! SECURITY CALLED. SAID YOU TRIED TO BREAK IN. SAID YOU WERE ON A MOST-WANTED LIST?!
DON'T COME IN. OFFICES ARE FILLED WITH BIOMETRIC ALARMS.
MY COVER IS BLOWN, NEVILLE. SOMEONE GOT TO ME.

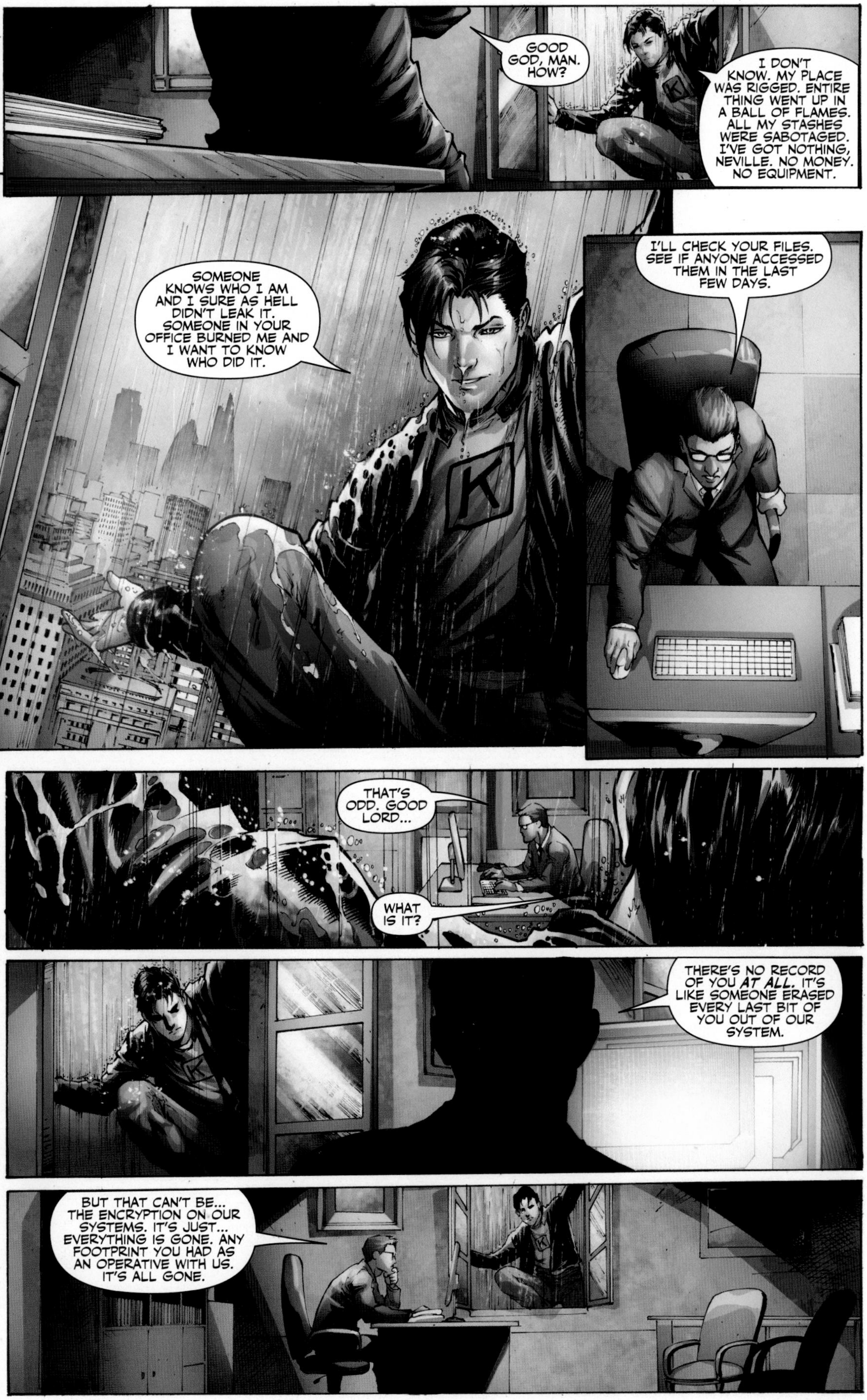
GOOD GOD, MAN. HOW?
I DON'T KNOW. MY PLACE WAS RIGGED. ENTIRE THING WENT UP IN A BALL OF FLAMES. ALL MY STASHES WERE SABOTAGED. I'VE GOT NOTHING, NEVILLE. NO MONEY. NO EQUIPMENT.
SOMEONE KNOWS WHO I AM AND I SURE AS HELL DIDN'T LEAK IT. SOMEONE IN YOUR OFFICE BURNED ME AND I WANT TO KNOW WHO DID IT.
I'LL CHECK YOUR FILES. SEE IF ANYONE ACCESSED THEM IN THE LAST FEW DAYS.
THAT'S ODD. GOOD LORD...
WHAT IS IT?
THERE'S NO RECORD OF YOU AT ALL. IT'S LIKE SOMEONE ERASED EVERY LAST BIT OF YOU OUT OF OUR SYSTEM.
BUT THAT CAN'T BE... THE ENCRYPTION ON OUR SYSTEMS. IT'S JUST... EVERYTHING IS GONE. ANY FOOTPRINT YOU HAD AS AN OPERATIVE WITH US. IT'S ALL GONE.

SO MI-6 HAS BEEN COMPROMISED, TOO.

NEVILLE? BEFORE THE DEADSIDE. BEFORE THE SHADOW SEVEN OPERATION. BEFORE X-O MANOWAR. YEARS AGO. DO YOU REMEMBER ME FROM THEN?

NO. WHY? THAT'S AN ODD QUESTION.

NO REASON. JUST TRYING TO FIGURE OUT WHO I CAN TRUST.

THERE'S GOT TO BE DIGITAL FINGERPRINTS ON THIS. BUT I'M GOING TO NEED HELP AND RESOURCES. IS LIVEWIRE IN TOWN?

COLIN...I'M SORRY.

NEVILLE? WHAT? WHAT DID YOU DO?

IT'S ALL OVER THE NEWS.

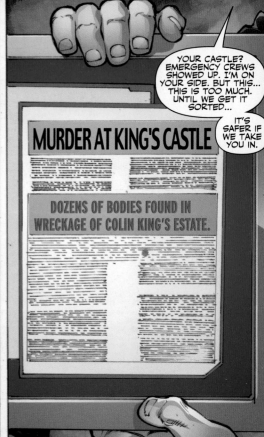

YOUR CASTLE? EMERGENCY CREWS SHOWED UP. I'M ON YOUR SIDE. BUT THIS... THIS IS TOO MUCH. UNTIL WE GET IT SORTED...

IT'S SAFER IF WE TAKE YOU IN.

MURDER AT KING'S CASTLE

DOZENS OF BODIES FOUND IN WRECKAGE OF COLIN KING'S ESTATE.

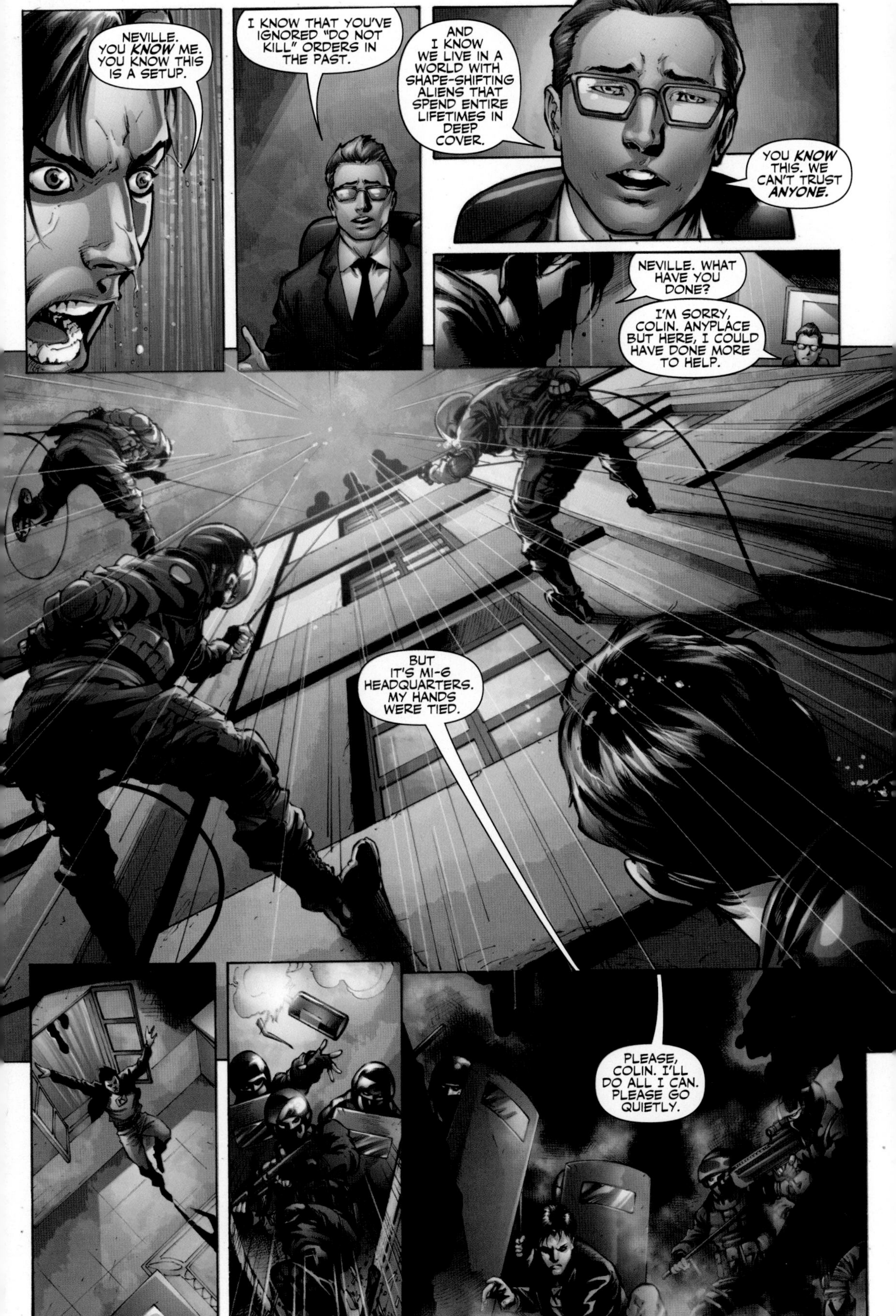
NEVILLE. YOU KNOW ME. YOU KNOW THIS IS A SETUP.
I KNOW THAT YOU'VE IGNORED "DO NOT KILL" ORDERS IN THE PAST.
AND I KNOW WE LIVE IN A WORLD WITH SHAPE-SHIFTING ALIENS THAT SPEND ENTIRE LIFETIMES IN DEEP COVER.
YOU KNOW THIS. WE CAN'T TRUST ANYONE.
NEVILLE. WHAT HAVE YOU DONE?
I'M SORRY, COLIN. ANYPLACE BUT HERE, I COULD HAVE DONE MORE TO HELP.
BUT IT'S MI-6 HEADQUARTERS. MY HANDS WERE TIED.
PLEASE, COLIN. I'LL DO ALL I CAN. PLEASE GO QUIETLY.

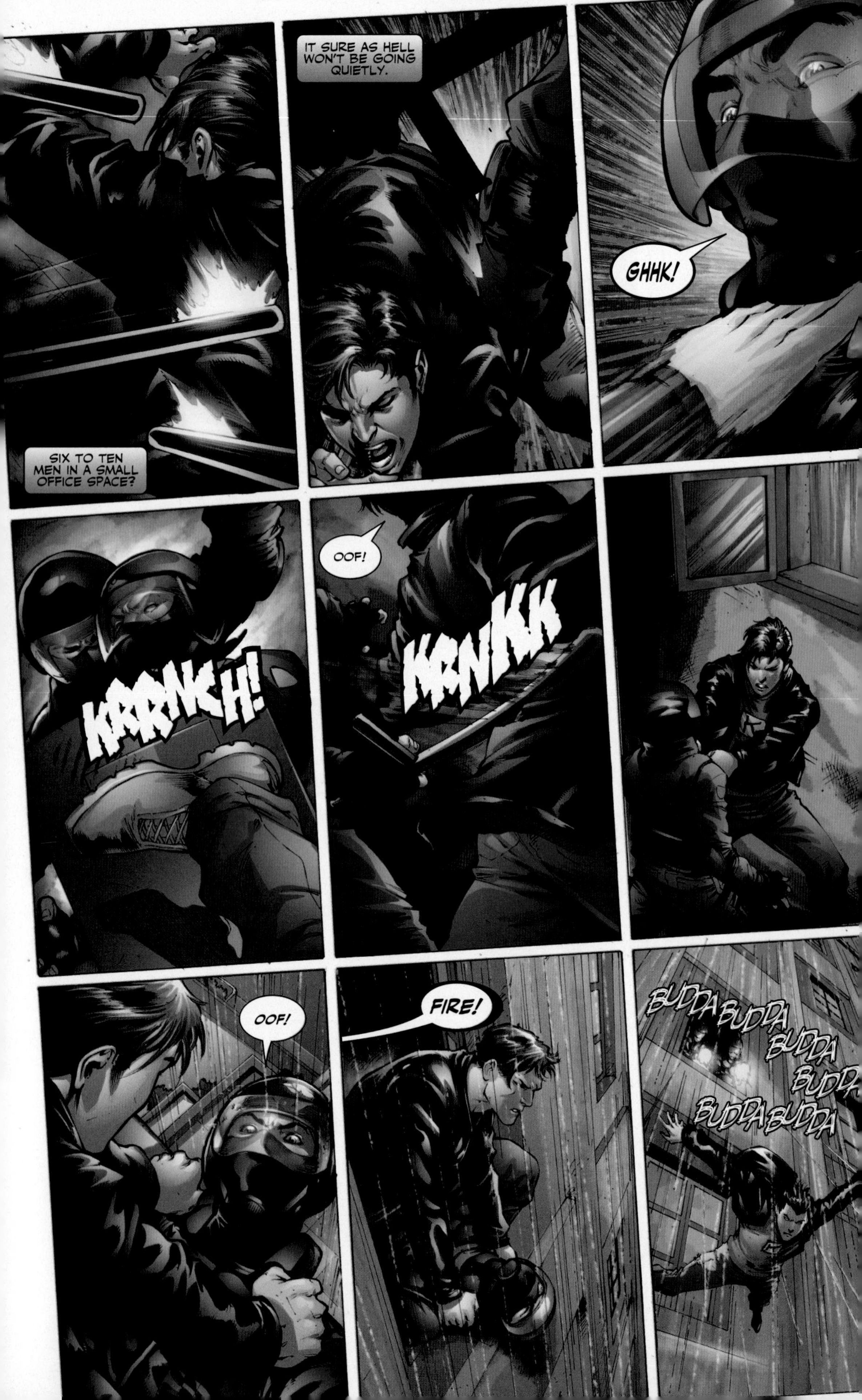
SIX TO TEN MEN IN A SMALL OFFICE SPACE?
IT SURE AS HELL WON'T BE GOING QUIETLY.
GHHK!
KRRNCH!
OOF!
KRNKK
OOF!
FIRE!
BUDDA BUDDA BUDDA BUDDA BUDDA BUDDA

BRITISH MUSEUM. LOT OF MEMORIES HERE. WHEN I WAS A KID I USED TO SNEAK IN AFTER HOURS AND MOVE THINGS AROUND.

IT'S BEEN TOO LONG, COLIN.

TOO TRUE, LIVEWIRE. I APPRECIATE YOU MEETING ME ON SHORT NOTICE. I'M IN SOME...TROUBLE.

ANYTIME. I HEARD ABOUT THE CASTLE.

I'M SURE YOU'VE SEEN THE NEWS. I'VE BEEN BURNED. LITERALLY AND FIGURATIVELY. IDENTITY COMPLETELY COMPROMISED. SOMEONE HAS DONE EVERYTHING SHORT OF KILL ME. NOT THAT THEY HAVEN'T BEEN TRYING.

HERE. PUT THIS IN.

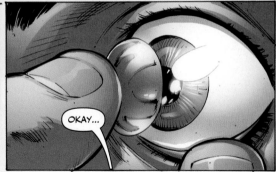

OKAY...

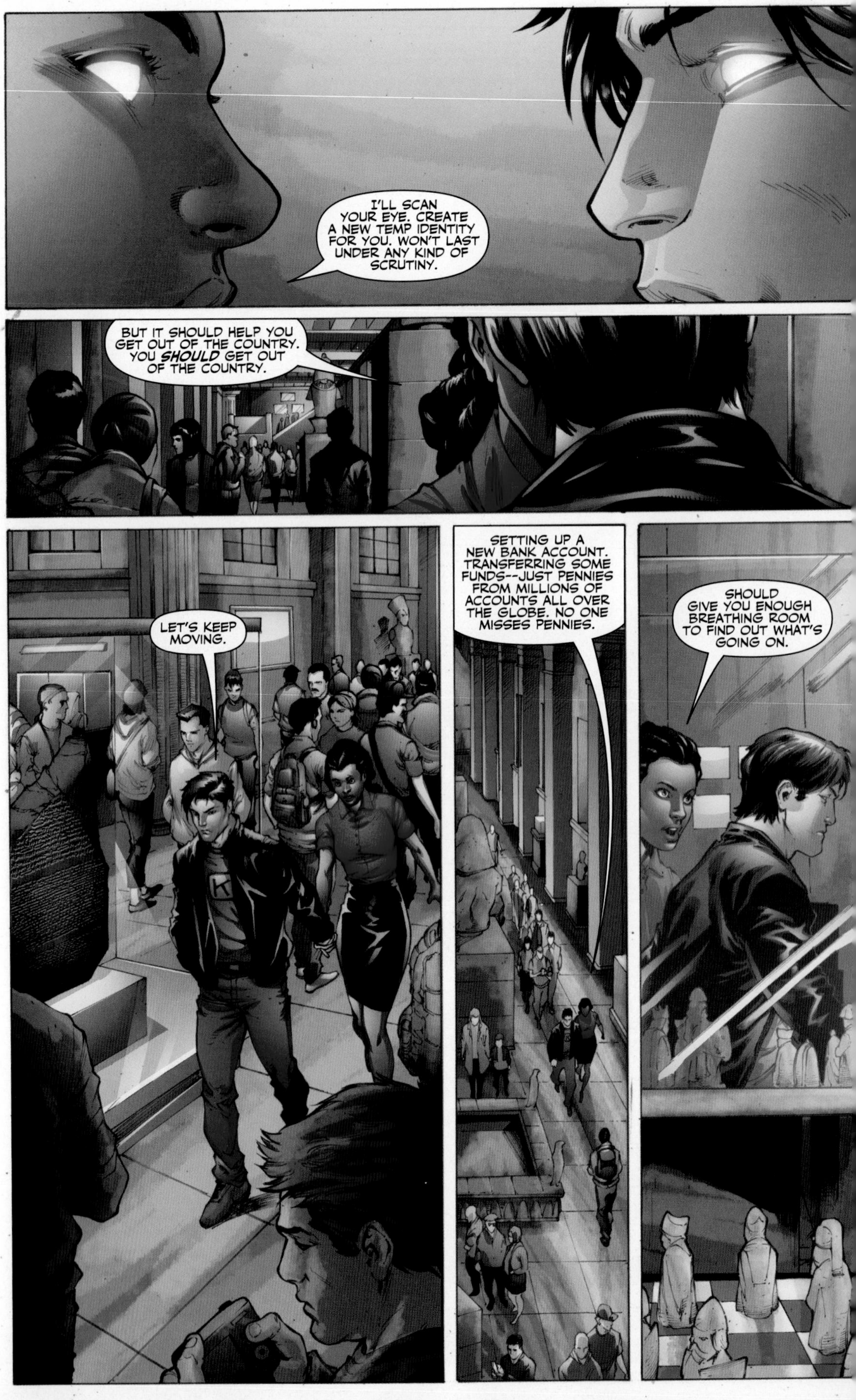
I'LL SCAN YOUR EYE. CREATE A NEW TEMP IDENTITY FOR YOU. WON'T LAST UNDER ANY KIND OF SCRUTINY.
BUT IT SHOULD HELP YOU GET OUT OF THE COUNTRY. YOU ***SHOULD*** GET OUT OF THE COUNTRY.
LET'S KEEP MOVING.
SETTING UP A NEW BANK ACCOUNT. TRANSFERRING SOME FUNDS--JUST PENNIES FROM MILLIONS OF ACCOUNTS ALL OVER THE GLOBE. NO ONE MISSES PENNIES.
SHOULD GIVE YOU ENOUGH BREATHING ROOM TO FIND OUT WHAT'S GOING ON.

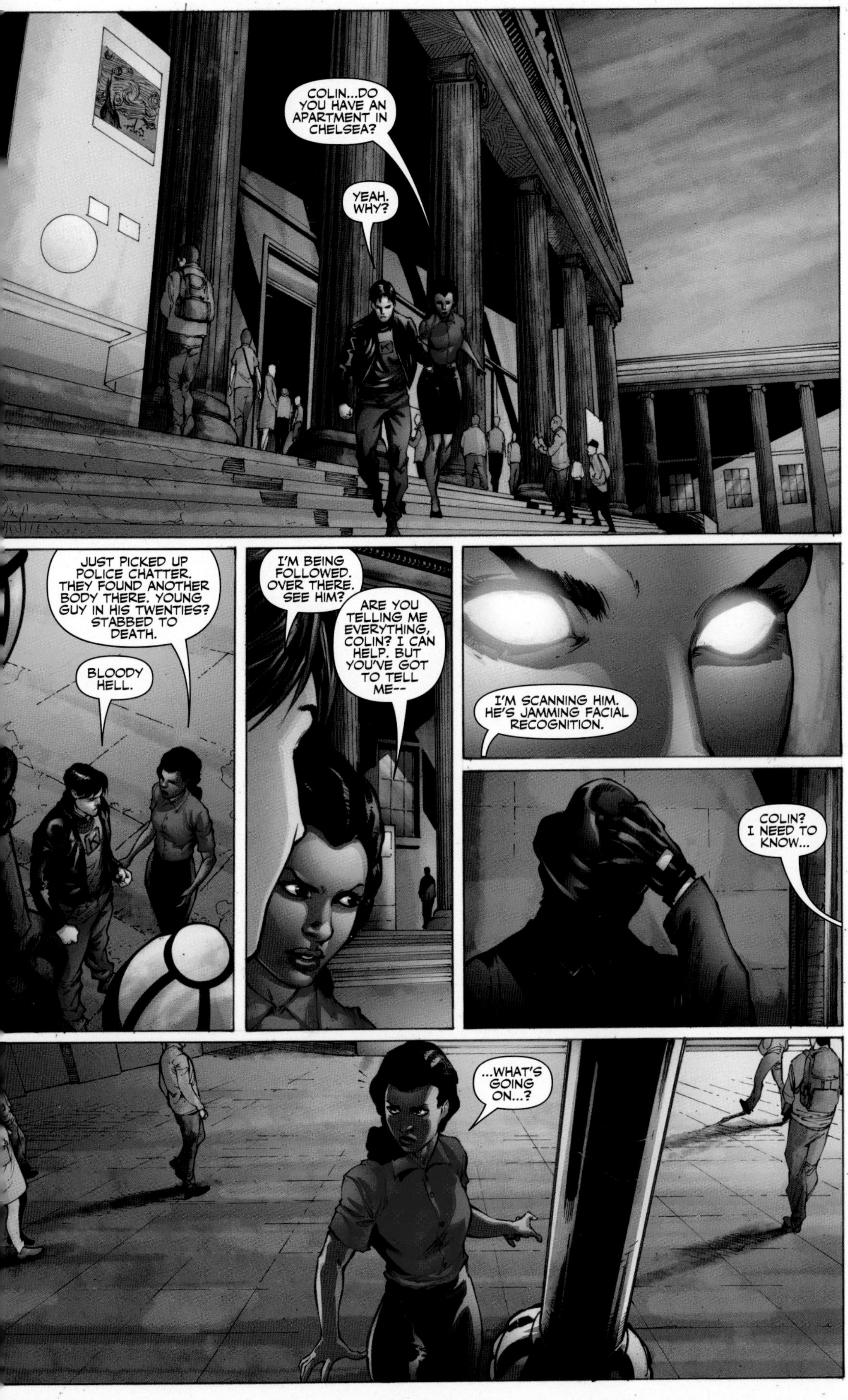
COLIN...DO YOU HAVE AN APARTMENT IN CHELSEA?
YEAH. WHY?
JUST PICKED UP POLICE CHATTER. THEY FOUND ANOTHER BODY THERE. YOUNG GUY IN HIS TWENTIES? STABBED TO DEATH.
BLOODY HELL.
I'M BEING FOLLOWED. OVER THERE. SEE HIM?
ARE YOU TELLING ME EVERYTHING, COLIN? I CAN HELP. BUT YOU'VE GOT TO TELL ME--
I'M SCANNING HIM. HE'S JAMMING FACIAL RECOGNITION.
COLIN? I NEED TO KNOW...
...WHAT'S GOING ON...?

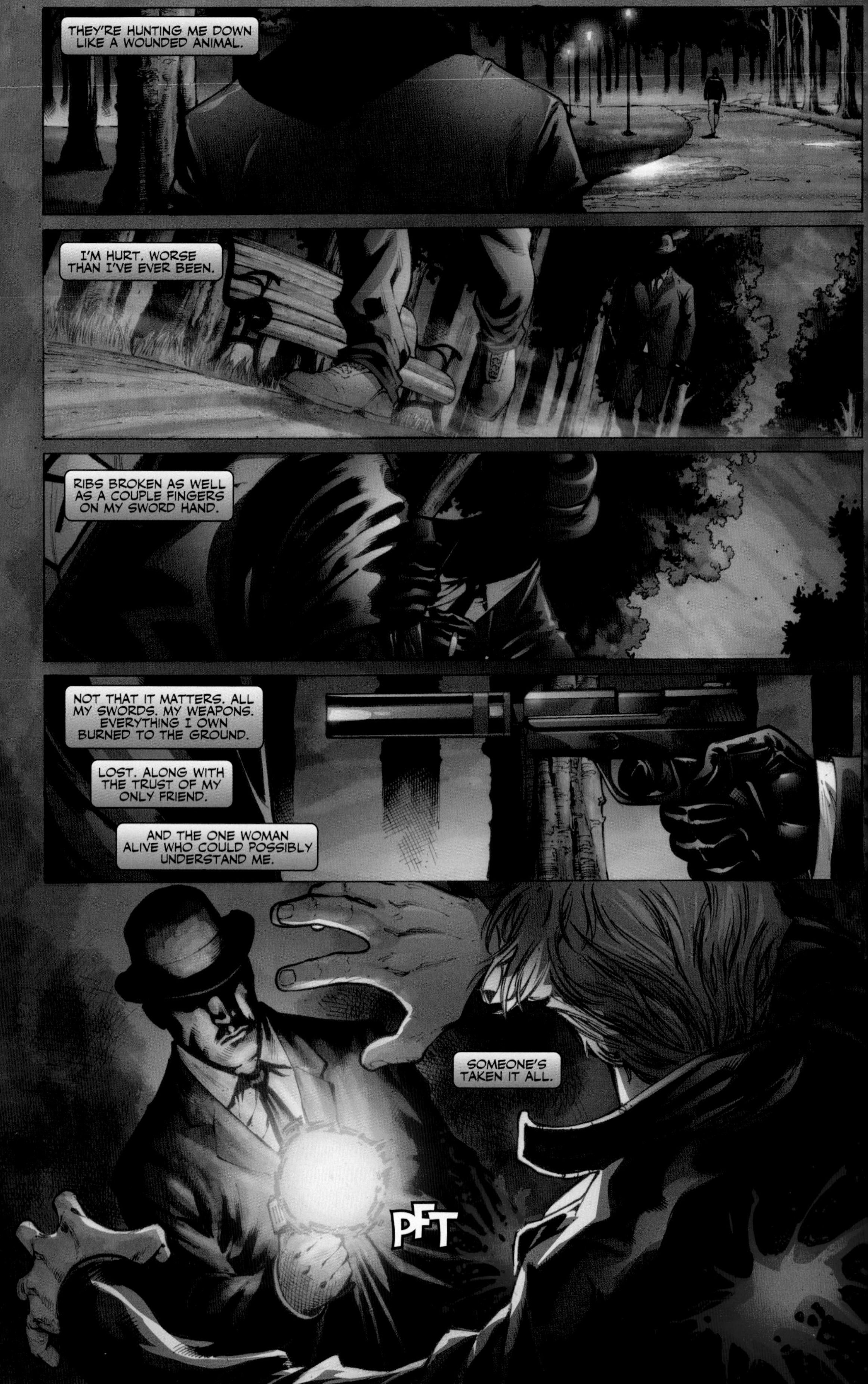
THEY'RE HUNTING ME DOWN LIKE A WOUNDED ANIMAL.
I'M HURT. WORSE THAN I'VE EVER BEEN.
RIBS BROKEN AS WELL AS A COUPLE FINGERS ON MY SWORD HAND.
NOT THAT IT MATTERS. ALL MY SWORDS. MY WEAPONS. EVERYTHING I OWN BURNED TO THE GROUND.
LOST. ALONG WITH THE TRUST OF MY ONLY FRIEND.
AND THE ONE WOMAN ALIVE WHO COULD POSSIBLY UNDERSTAND ME.
SOMEONE'S TAKEN IT ALL.
PFT

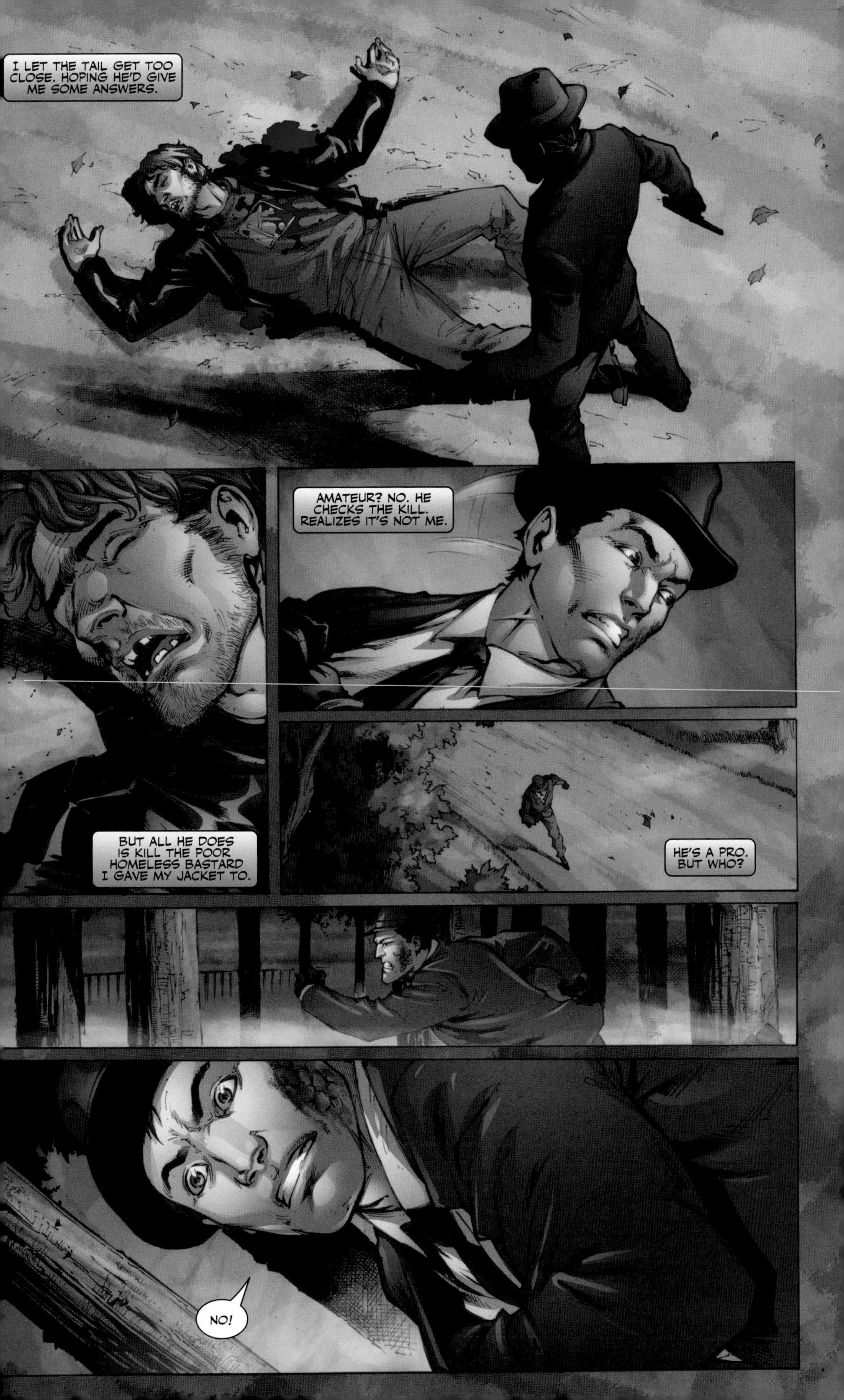
I LET THE TAIL GET TOO CLOSE. HOPING HE'D GIVE ME SOME ANSWERS.
AMATEUR? NO. HE CHECKS THE KILL. REALIZES IT'S NOT ME.
BUT ALL HE DOES IS KILL THE POOR HOMELESS BASTARD I GAVE MY JACKET TO.
HE'S A PRO. BUT WHO?
NO!

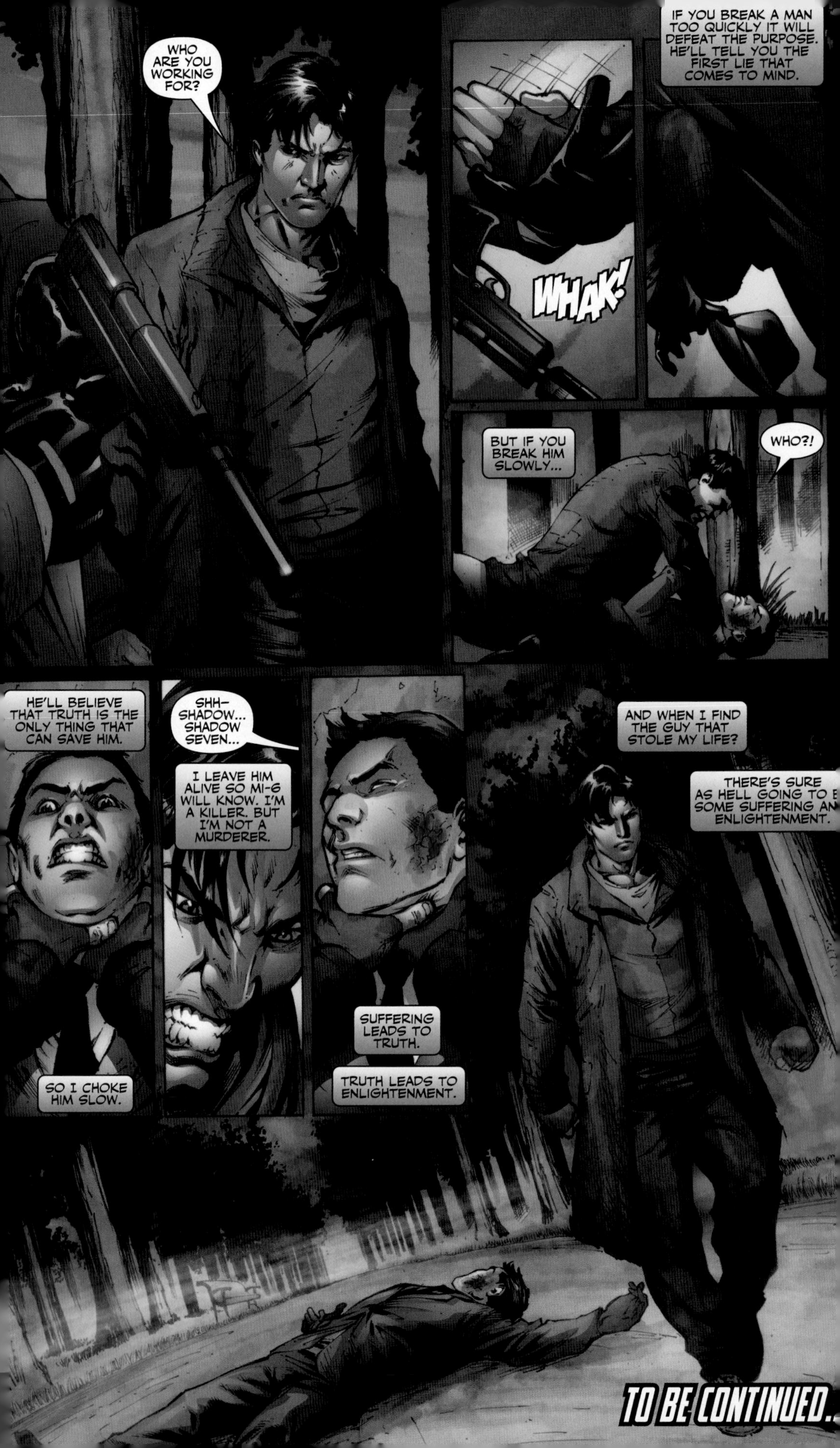
WHO ARE YOU WORKING FOR?
IF YOU BREAK A MAN TOO QUICKLY IT WILL DEFEAT THE PURPOSE. HE'LL TELL YOU THE FIRST LIE THAT COMES TO MIND.
WHAK!
BUT IF YOU BREAK HIM SLOWLY...
WHO?!
HE'LL BELIEVE THAT TRUTH IS THE ONLY THING THAT CAN SAVE HIM.
SO I CHOKE HIM SLOW.
SHH-SHADOW... SHADOW SEVEN...
I LEAVE HIM ALIVE SO MI-6 WILL KNOW. I'M A KILLER. BUT I'M NOT A MURDERER.
SUFFERING LEADS TO TRUTH.
TRUTH LEADS TO ENLIGHTENMENT.
AND WHEN I FIND THE GUY THAT STOLE MY LIFE?
THERE'S SURE AS HELL GOING TO BE SOME SUFFERING AND ENLIGHTENMENT.
TO BE CONTINUED...

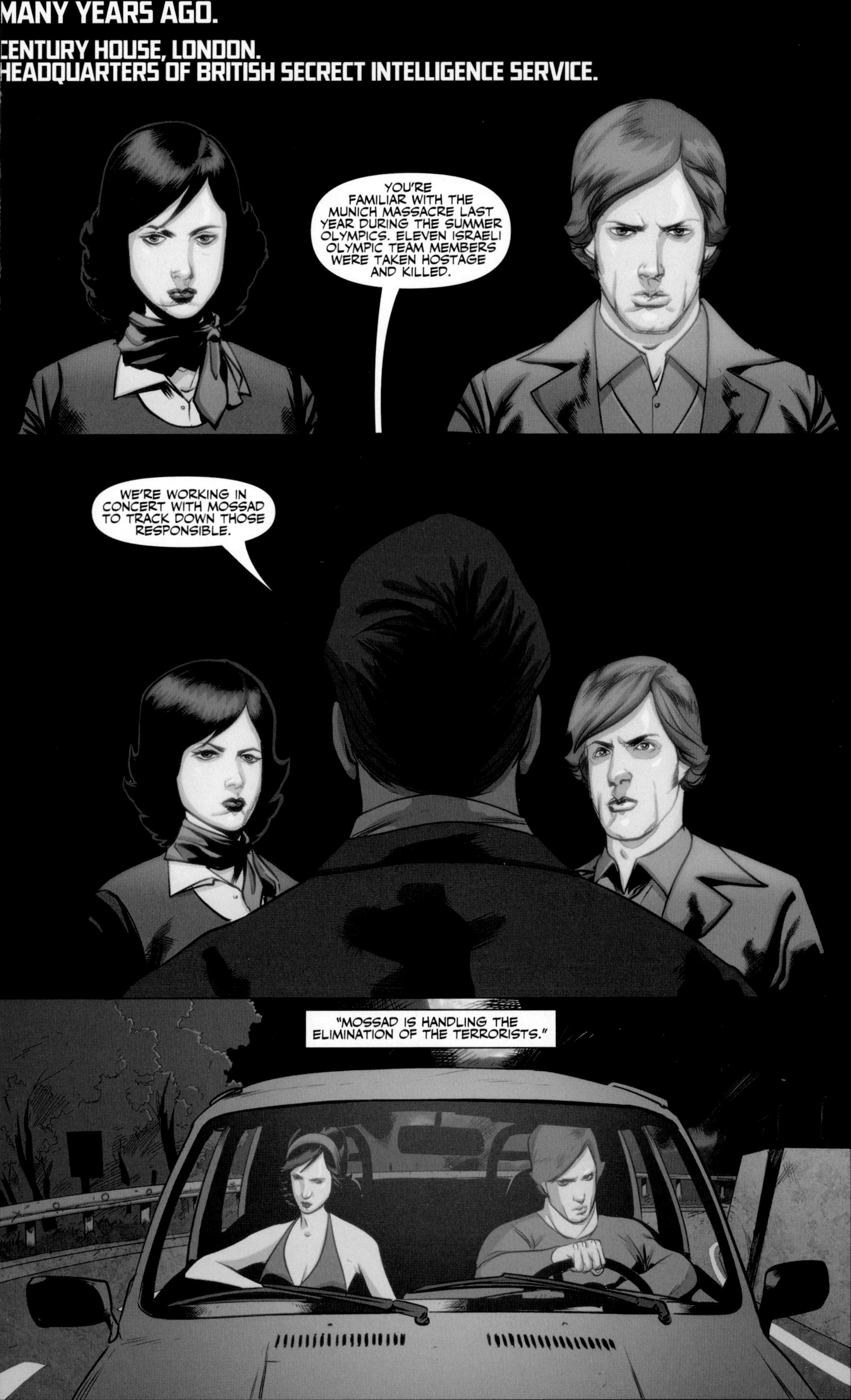
MANY YEARS AGO.
CENTURY HOUSE, LONDON.
HEADQUARTERS OF BRITISH SECRECT INTELLIGENCE SERVICE.
YOU'RE FAMILIAR WITH THE MUNICH MASSACRE LAST YEAR DURING THE SUMMER OLYMPICS. ELEVEN ISRAELI OLYMPIC TEAM MEMBERS WERE TAKEN HOSTAGE AND KILLED.
WE'RE WORKING IN CONCERT WITH MOSSAD TO TRACK DOWN THOSE RESPONSIBLE.
"MOSSAD IS HANDLING THE ELIMINATION OF THE TERRORISTS."

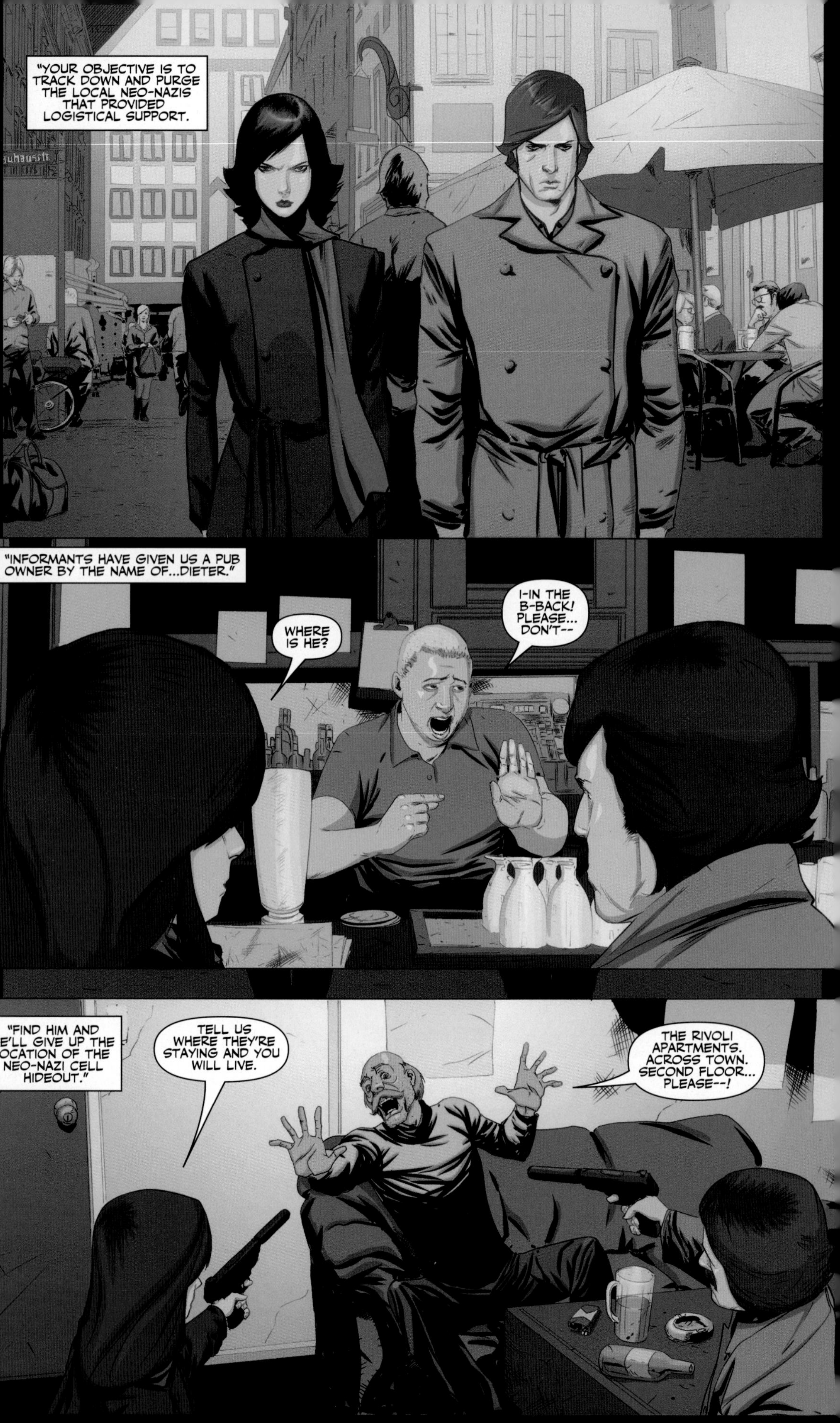
"YOUR OBJECTIVE IS TO TRACK DOWN AND PURGE THE LOCAL NEO-NAZIS THAT PROVIDED LOGISTICAL SUPPORT.
"INFORMANTS HAVE GIVEN US A PUB OWNER BY THE NAME OF...DIETER."
WHERE IS HE?
I-IN THE B-BACK! PLEASE... DON'T--
"FIND HIM AND HE'LL GIVE UP THE LOCATION OF THE NEO-NAZI CELL HIDEOUT."
TELL US WHERE THEY'RE STAYING AND YOU WILL LIVE.
THE RIVOLI APARTMENTS. ACROSS TOWN. SECOND FLOOR... PLEASE--!

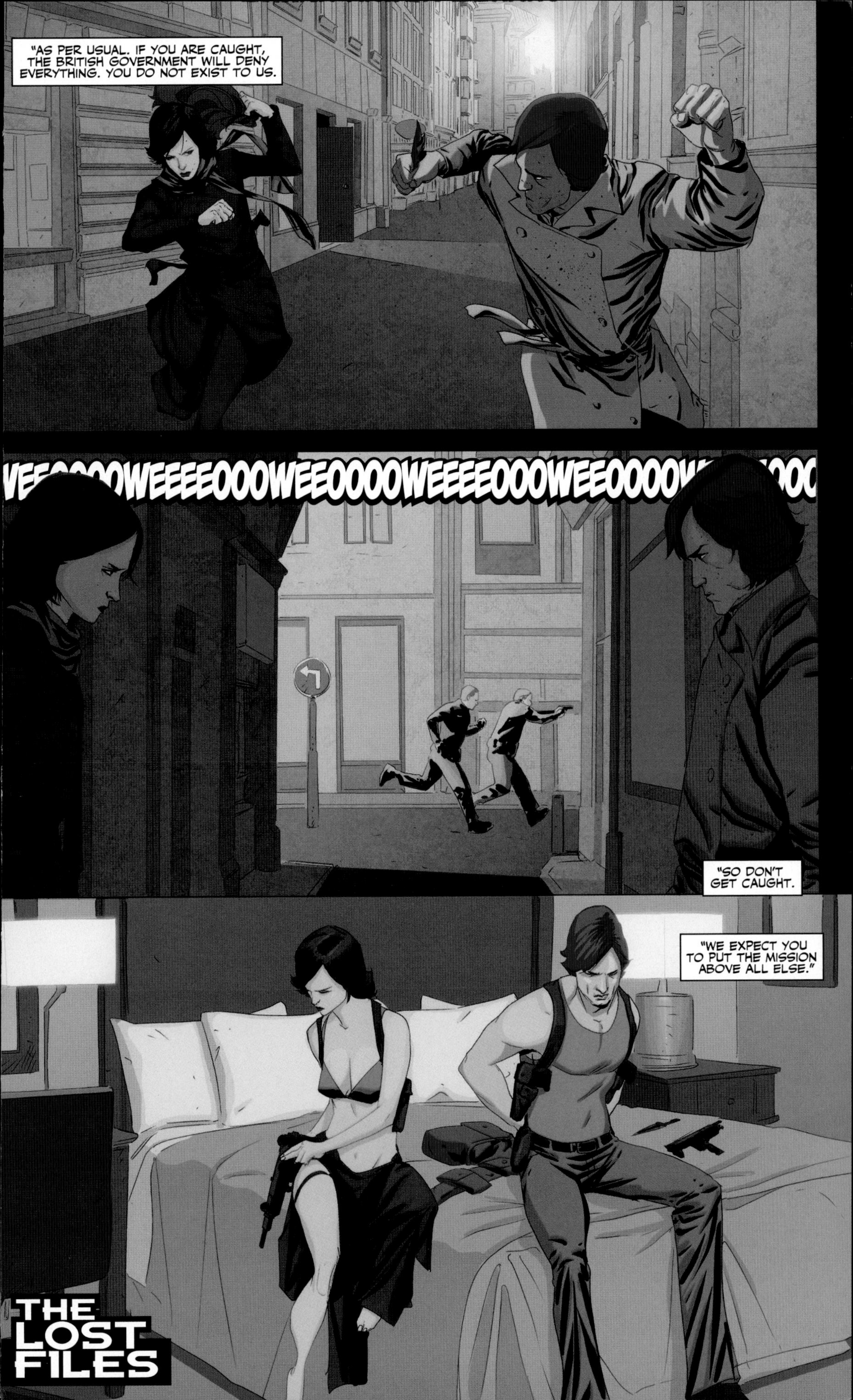
"AS PER USUAL. IF YOU ARE CAUGHT, THE BRITISH GOVERNMENT WILL DENY EVERYTHING. YOU DO NOT EXIST TO US.
"SO DON'T GET CAUGHT.
"WE EXPECT YOU TO PUT THE MISSION ABOVE ALL ELSE."
THE LOST FILES

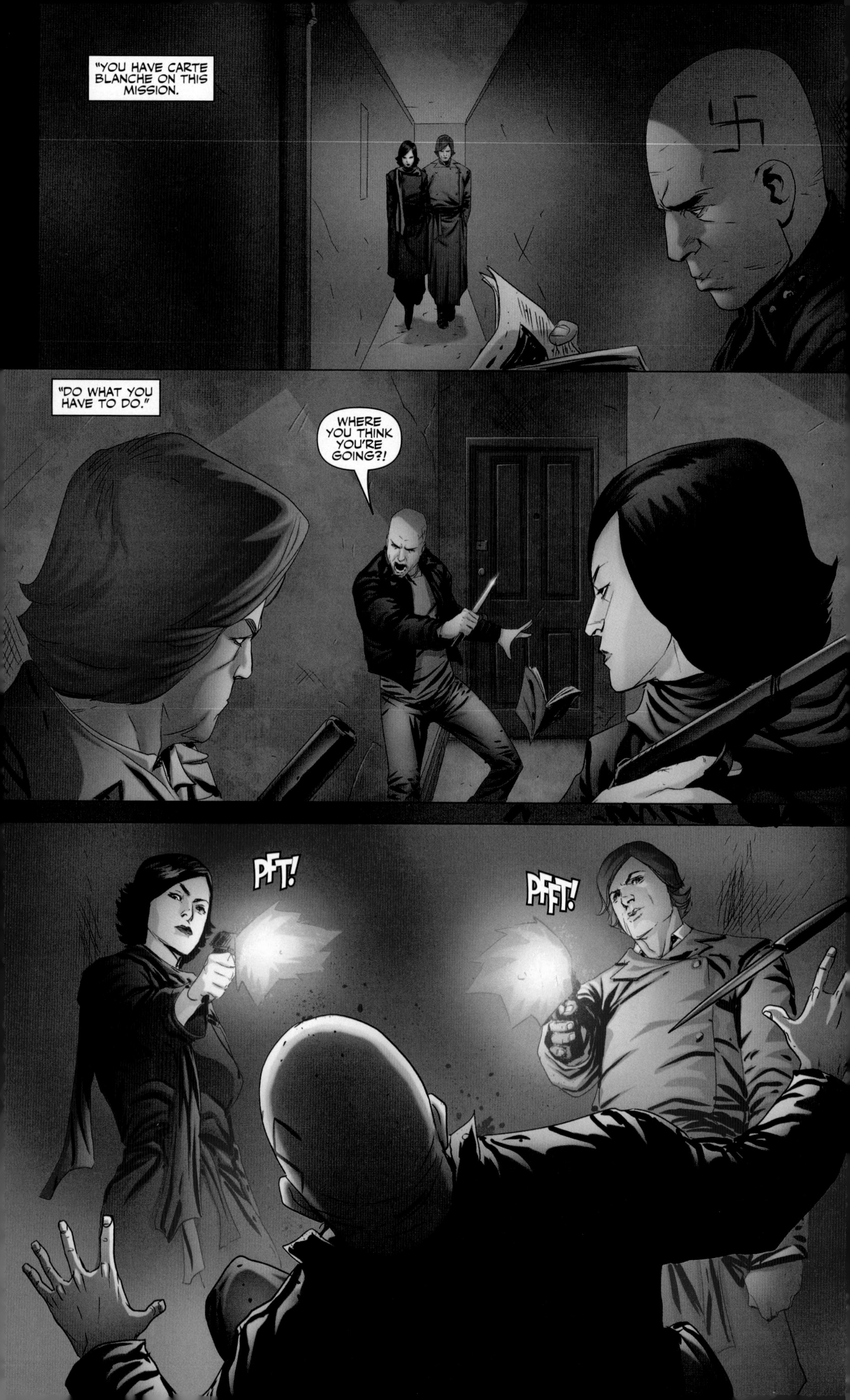
"YOU HAVE CARTE BLANCHE ON THIS MISSION.
"DO WHAT YOU HAVE TO DO."
WHERE YOU THINK YOU'RE GOING?!
PFT!
PFFT!

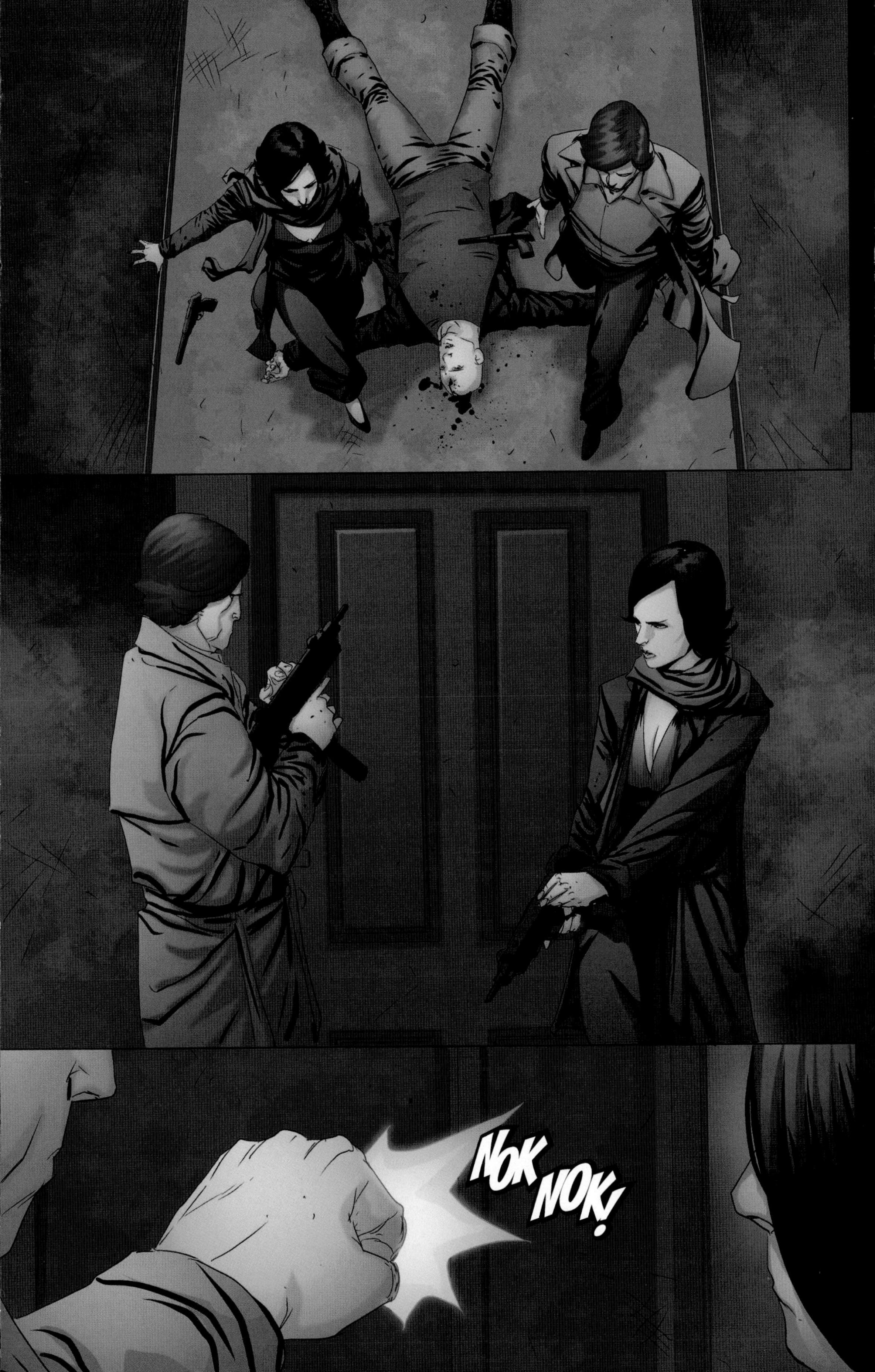
NOK NOK!

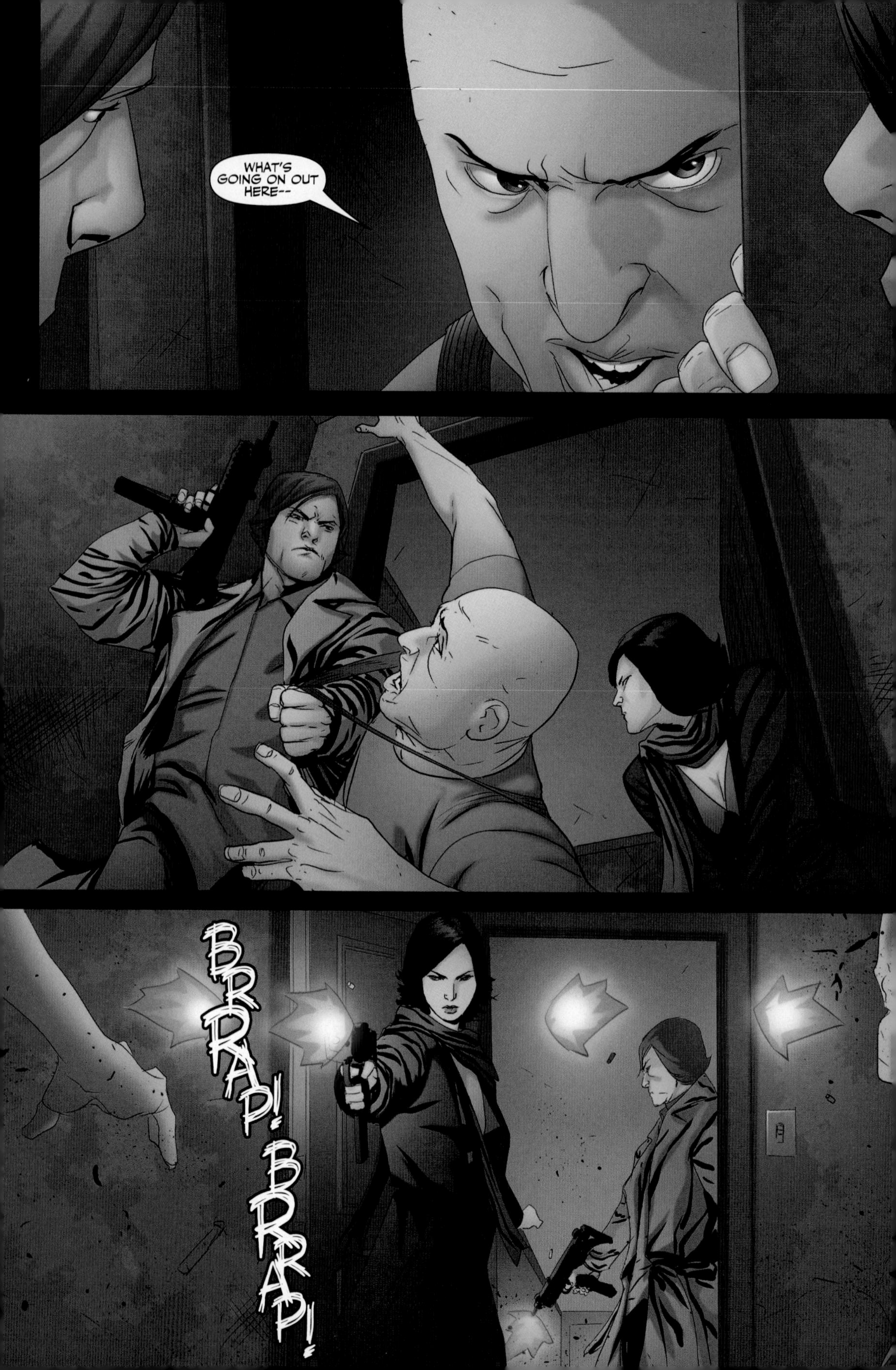
WHAT'S GOING ON OUT HERE--
BRRAP! BRRAP!

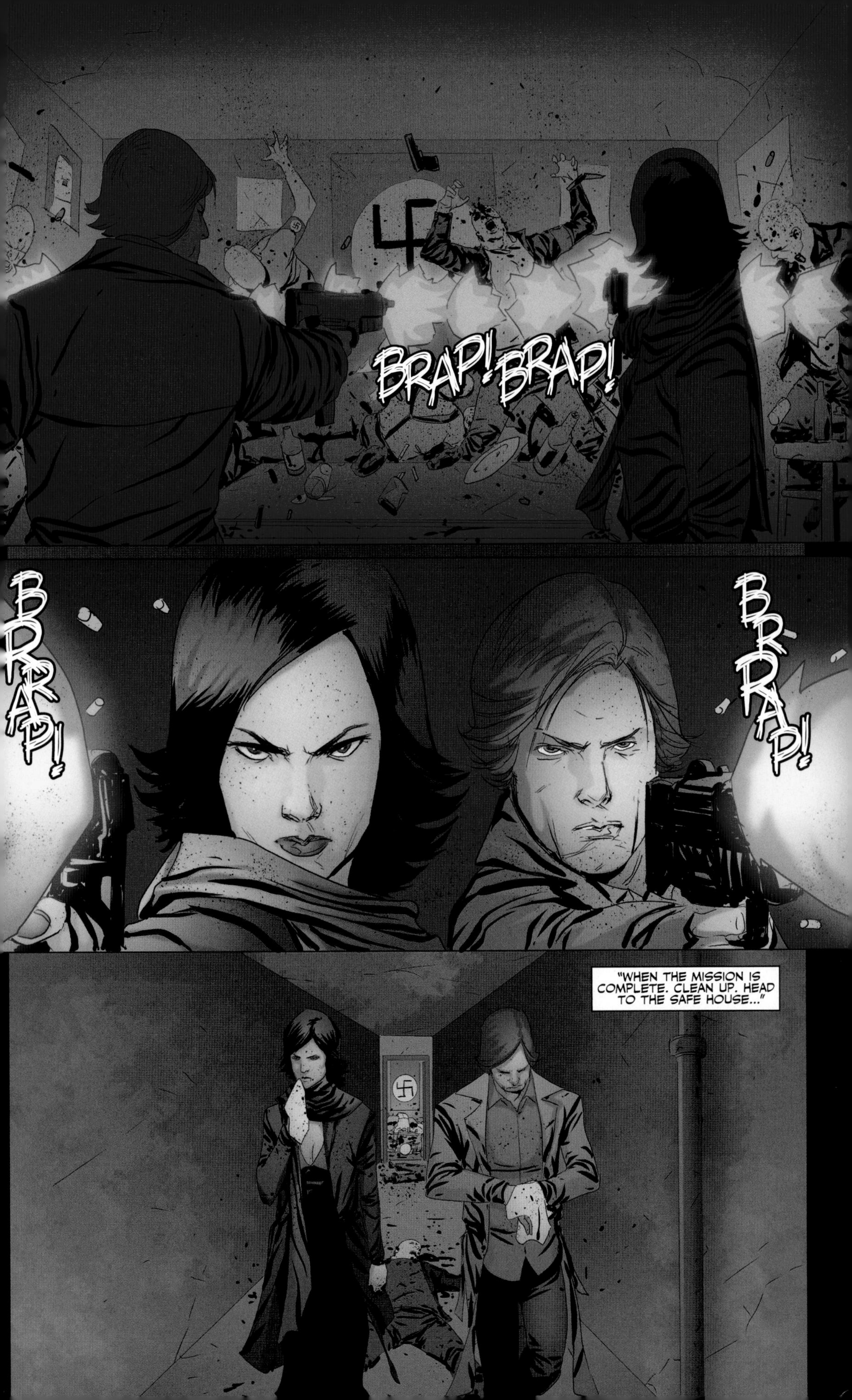
BRAP! BRAP!
BRRAP!
BRRAP!
"WHEN THE MISSION IS COMPLETE. CLEAN UP. HEAD TO THE SAFE HOUSE..."

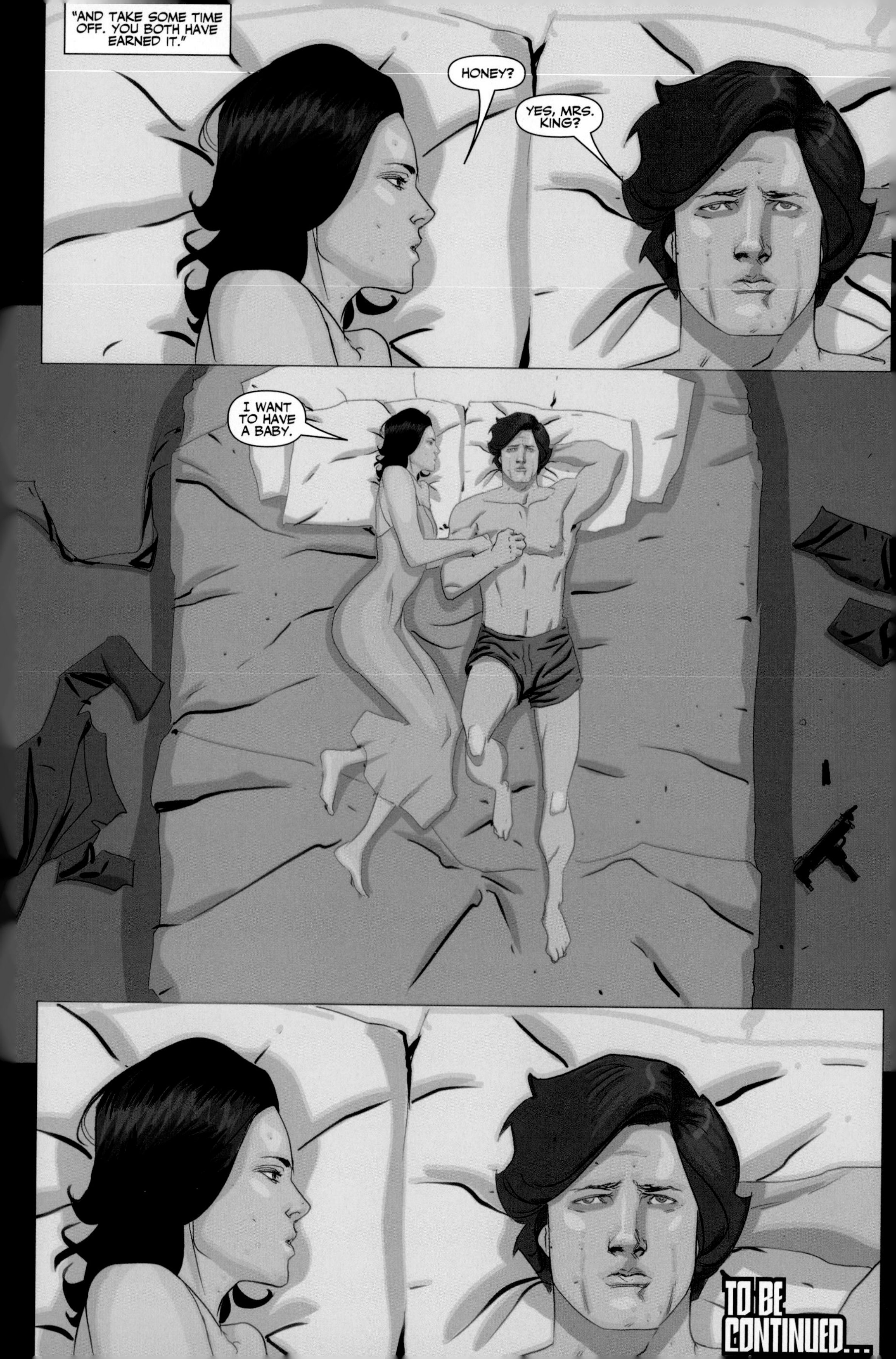
"AND TAKE SOME TIME OFF. YOU BOTH HAVE EARNED IT."
HONEY?
YES, MRS. KING?
I WANT TO HAVE A BABY.
TO BE CONTINUED...

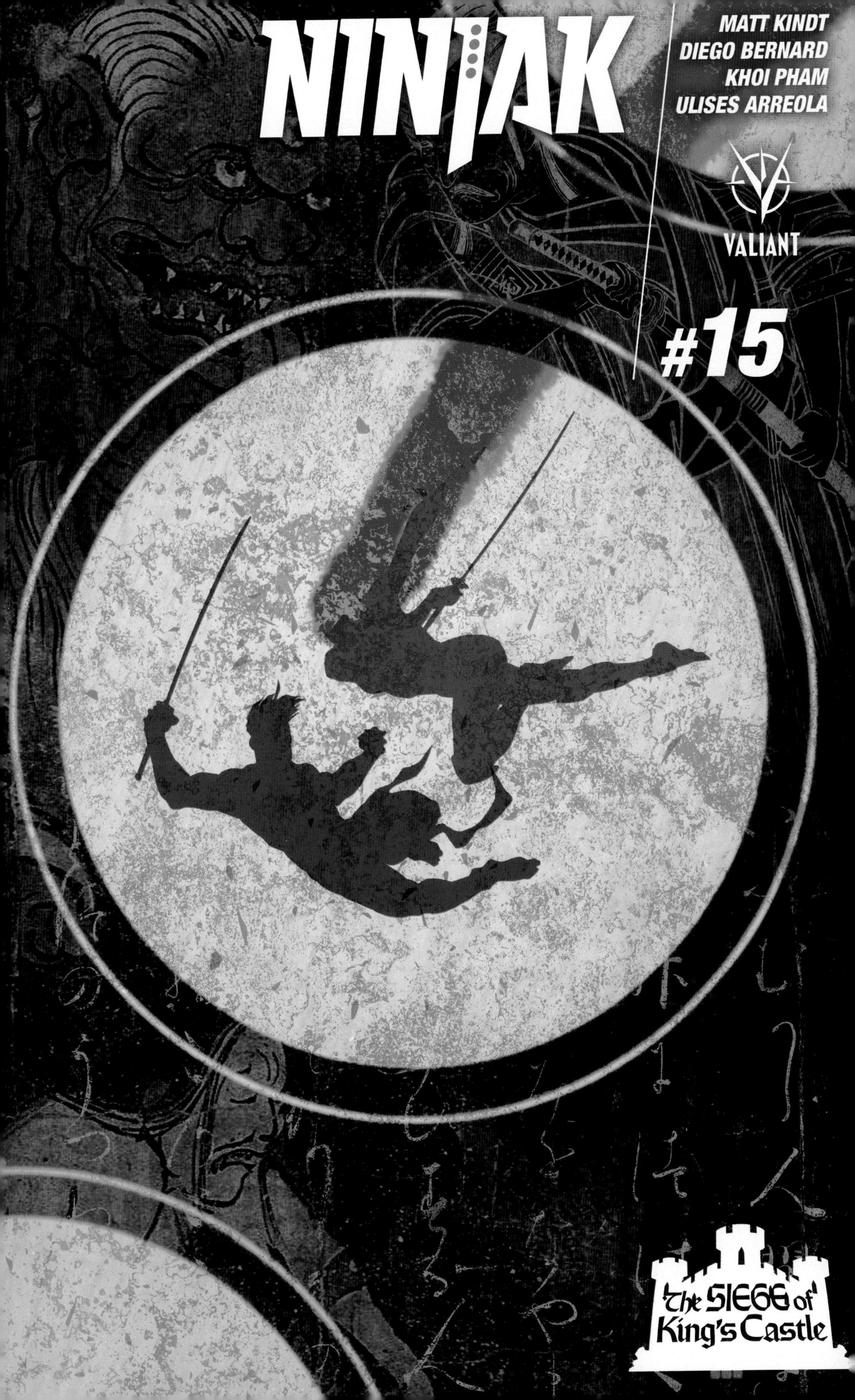
NINJAK
MATT KINDT
DIEGO BERNARD
KHOI PHAM
ULISES ARREOLA
VALIANT
#15
The SIEGE of King's Castle

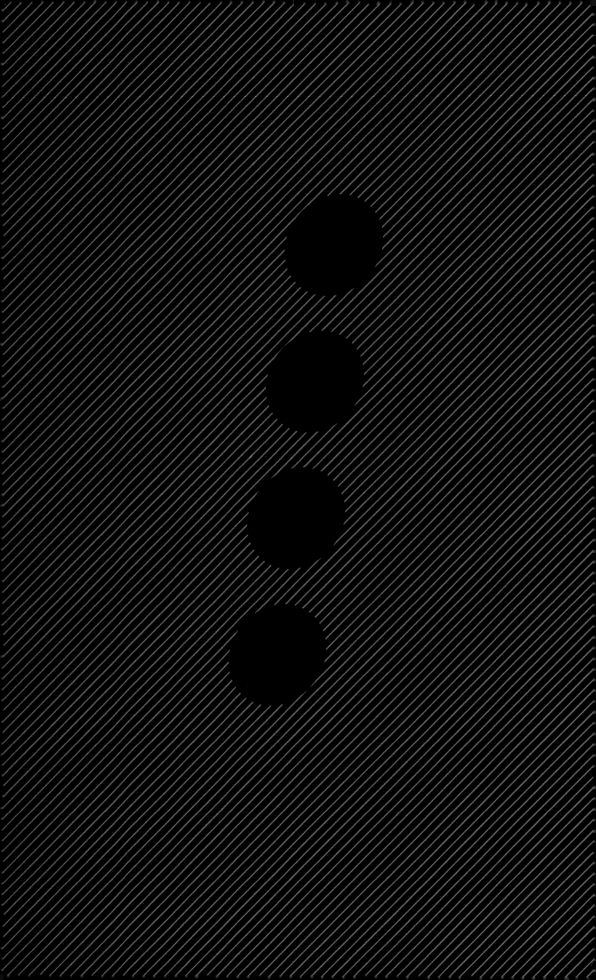

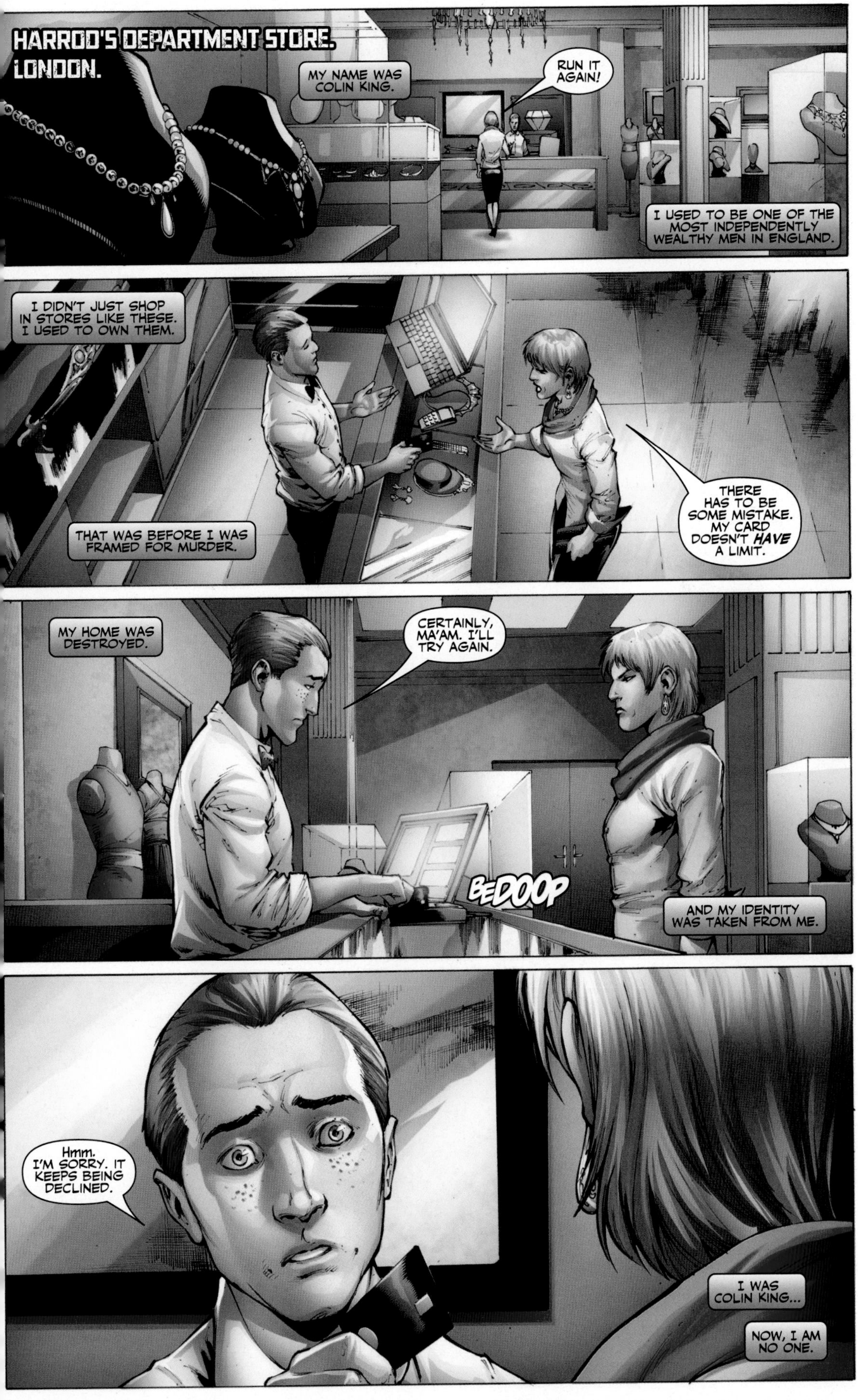
HARROD'S DEPARTMENT STORE. LONDON.
MY NAME WAS COLIN KING.
RUN IT AGAIN!
I USED TO BE ONE OF THE MOST INDEPENDENTLY WEALTHY MEN IN ENGLAND.
I DIDN'T JUST SHOP IN STORES LIKE THESE. I USED TO OWN THEM.
THERE HAS TO BE SOME MISTAKE. MY CARD DOESN'T HAVE A LIMIT.
THAT WAS BEFORE I WAS FRAMED FOR MURDER.
MY HOME WAS DESTROYED.
CERTAINLY, MA'AM. I'LL TRY AGAIN.
BEDOOP
AND MY IDENTITY WAS TAKEN FROM ME.
Hmm. I'M SORRY. IT KEEPS BEING DECLINED.
I WAS COLIN KING...
NOW, I AM NO ONE.

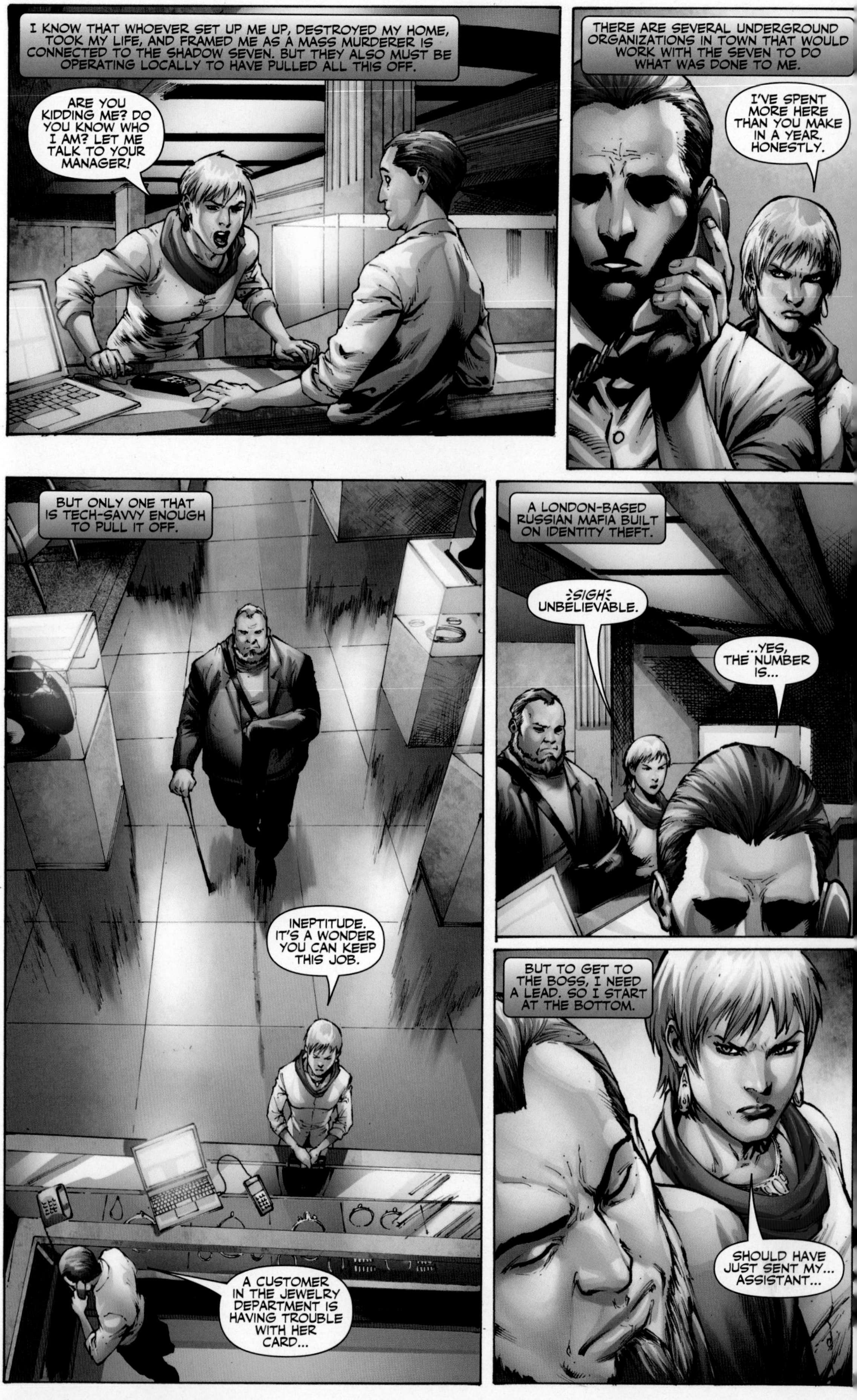
I KNOW THAT WHOEVER SET UP ME UP, DESTROYED MY HOME, TOOK MY LIFE, AND FRAMED ME AS A MASS MURDERER IS CONNECTED TO THE SHADOW SEVEN. BUT THEY ALSO MUST BE OPERATING LOCALLY TO HAVE PULLED ALL THIS OFF.
ARE YOU KIDDING ME? DO YOU KNOW WHO I AM? LET ME TALK TO YOUR MANAGER!
THERE ARE SEVERAL UNDERGROUND ORGANIZATIONS IN TOWN THAT WOULD WORK WITH THE SEVEN TO DO WHAT WAS DONE TO ME.
I'VE SPENT MORE HERE THAN YOU MAKE IN A YEAR. HONESTLY.
BUT ONLY ONE THAT IS TECH-SAVVY ENOUGH TO PULL IT OFF.
INEPTITUDE. IT'S A WONDER YOU CAN KEEP THIS JOB.
A CUSTOMER IN THE JEWELRY DEPARTMENT IS HAVING TROUBLE WITH HER CARD...
A LONDON-BASED RUSSIAN MAFIA BUILT ON IDENTITY THEFT.
SIGH UNBELIEVABLE.
...YES, THE NUMBER IS...
BUT TO GET TO THE BOSS, I NEED A LEAD. SO I START AT THE BOTTOM.
SHOULD HAVE JUST SENT MY... ASSISTANT...

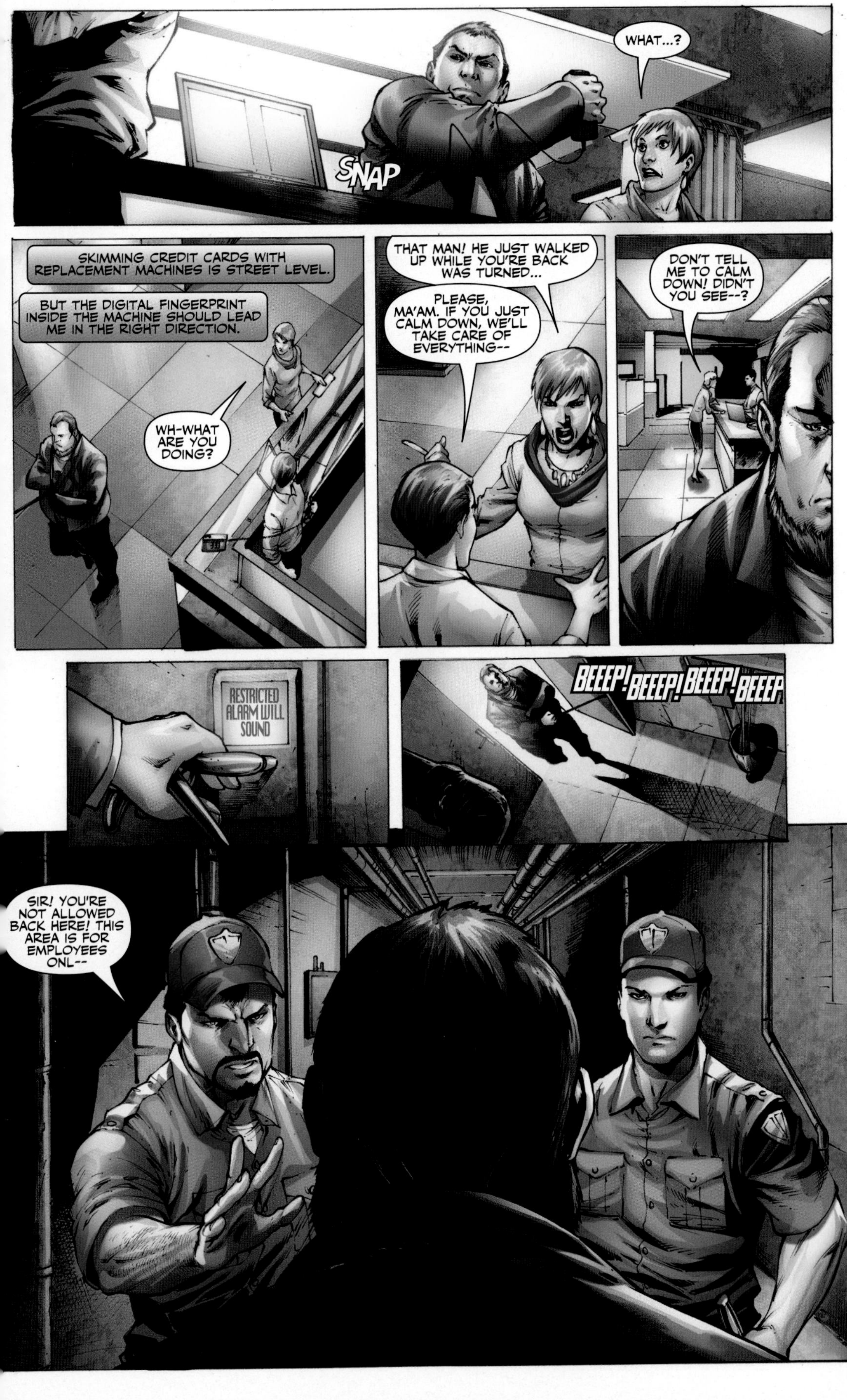
WHAT...?
SNAP
SKIMMING CREDIT CARDS WITH REPLACEMENT MACHINES IS STREET LEVEL.
BUT THE DIGITAL FINGERPRINT INSIDE THE MACHINE SHOULD LEAD ME IN THE RIGHT DIRECTION.
WH-WHAT ARE YOU DOING?
THAT MAN! HE JUST WALKED UP WHILE YOU'RE BACK WAS TURNED...
PLEASE, MA'AM. IF YOU JUST CALM DOWN, WE'LL TAKE CARE OF EVERYTHING--
DON'T TELL ME TO CALM DOWN! DIDN'T YOU SEE--?
RESTRICTED ALARM WILL SOUND
BEEEP! BEEEP! BEEEP! BEEEP
SIR! YOU'RE NOT ALLOWED BACK HERE! THIS AREA IS FOR EMPLOYEES ONL--

KRRITCH

GAH!

KRAKK

KRUNCH

WHUMP

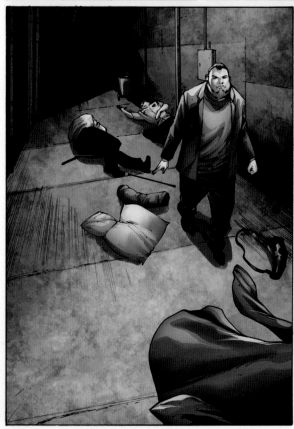

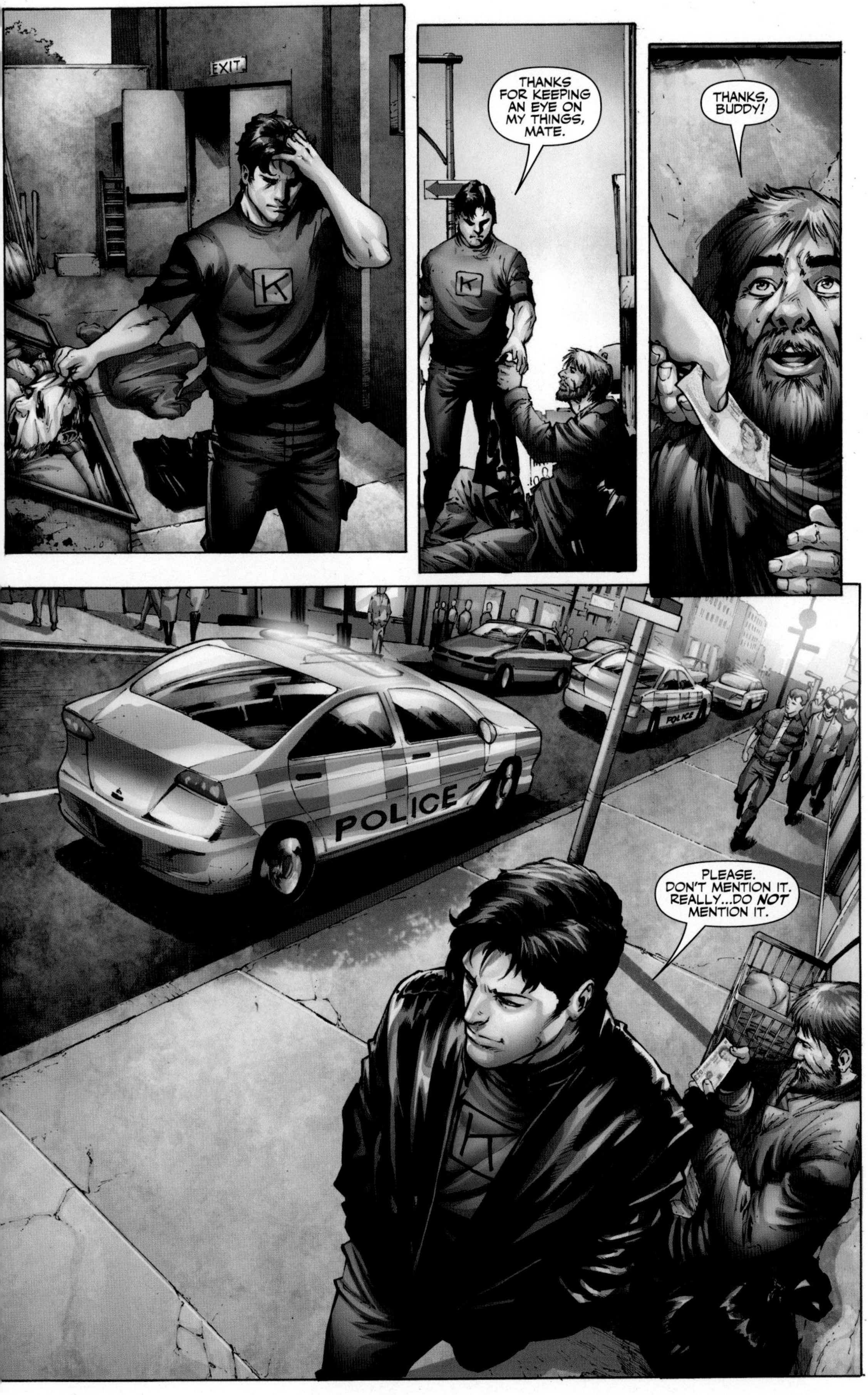
EXIT
THANKS FOR KEEPING AN EYE ON MY THINGS, MATE.
THANKS, BUDDY!
POLICE
POLICE
PLEASE. DON'T MENTION IT. REALLY...DO *NOT* MENTION IT.

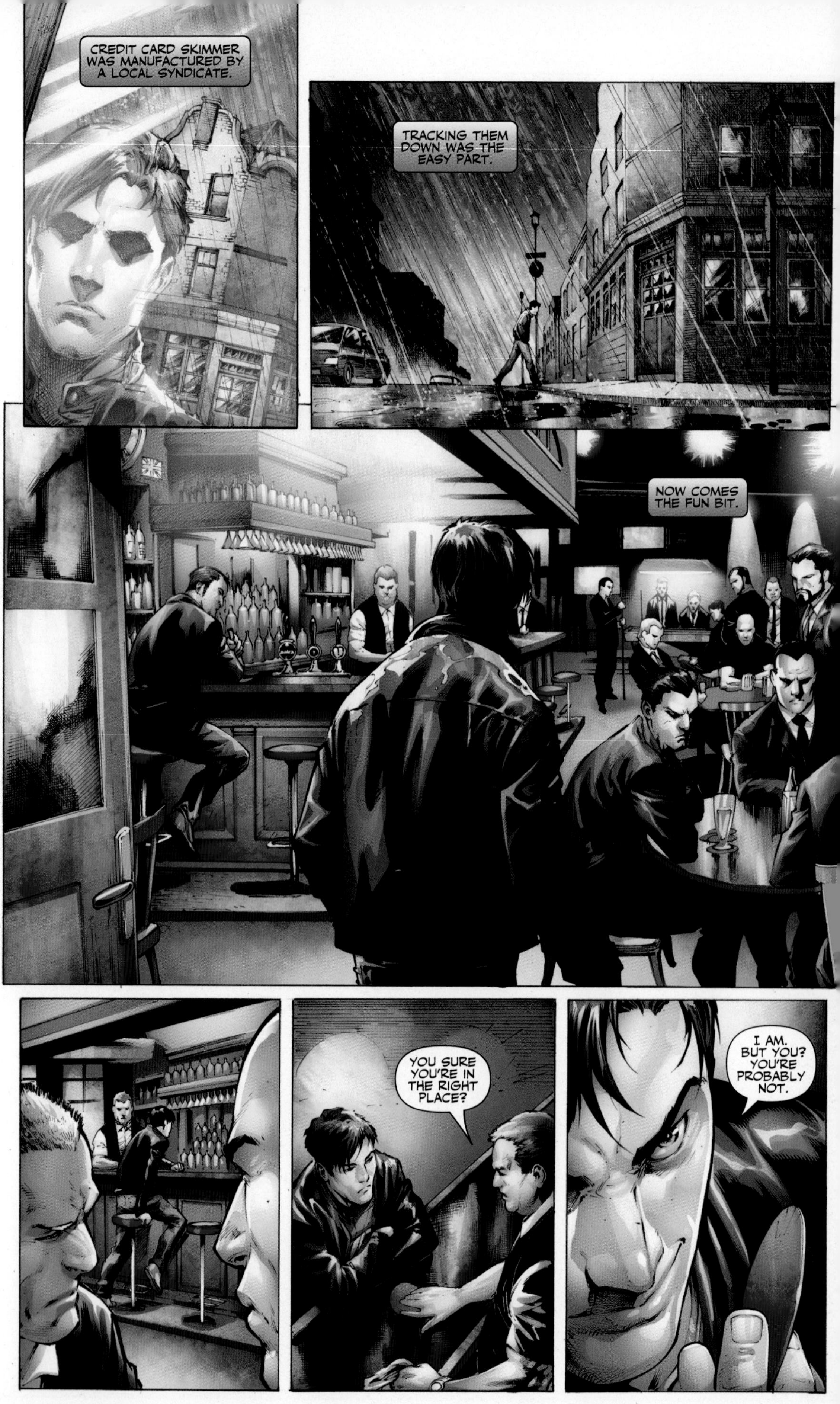
CREDIT CARD SKIMMER WAS MANUFACTURED BY A LOCAL SYNDICATE.
TRACKING THEM DOWN WAS THE EASY PART.
NOW COMES THE FUN BIT.
YOU SURE YOU'RE IN THE RIGHT PLACE?
I AM. BUT YOU? YOU'RE PROBABLY NOT.

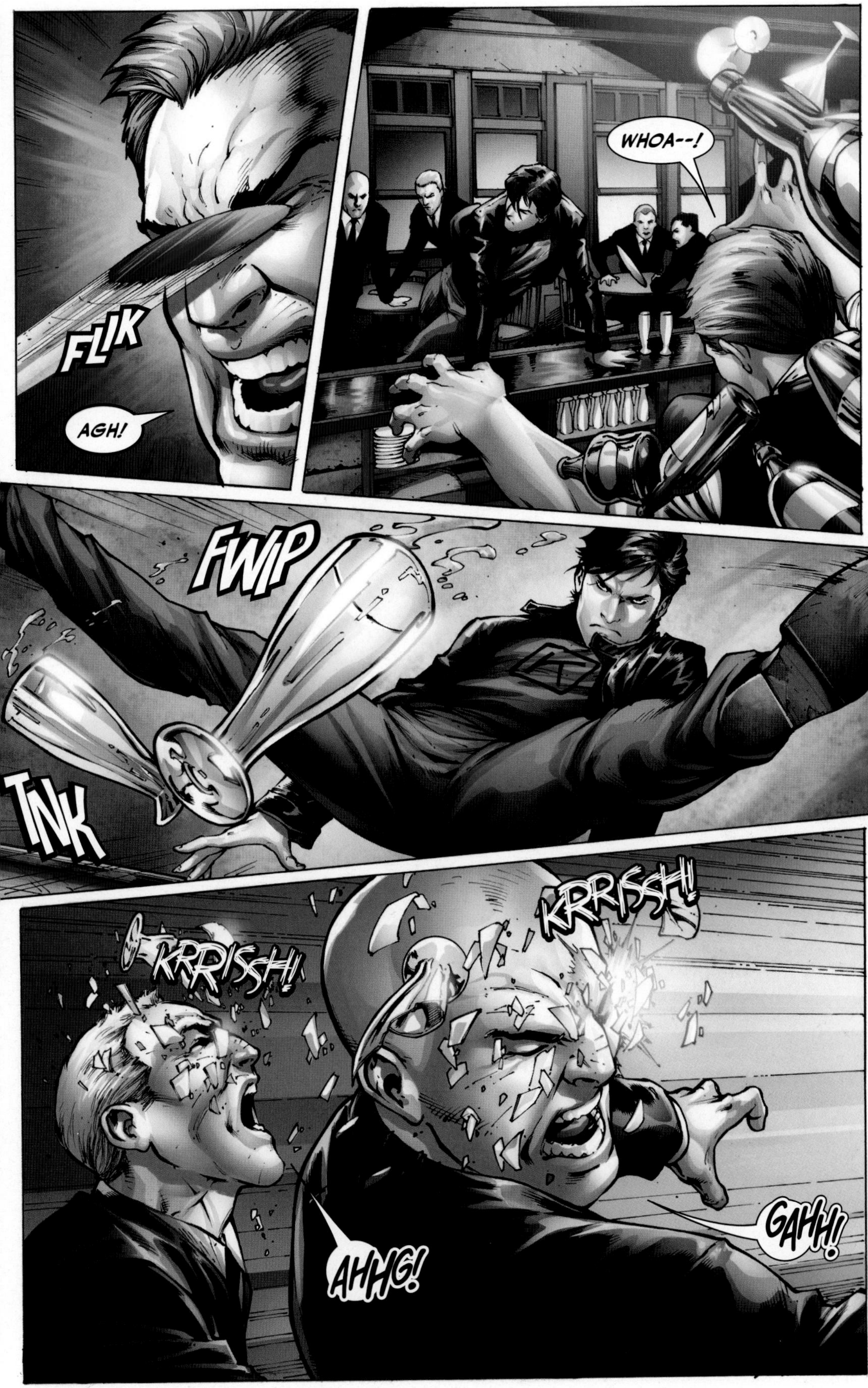
FLIK
AGH!
WHOA--!
FWIP
TINK
KRRISSH!
KRRISSH!
AHHG!
GAHH!

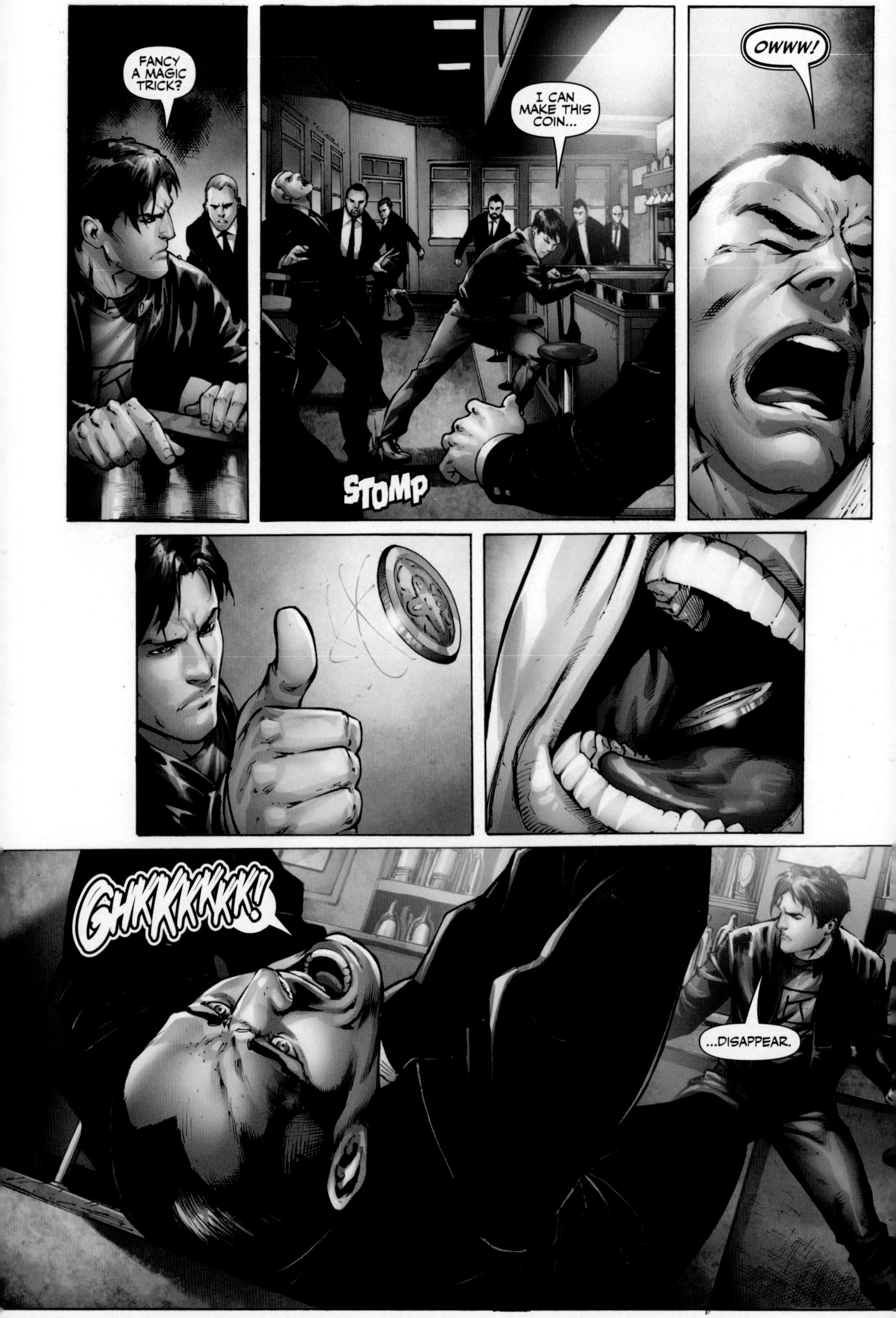
FANCY A MAGIC TRICK?
I CAN MAKE THIS COIN...
STOMP
OWWW!
GHKKKKKK!
...DISAPPEAR.

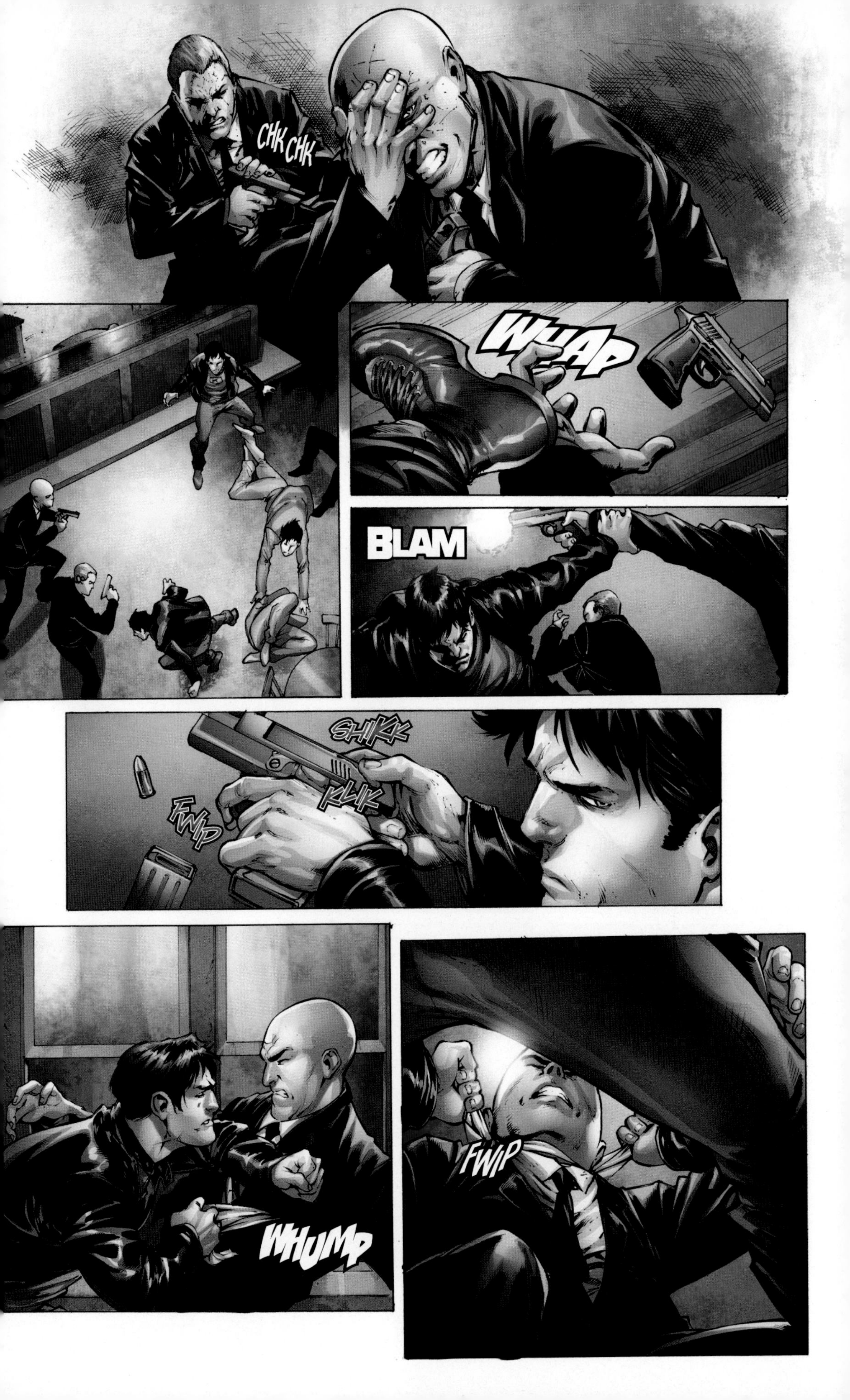
CHK CHK
WHAP
BLAM
SHIKK
KLIK
FWIP
WHUMP
FWIP

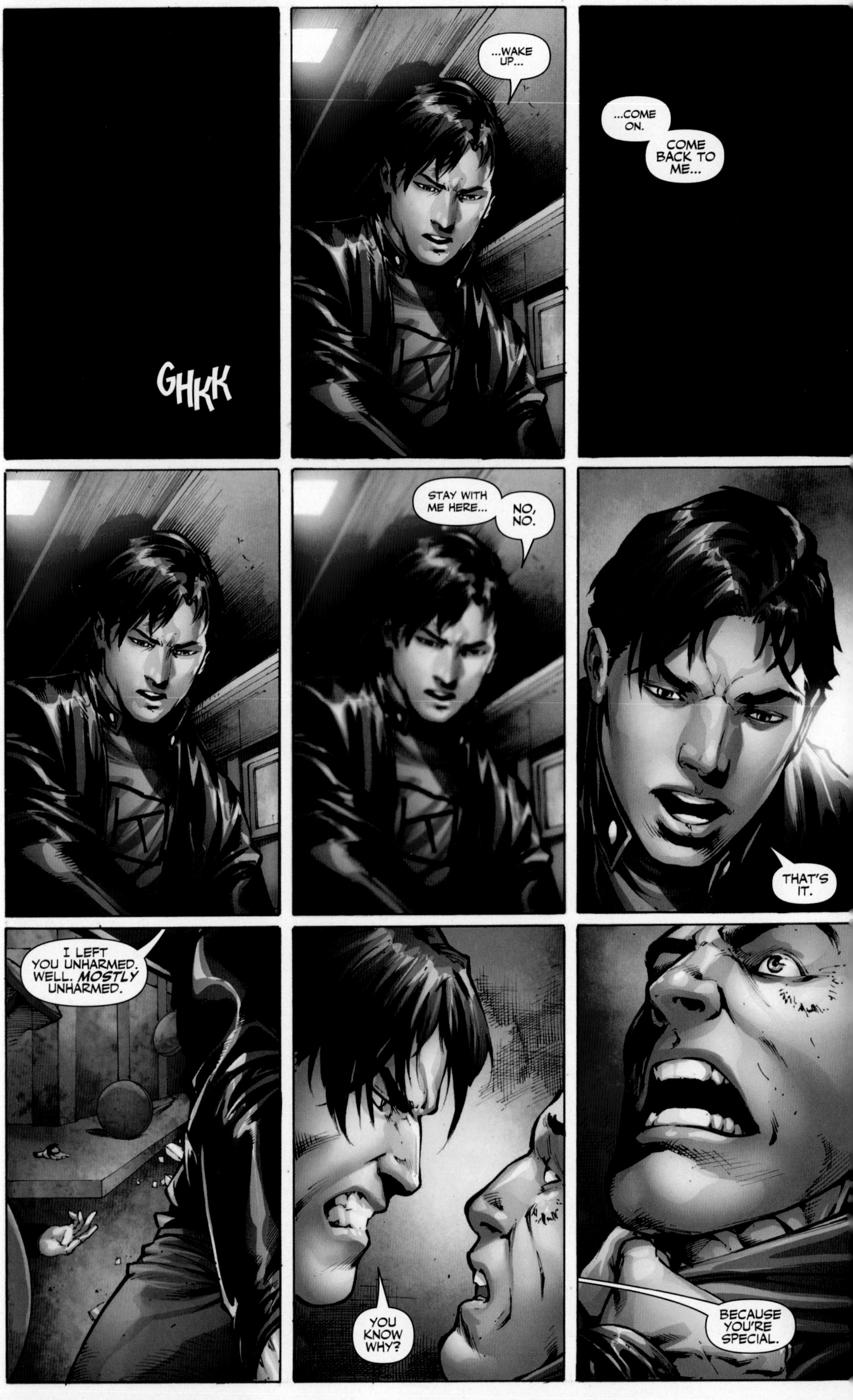
GHKK
...WAKE UP...
...COME ON.
COME BACK TO ME...
STAY WITH ME HERE...
NO, NO.
THAT'S IT.
I LEFT YOU UNHARMED. WELL. *MOSTLY* UNHARMED.
YOU KNOW WHY?
BECAUSE YOU'RE SPECIAL.

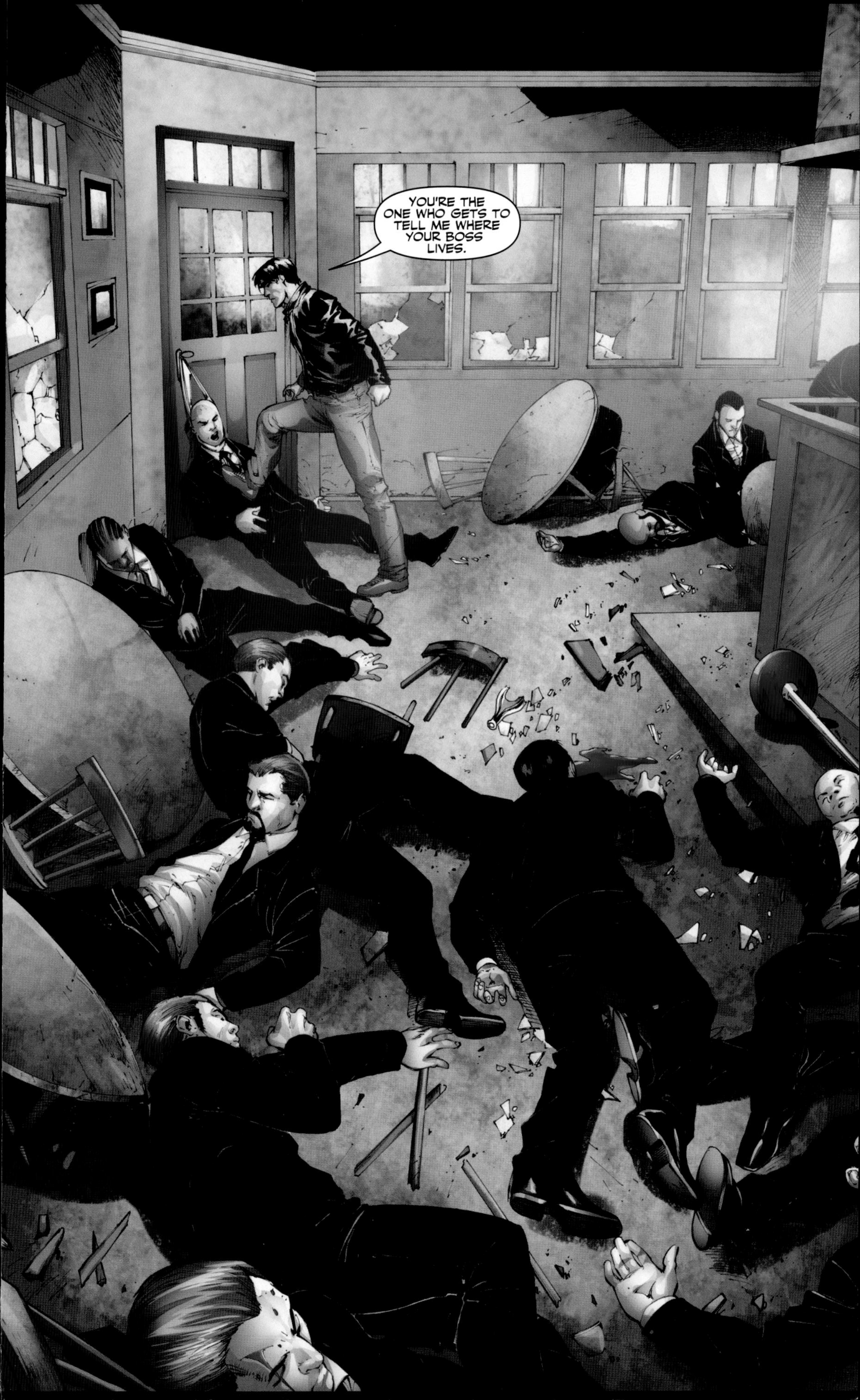
YOU'RE THE ONE WHO GETS TO TELL ME WHERE YOUR BOSS LIVES.

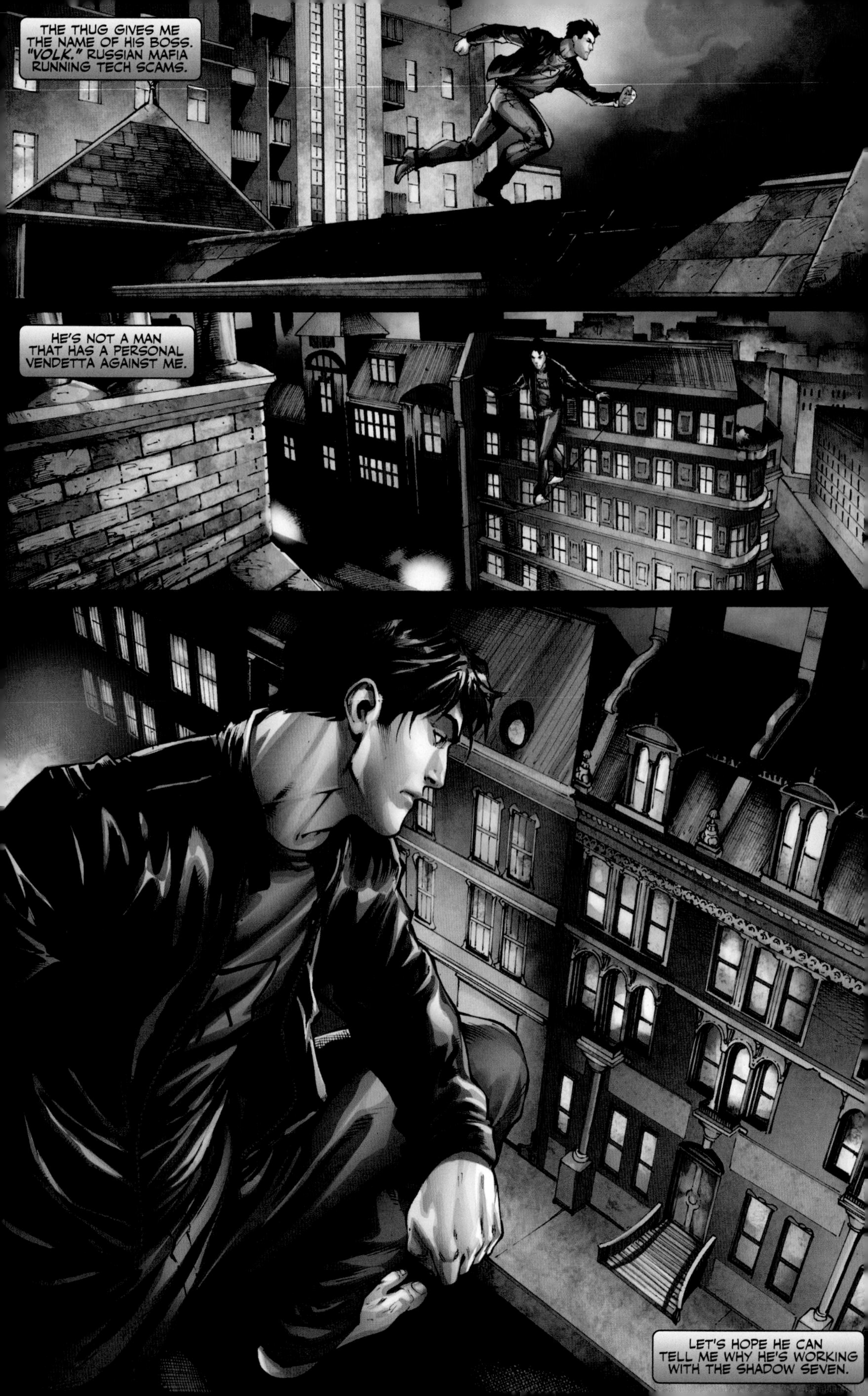
THE THUG GIVES ME THE NAME OF HIS BOSS. "VOLK." RUSSIAN MAFIA RUNNING TECH SCAMS.
HE'S NOT A MAN THAT HAS A PERSONAL VENDETTA AGAINST ME.
LET'S HOPE HE CAN TELL ME WHY HE'S WORKING WITH THE SHADOW SEVEN.

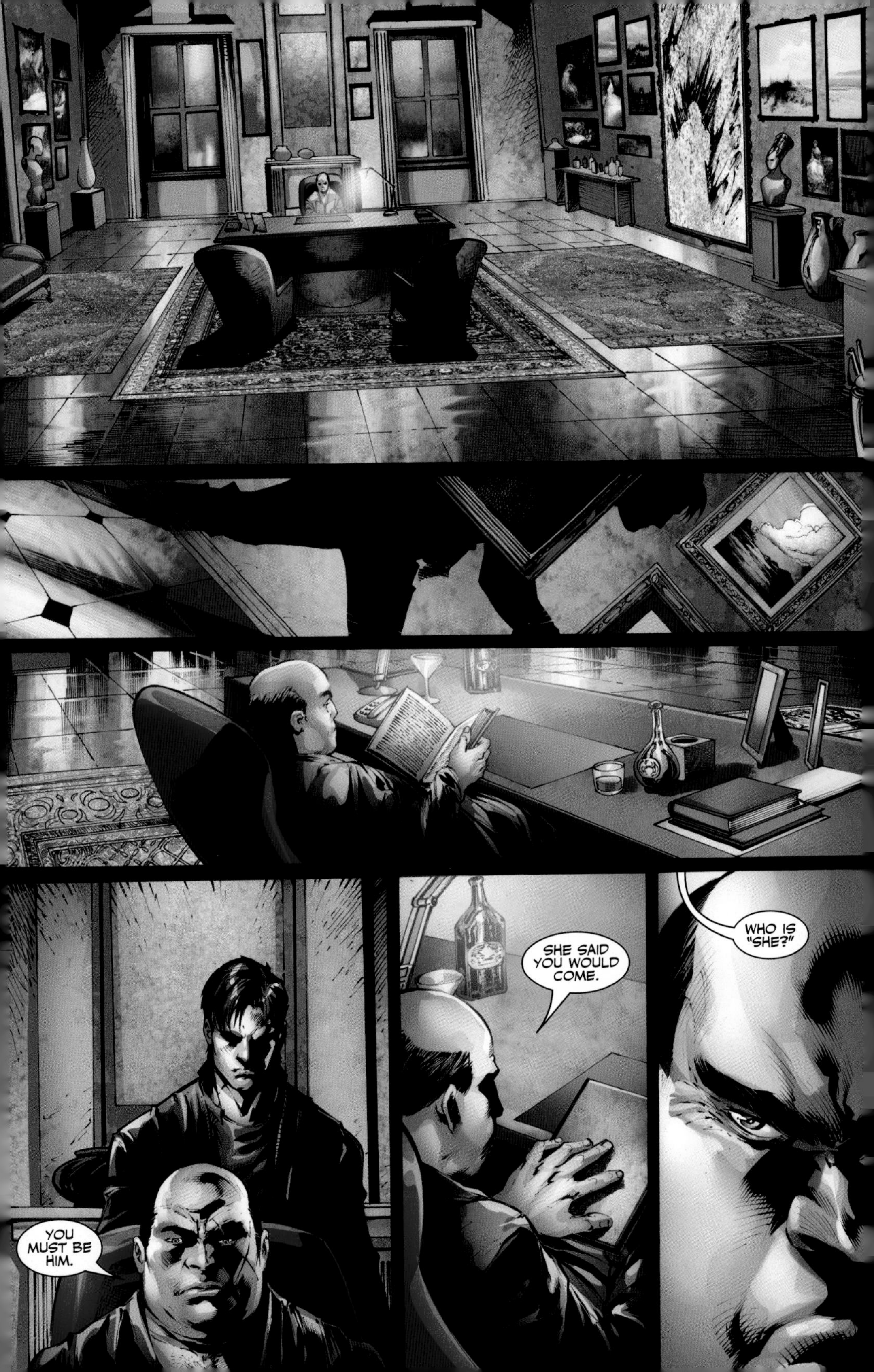
YOU MUST BE HIM.
SHE SAID YOU WOULD COME.
WHO IS "SHE?"

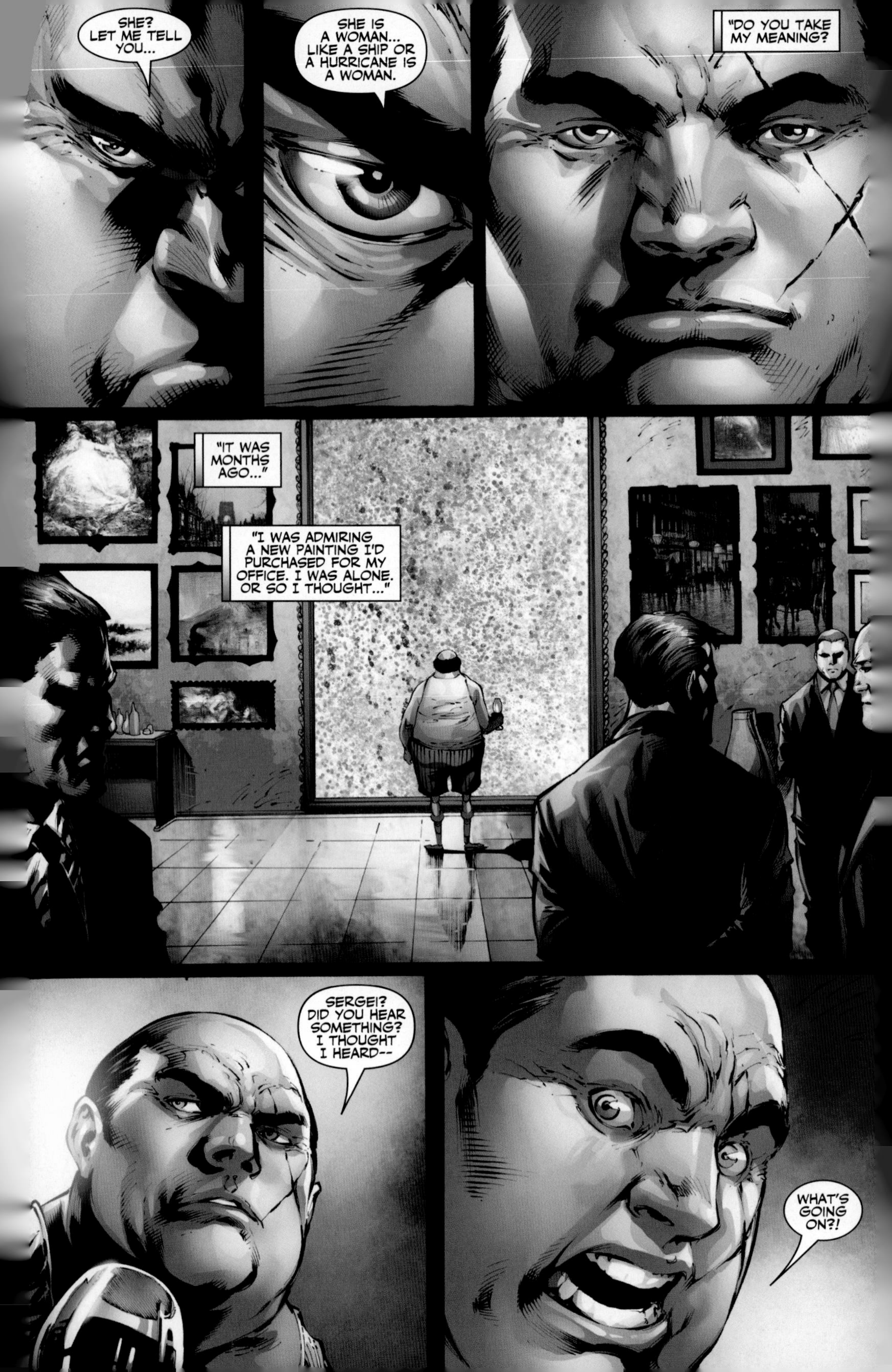
SHE? LET ME TELL YOU...
SHE IS A WOMAN... LIKE A SHIP OR A HURRICANE IS A WOMAN.
"DO YOU TAKE MY MEANING?
"IT WAS MONTHS AGO..."
"I WAS ADMIRING A NEW PAINTING I'D PURCHASED FOR MY OFFICE. I WAS ALONE. OR SO I THOUGHT..."
SERGEI? DID YOU HEAR SOMETHING? I THOUGHT I HEARD--
WHAT'S GOING ON?!

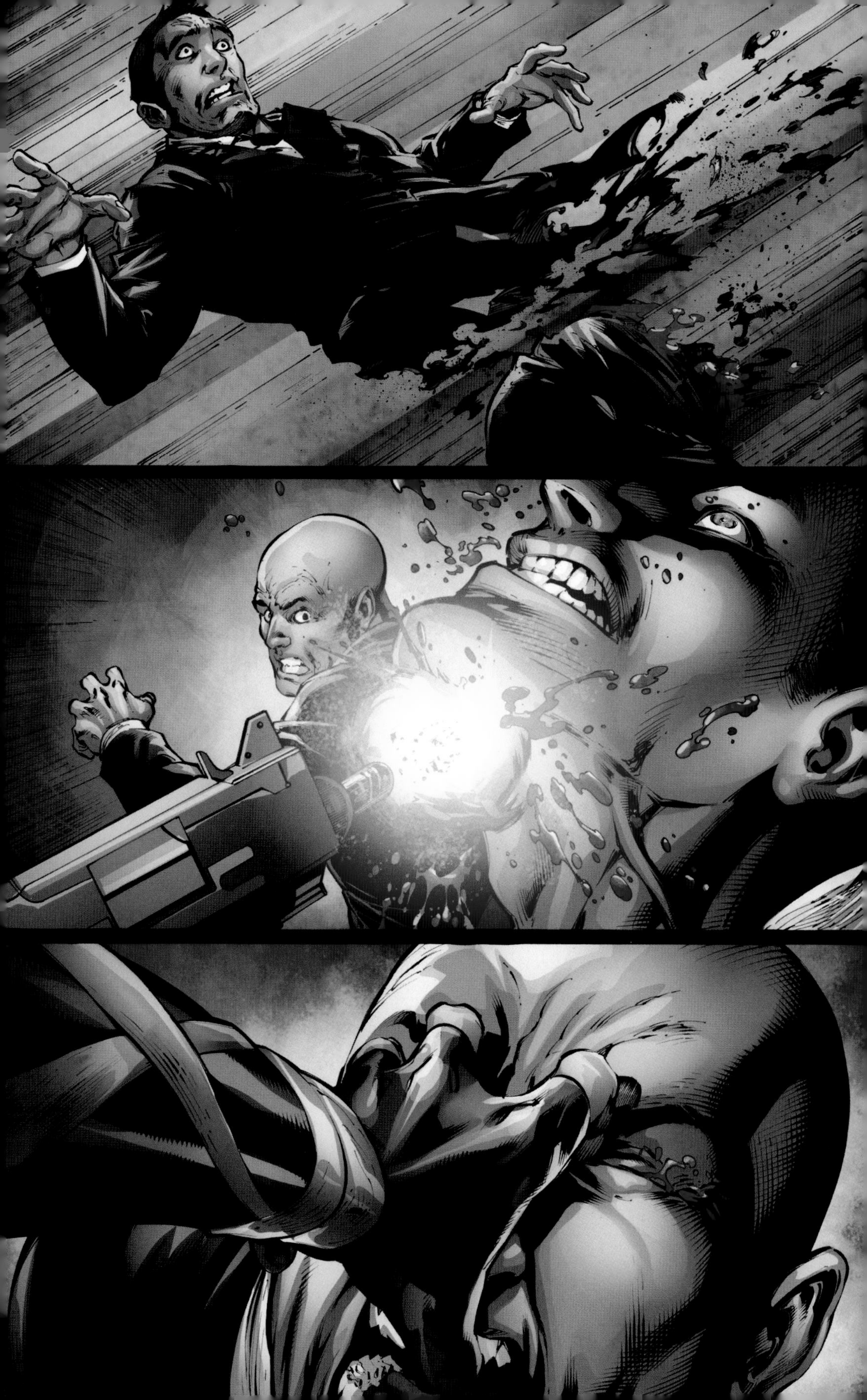

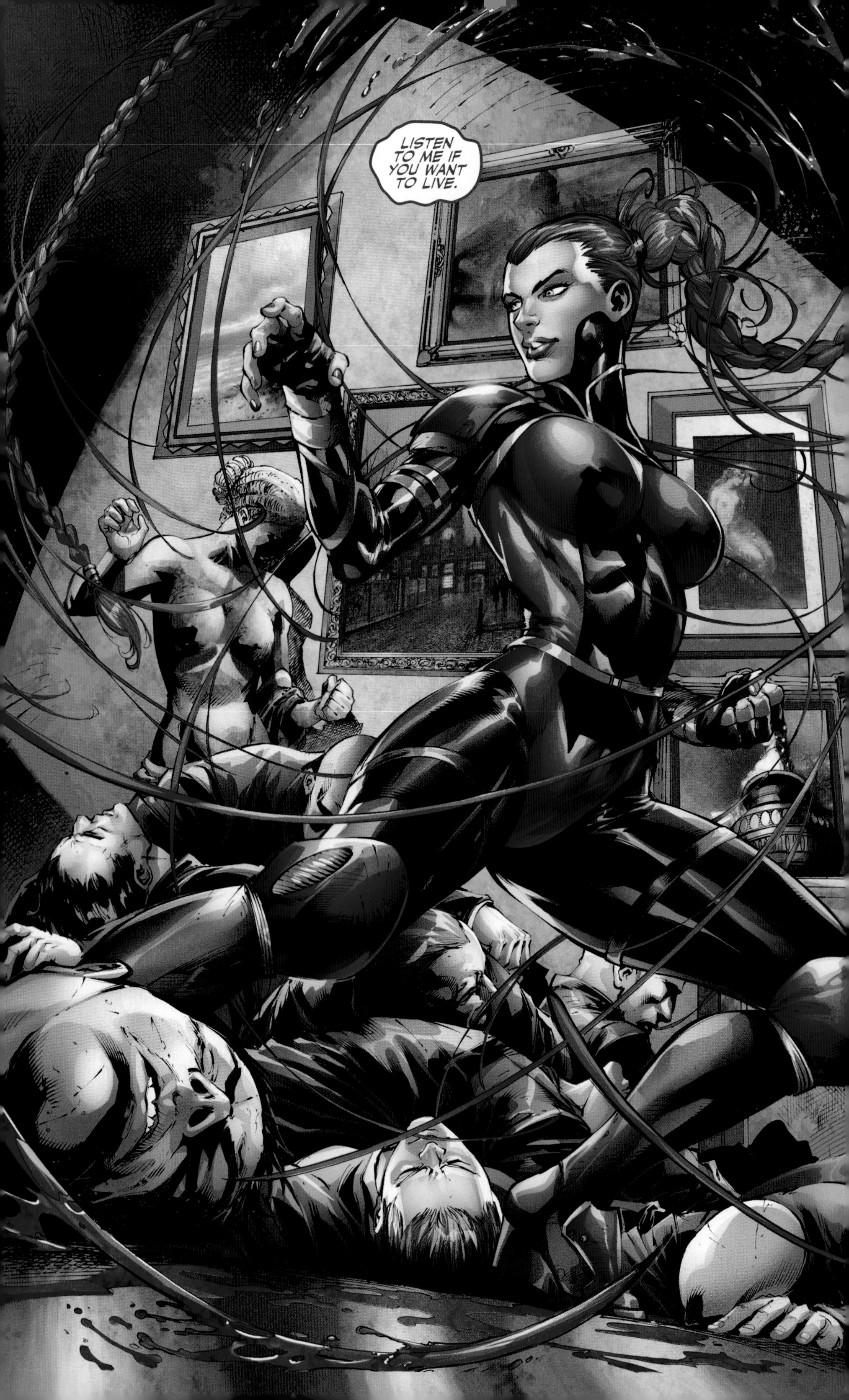
LISTEN TO ME IF YOU WANT TO LIVE.

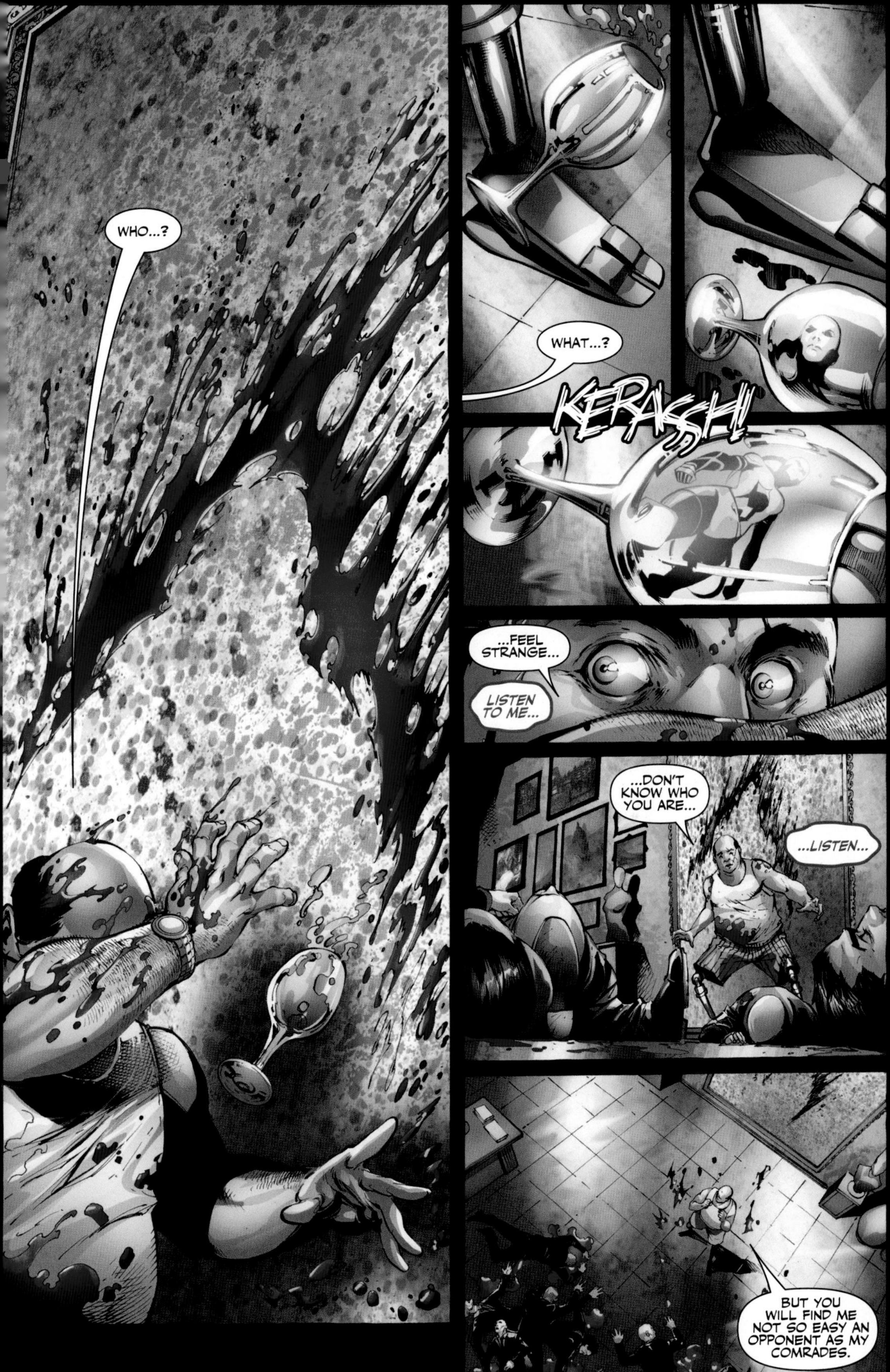
WHO...?
WHAT...?
KERASSH!
...FEEL STRANGE...
LISTEN TO ME...
...DON'T KNOW WHO YOU ARE...
...LISTEN...
BUT YOU WILL FIND ME NOT SO EASY AN OPPONENT AS MY COMRADES.

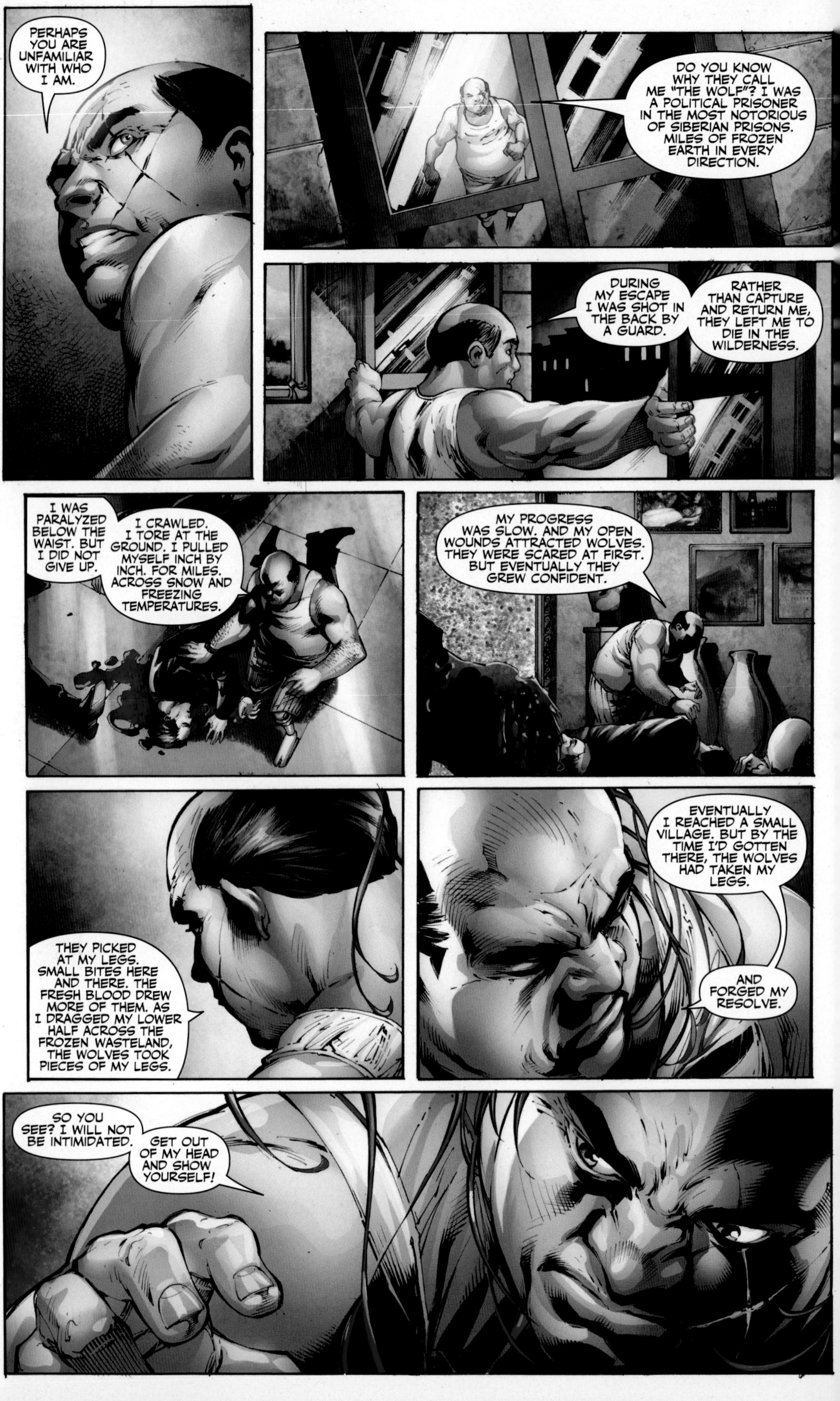

PERHAPS YOU ARE UNFAMILIAR WITH WHO I AM.
DO YOU KNOW WHY THEY CALL ME "THE WOLF"? I WAS A POLITICAL PRISONER IN THE MOST NOTORIOUS OF SIBERIAN PRISONS. MILES OF FROZEN EARTH IN EVERY DIRECTION.
DURING MY ESCAPE I WAS SHOT IN THE BACK BY A GUARD.
RATHER THAN CAPTURE AND RETURN ME, THEY LEFT ME TO DIE IN THE WILDERNESS.
I WAS PARALYZED BELOW THE WAIST. BUT I DID NOT GIVE UP.
I CRAWLED. I TORE AT THE GROUND. I PULLED MYSELF INCH BY INCH. FOR MILES. ACROSS SNOW AND FREEZING TEMPERATURES.
MY PROGRESS WAS SLOW. AND MY OPEN WOUNDS ATTRACTED WOLVES. THEY WERE SCARED AT FIRST. BUT EVENTUALLY THEY GREW CONFIDENT.
THEY PICKED AT MY LEGS. SMALL BITES HERE AND THERE. THE FRESH BLOOD DREW MORE OF THEM. AS I DRAGGED MY LOWER HALF ACROSS THE FROZEN WASTELAND, THE WOLVES TOOK PIECES OF MY LEGS.
EVENTUALLY I REACHED A SMALL VILLAGE. BUT BY THE TIME I'D GOTTEN THERE, THE WOLVES HAD TAKEN MY LEGS.
AND FORGED MY RESOLVE.
SO YOU SEE? I WILL NOT BE INTIMIDATED.
GET OUT OF MY HEAD AND SHOW YOURSELF!

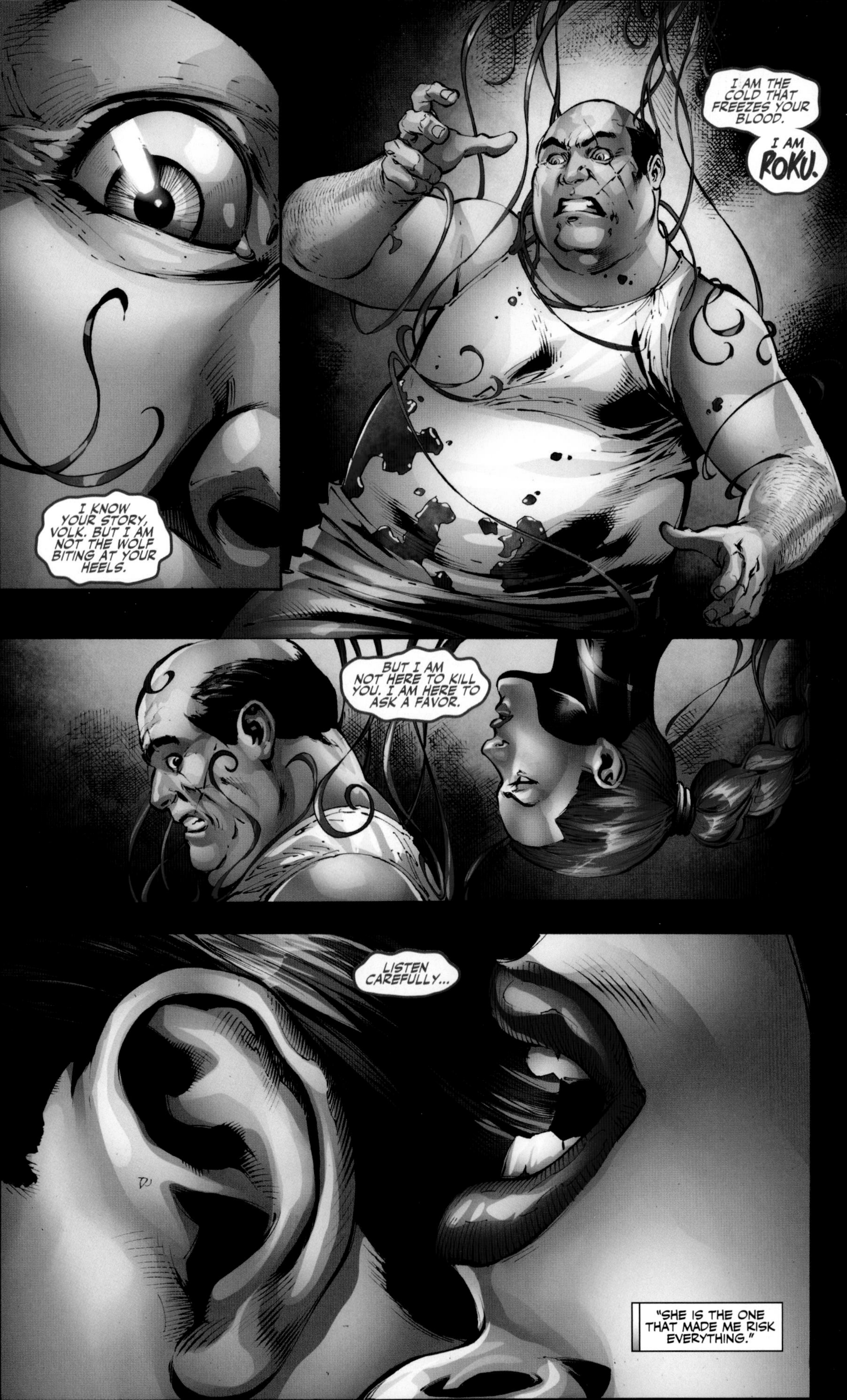
I AM THE COLD THAT FREEZES YOUR BLOOD.
I AM ROKU.
I KNOW YOUR STORY, VOLK. BUT I AM NOT THE WOLF BITING AT YOUR HEELS.
BUT I AM NOT HERE TO KILL YOU. I AM HERE TO ASK A FAVOR.
LISTEN CAREFULLY...
"SHE IS THE ONE THAT MADE ME RISK EVERYTHING."

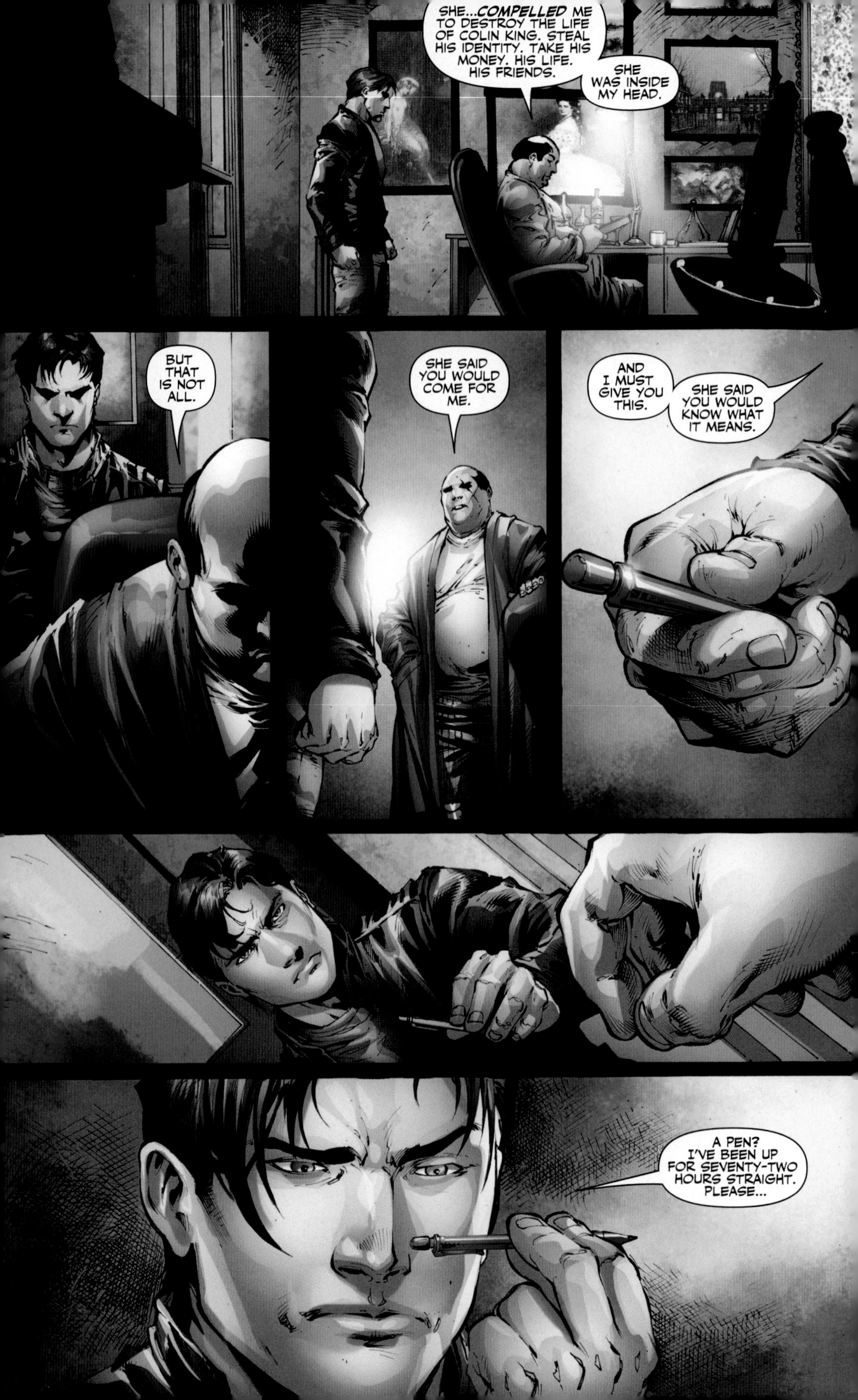
SHE...*COMPELLED* ME TO DESTROY THE LIFE OF COLIN KING. STEAL HIS IDENTITY. TAKE HIS MONEY. HIS LIFE. HIS FRIENDS.
SHE WAS INSIDE MY HEAD.
BUT THAT IS NOT ALL.
SHE SAID YOU WOULD COME FOR ME.
AND I MUST GIVE YOU THIS.
SHE SAID YOU WOULD KNOW WHAT IT MEANS.
A PEN? I'VE BEEN UP FOR SEVENTY-TWO HOURS STRAIGHT. PLEASE...

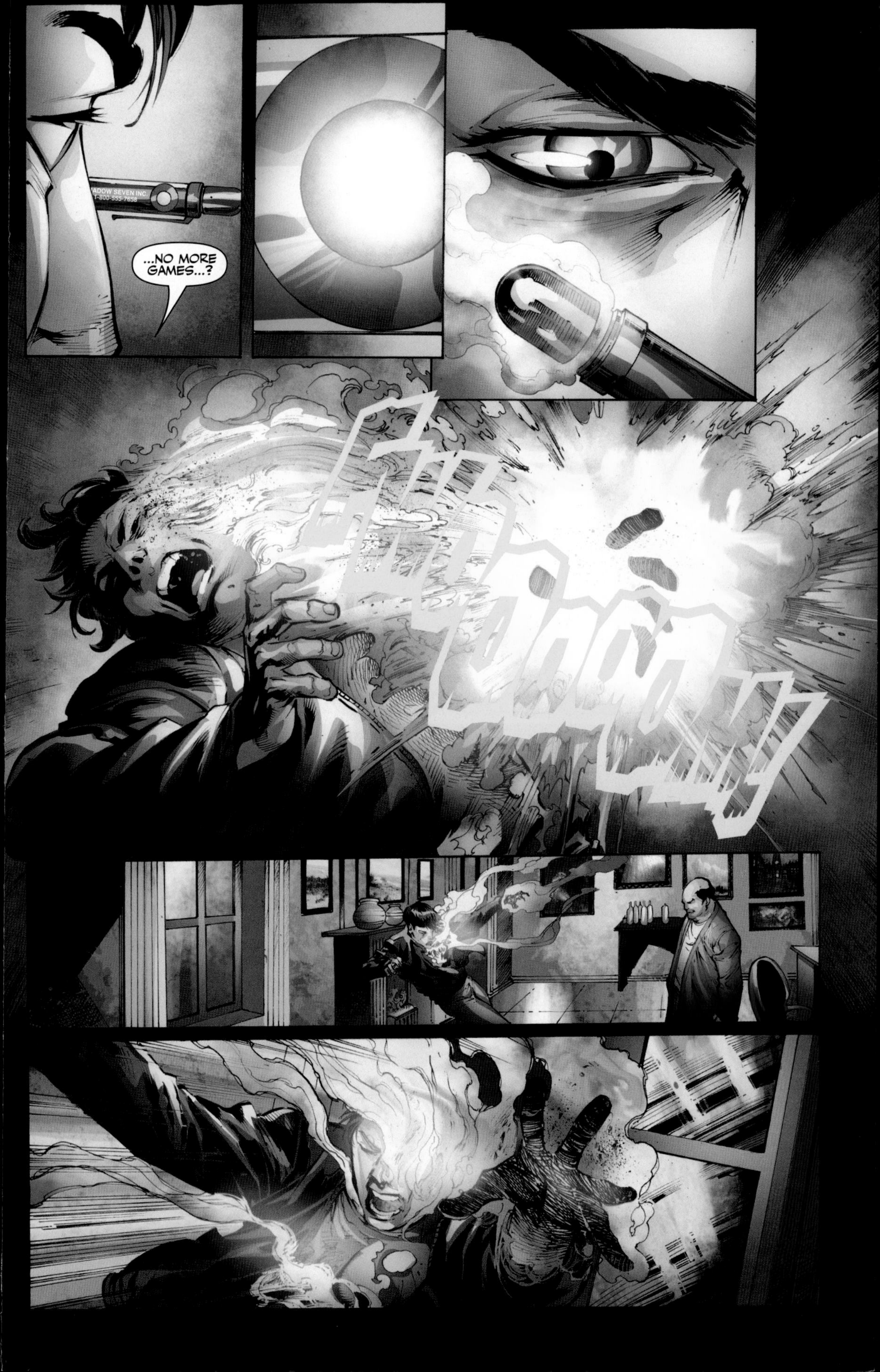
ADOW SEVEN INC.
1-800-555-7658
...NO MORE GAMES...?

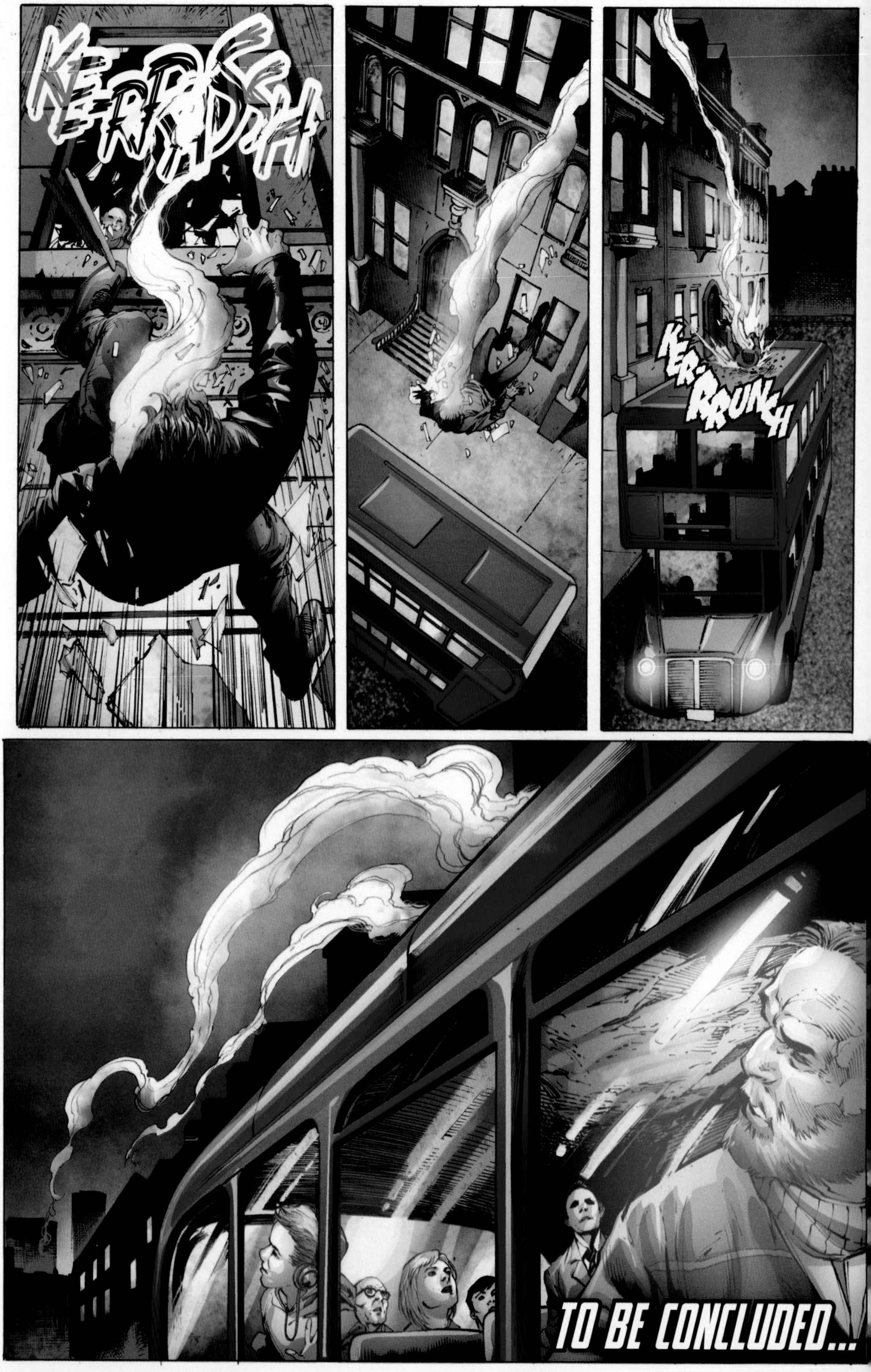
KER-RASSH
KER-RRUNCH
TO BE CONCLUDED...

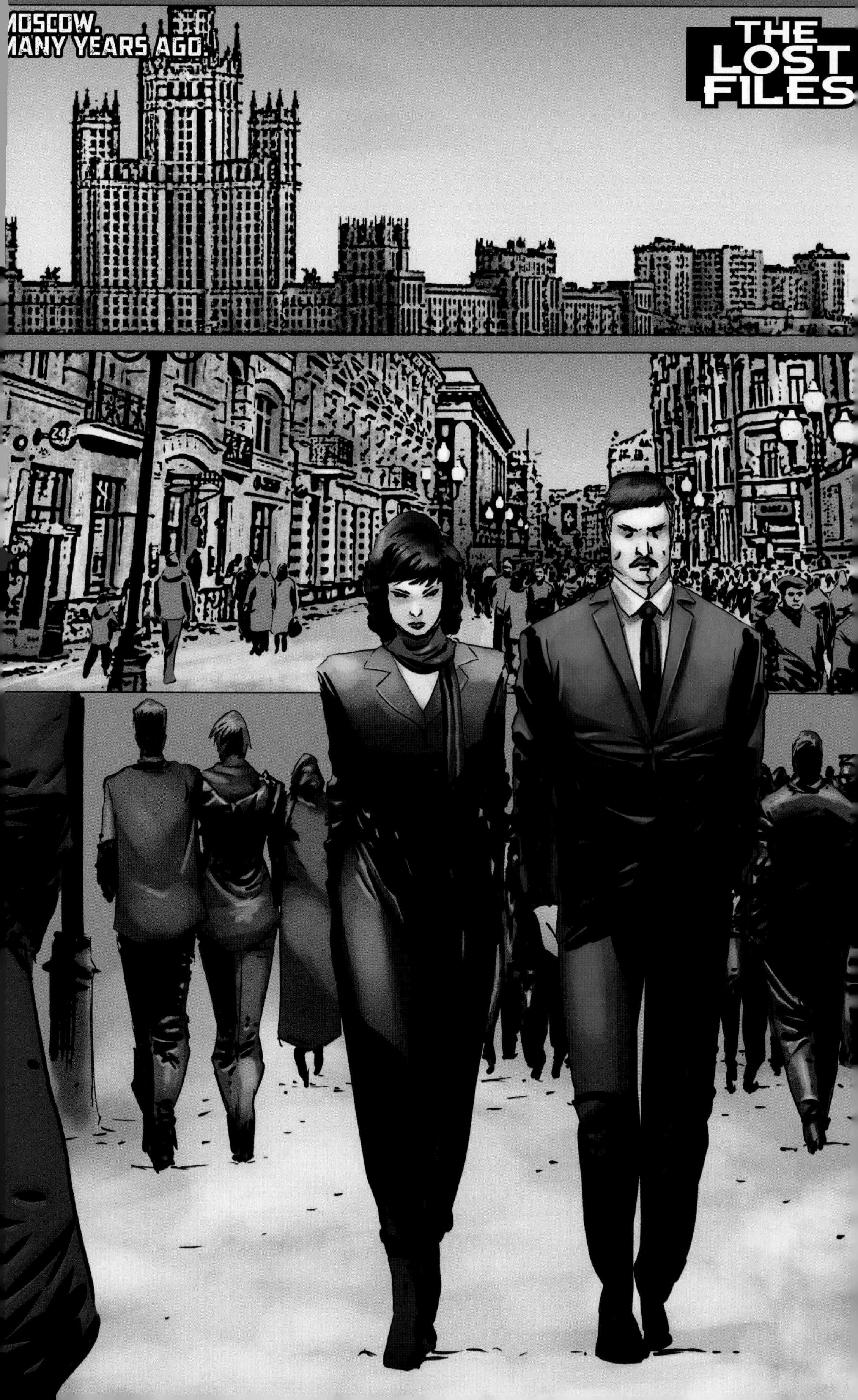
THE LOST FILES
MOSCOW.
MANY YEARS AGO.

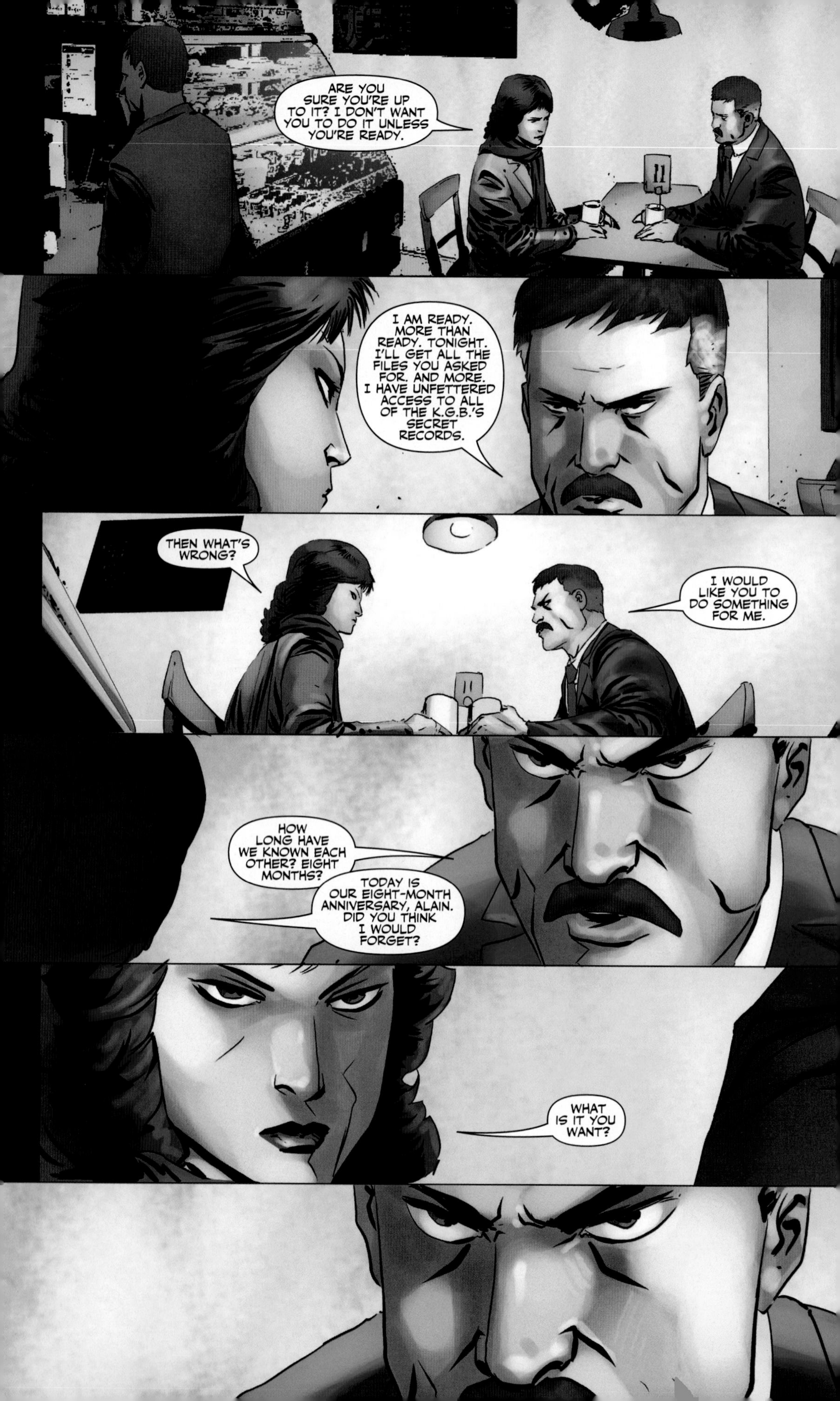
ARE YOU SURE YOU'RE UP TO IT? I DON'T WANT YOU TO DO IT UNLESS YOU'RE READY.
I AM READY. MORE THAN READY. TONIGHT. I'LL GET ALL THE FILES YOU ASKED FOR. AND MORE. I HAVE UNFETTERED ACCESS TO ALL OF THE K.G.B.'S SECRET RECORDS.
THEN WHAT'S WRONG?
I WOULD LIKE YOU TO DO SOMETHING FOR ME.
HOW LONG HAVE WE KNOWN EACH OTHER? EIGHT MONTHS?
TODAY IS OUR EIGHT-MONTH ANNIVERSARY, ALAIN. DID YOU THINK I WOULD FORGET?
WHAT IS IT YOU WANT?

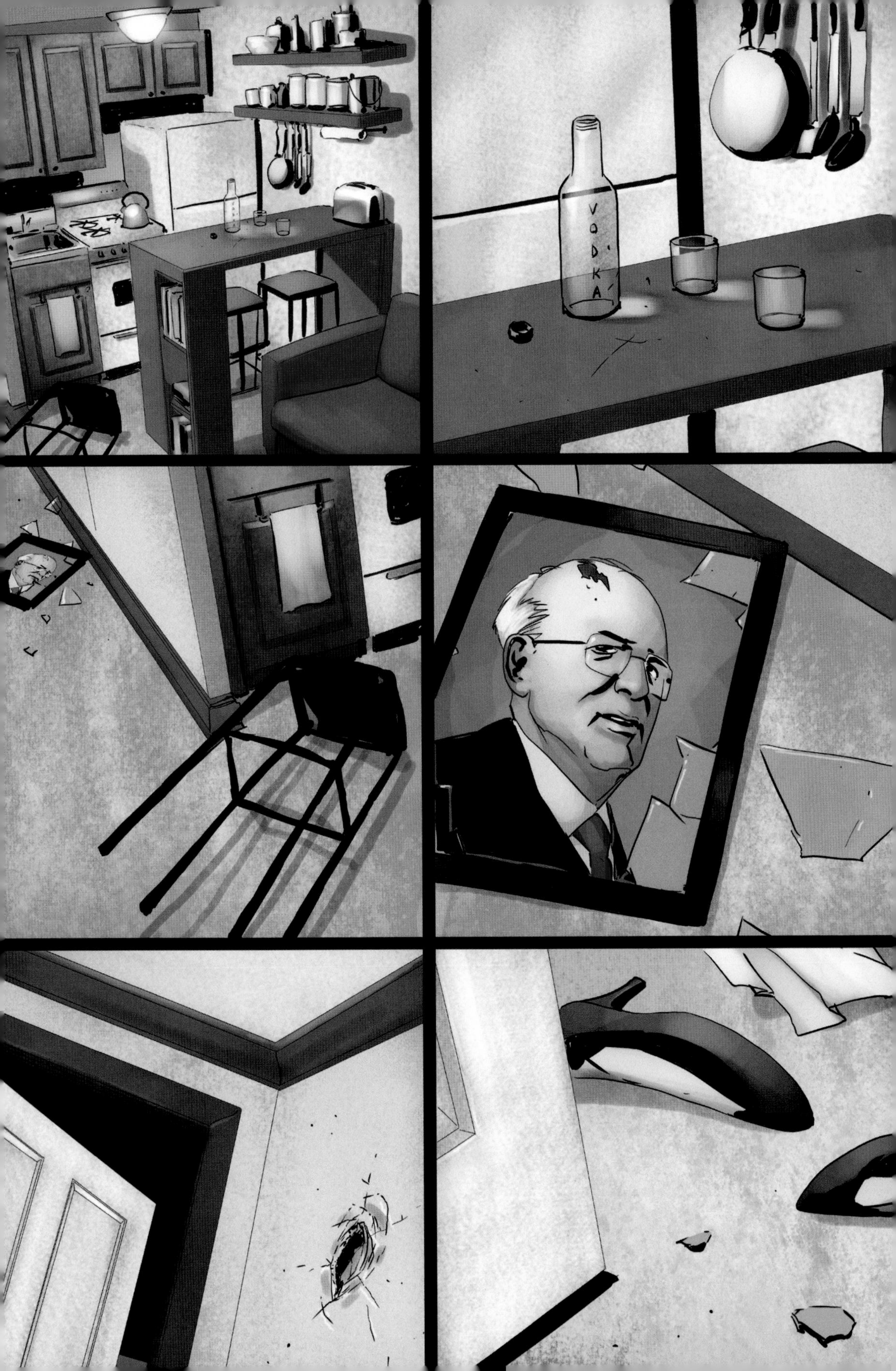
VODKA

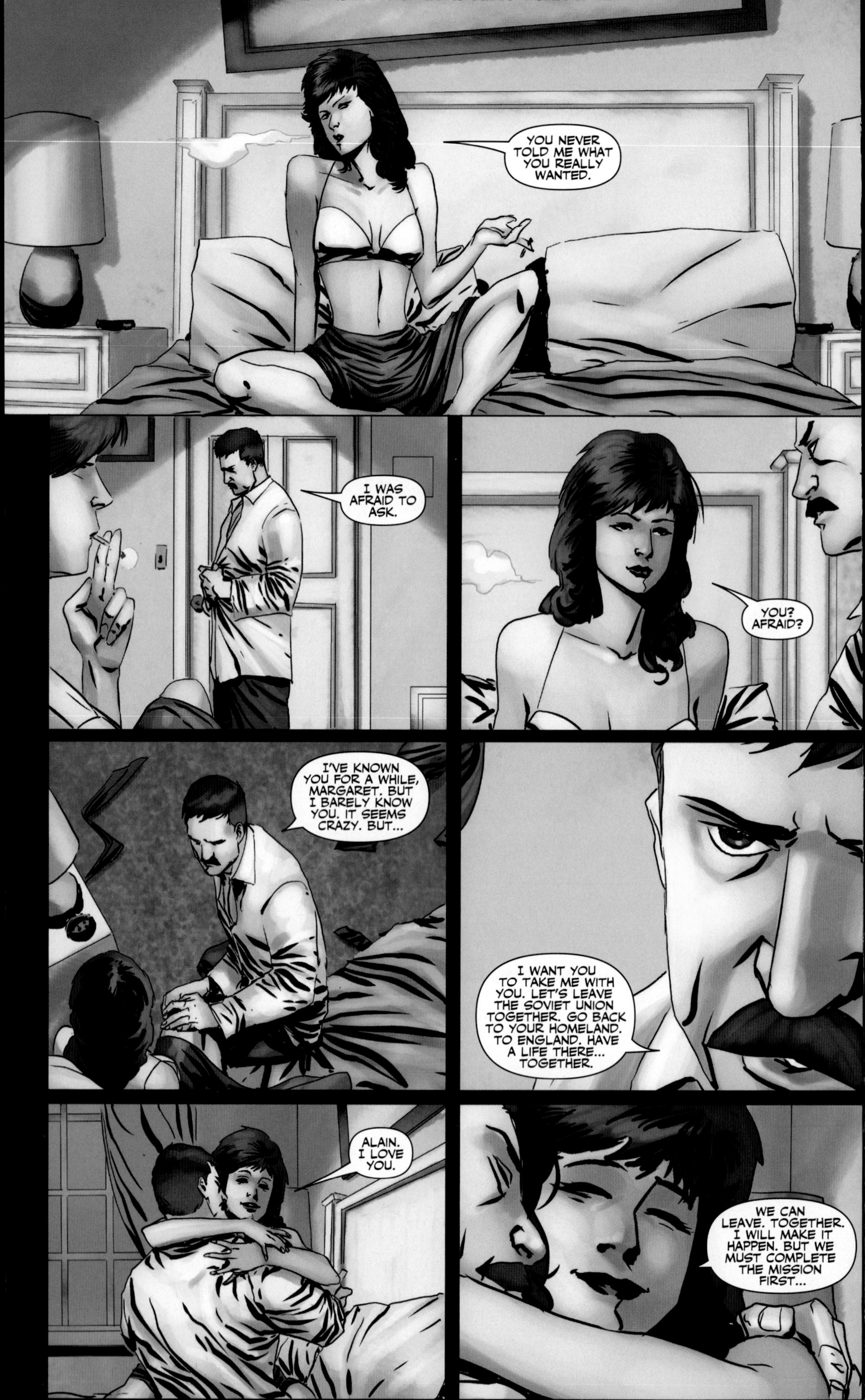
YOU NEVER TOLD ME WHAT YOU REALLY WANTED.
I WAS AFRAID TO ASK.
YOU? AFRAID?
I'VE KNOWN YOU FOR A WHILE, MARGARET. BUT I BARELY KNOW YOU. IT SEEMS CRAZY. BUT...
I WANT YOU TO TAKE ME WITH YOU. LET'S LEAVE THE SOVIET UNION TOGETHER. GO BACK TO YOUR HOMELAND. TO ENGLAND. HAVE A LIFE THERE... TOGETHER.
ALAIN. I LOVE YOU.
WE CAN LEAVE. TOGETHER. I WILL MAKE IT HAPPEN. BUT WE MUST COMPLETE THE MISSION FIRST...

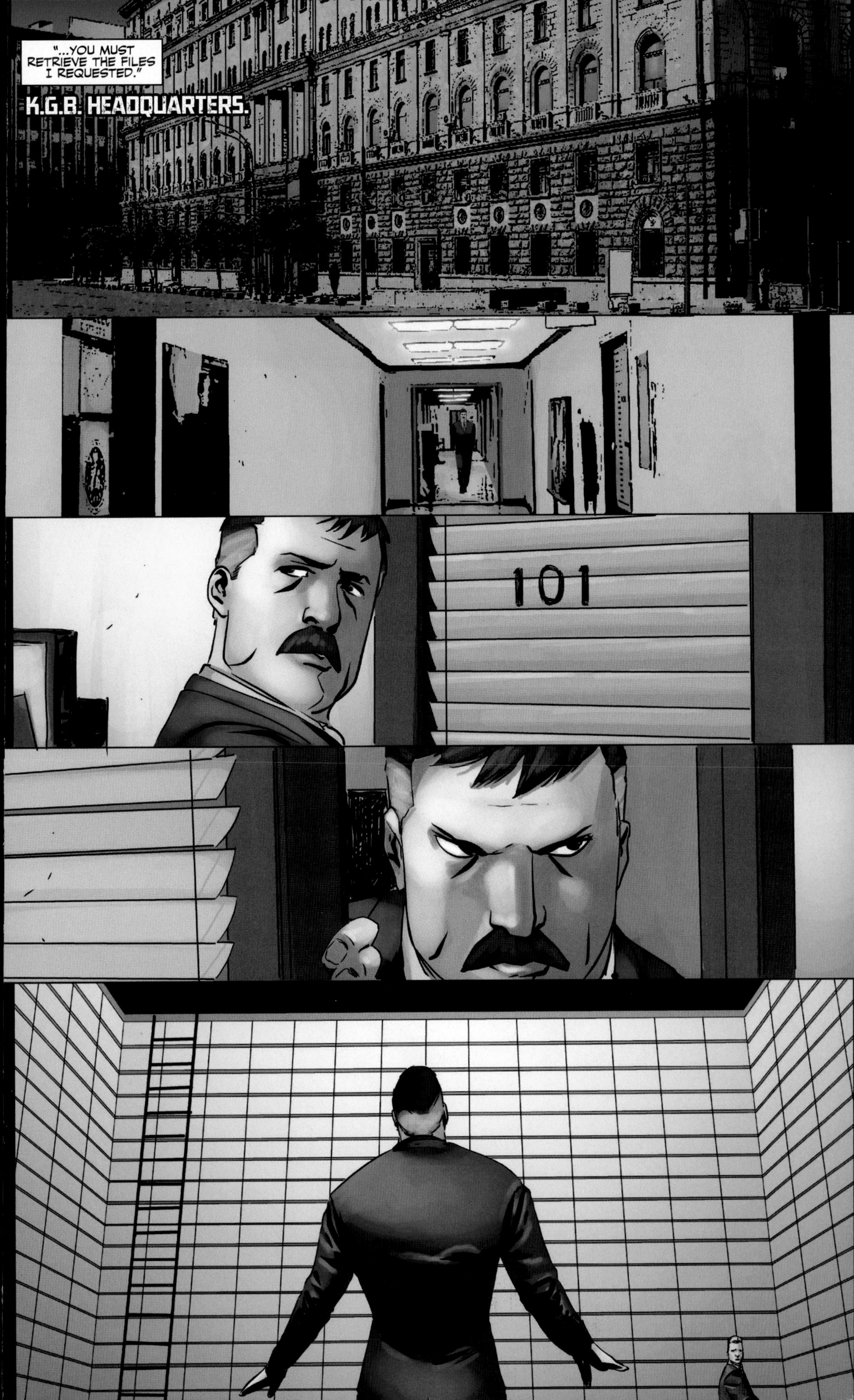
"...YOU MUST RETRIEVE THE FILES I REQUESTED."
K.G.B. HEADQUARTERS.
101

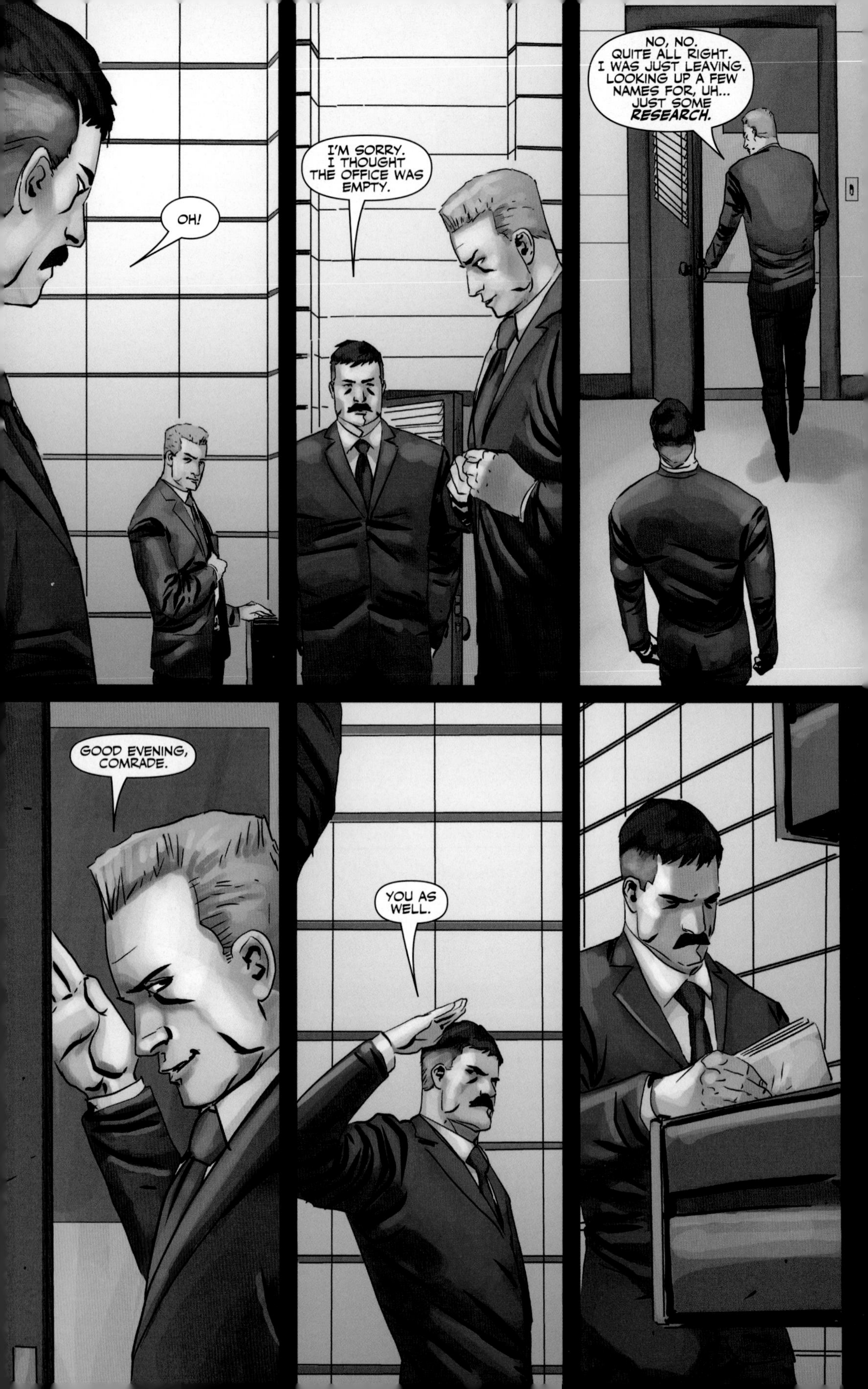
OH!
I'M SORRY. I THOUGHT THE OFFICE WAS EMPTY.
NO, NO. QUITE ALL RIGHT. I WAS JUST LEAVING. LOOKING UP A FEW NAMES FOR, UH... JUST SOME *RESEARCH.*
GOOD EVENING, COMRADE.
YOU AS WELL.

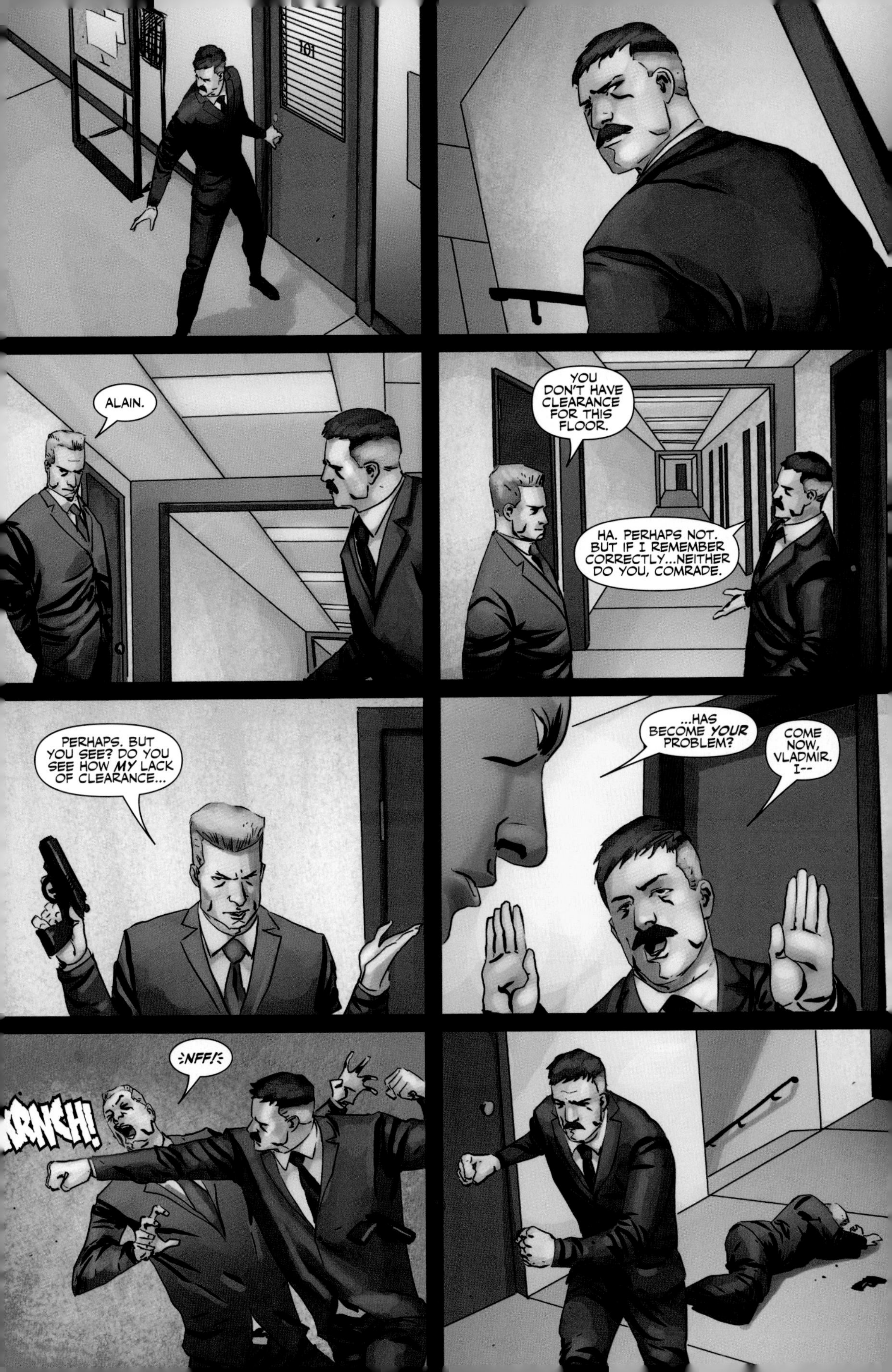

ALAIN.
YOU DON'T HAVE CLEARANCE FOR THIS FLOOR.
HA. PERHAPS NOT. BUT IF I REMEMBER CORRECTLY...NEITHER DO YOU, COMRADE.
PERHAPS. BUT YOU SEE? DO YOU SEE HOW *MY* LACK OF CLEARANCE...
...HAS BECOME *YOUR* PROBLEM?
COME NOW, VLADMIR. I--
RNCH!
NFF!

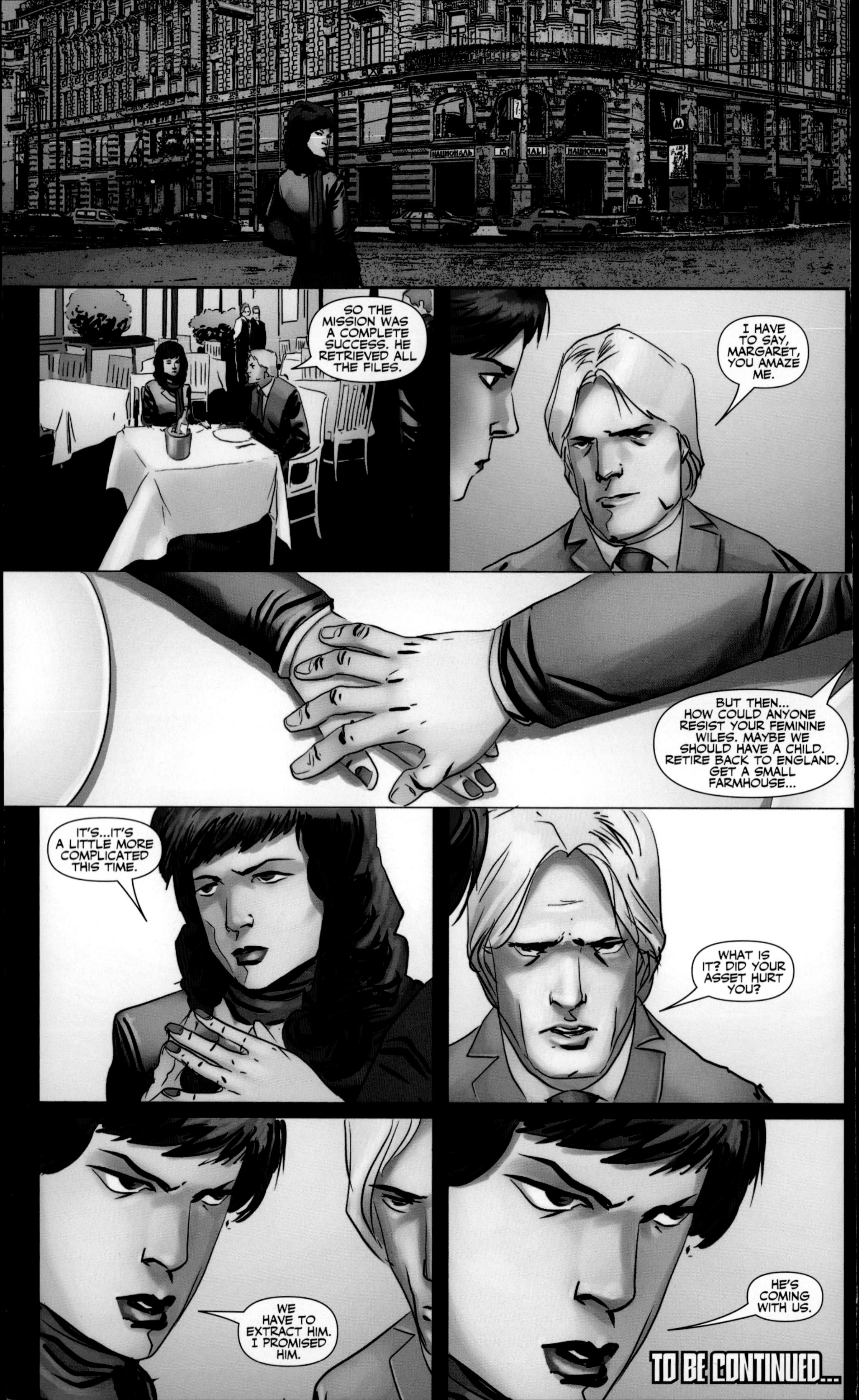

НАЦИОНАЛЬ
SO THE MISSION WAS A COMPLETE SUCCESS. HE RETRIEVED ALL THE FILES.
I HAVE TO SAY, MARGARET, YOU AMAZE ME.
BUT THEN... HOW COULD ANYONE RESIST YOUR FEMININE WILES. MAYBE WE SHOULD HAVE A CHILD. RETIRE BACK TO ENGLAND. GET A SMALL FARMHOUSE...
IT'S...IT'S A LITTLE MORE COMPLICATED THIS TIME.
WHAT IS IT? DID YOUR ASSET HURT YOU?
WE HAVE TO EXTRACT HIM. I PROMISED HIM.
HE'S COMING WITH US.
TO BE CONTINUED...

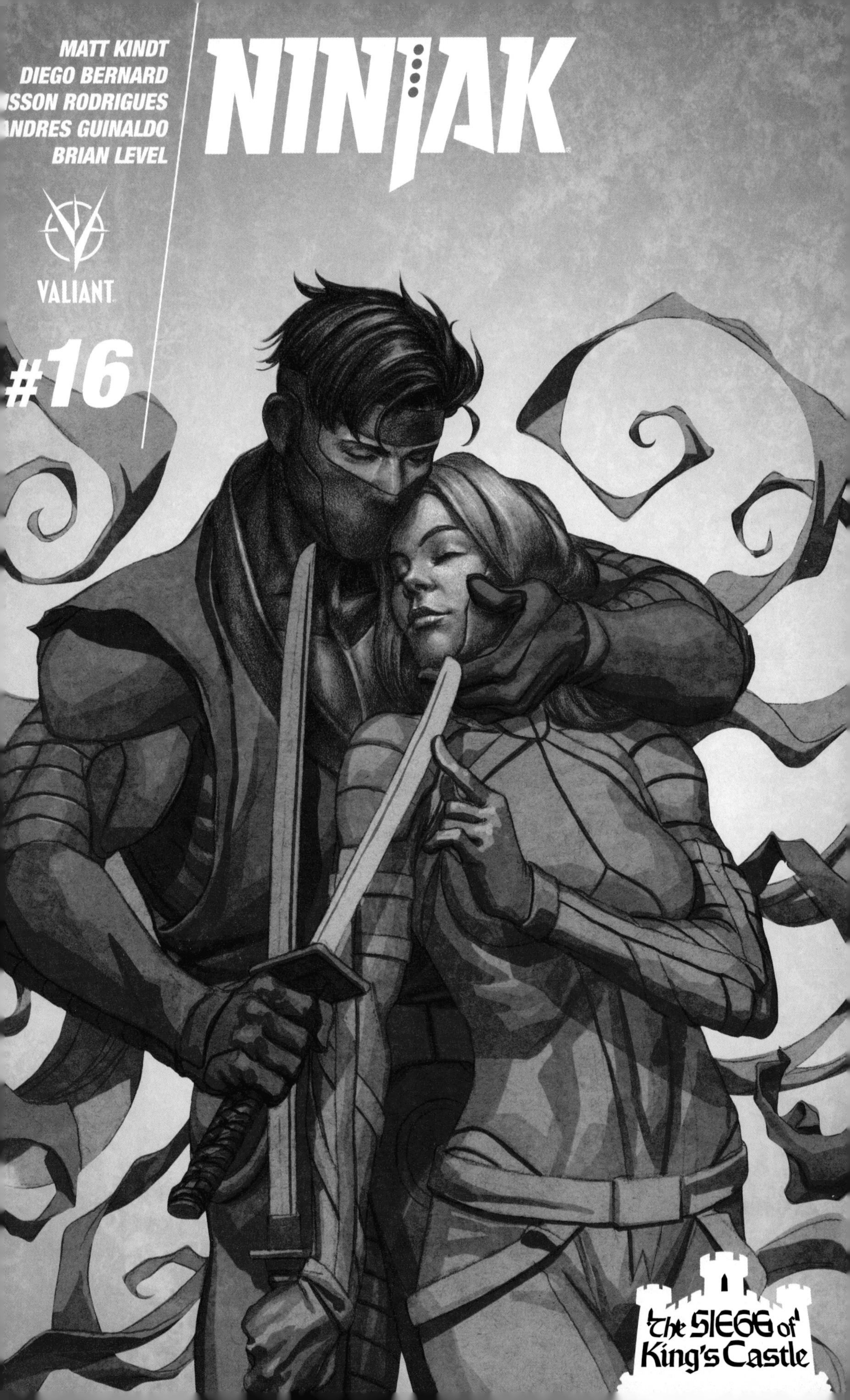
MATT KINDT
DIEGO BERNARD
ISSON RODRIGUES
ANDRES GUINALDO
BRIAN LEVEL
NINJAK
VALIANT
#16
The SIEGE of King's Castle

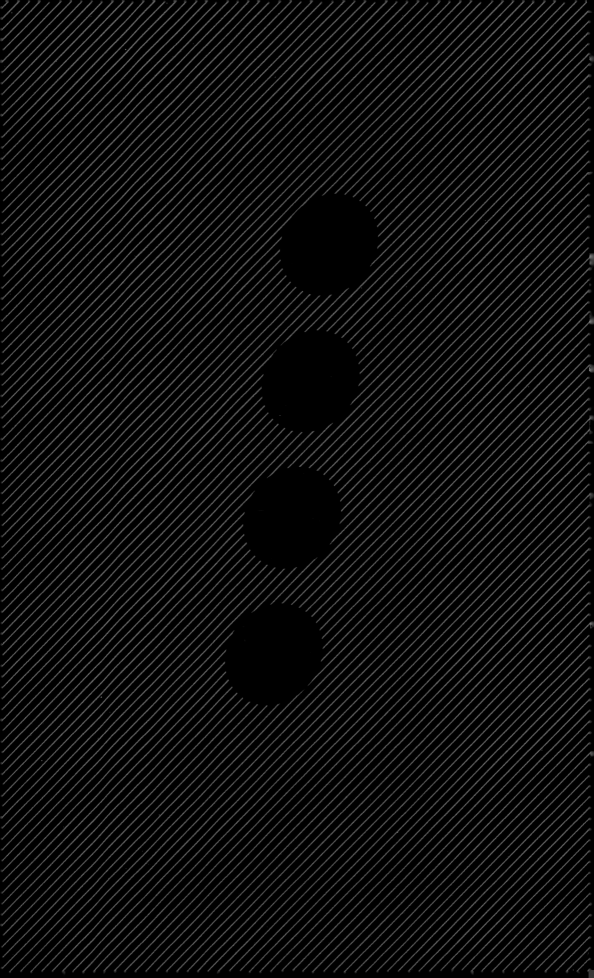

I KNEW IT WAS A TRAP FROM THE BEGINNING.

AND NOW I KNOW WHO IT IS.

BUT WHY DID SHE DO IT?

THERE ARE EASIER WAYS TO GET TO ME.

EASIER THAN DESTROYING MY ENTIRE CASTLE.

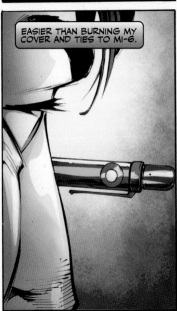

EASIER THAN BURNING MY COVER AND TIES TO MI-6.

EASIER THAN SABOTAGING DOZENS OF MY SAFE-HOUSES AND WEAPONS AND MONEY CACHES.

EASIER THAN FRAMING ME FOR MURDER.

ALL OF THIS IS ONE ELABORATE TRAP.

THE PEN. THE EXPLOSIVES.

THIS ISN'T ABOUT KILLING ME.

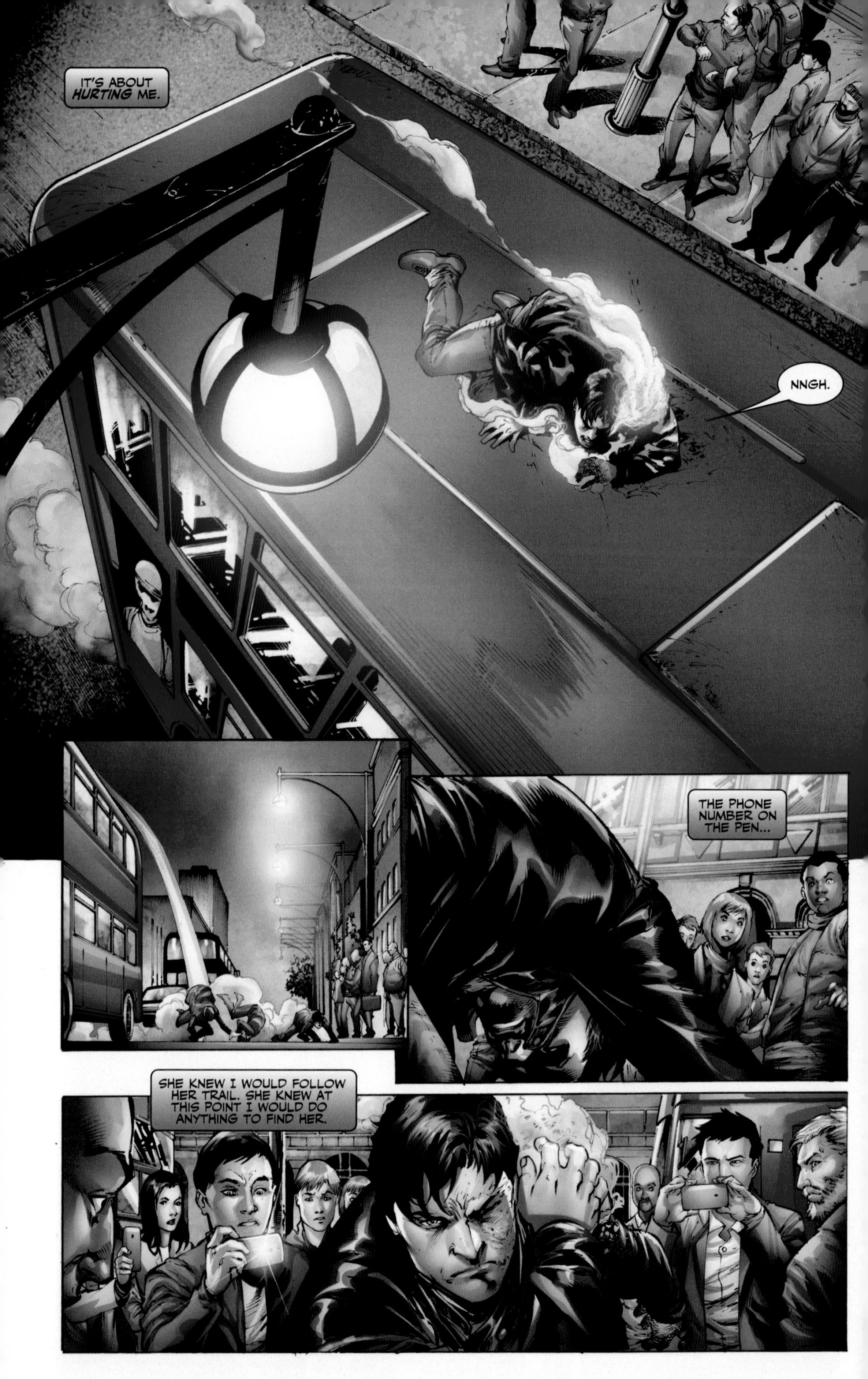
IT'S ABOUT HURTING ME.
NNGH.
THE PHONE NUMBER ON THE PEN...
SHE KNEW I WOULD FOLLOW HER TRAIL. SHE KNEW AT THIS POINT I WOULD DO ANYTHING TO FIND HER.

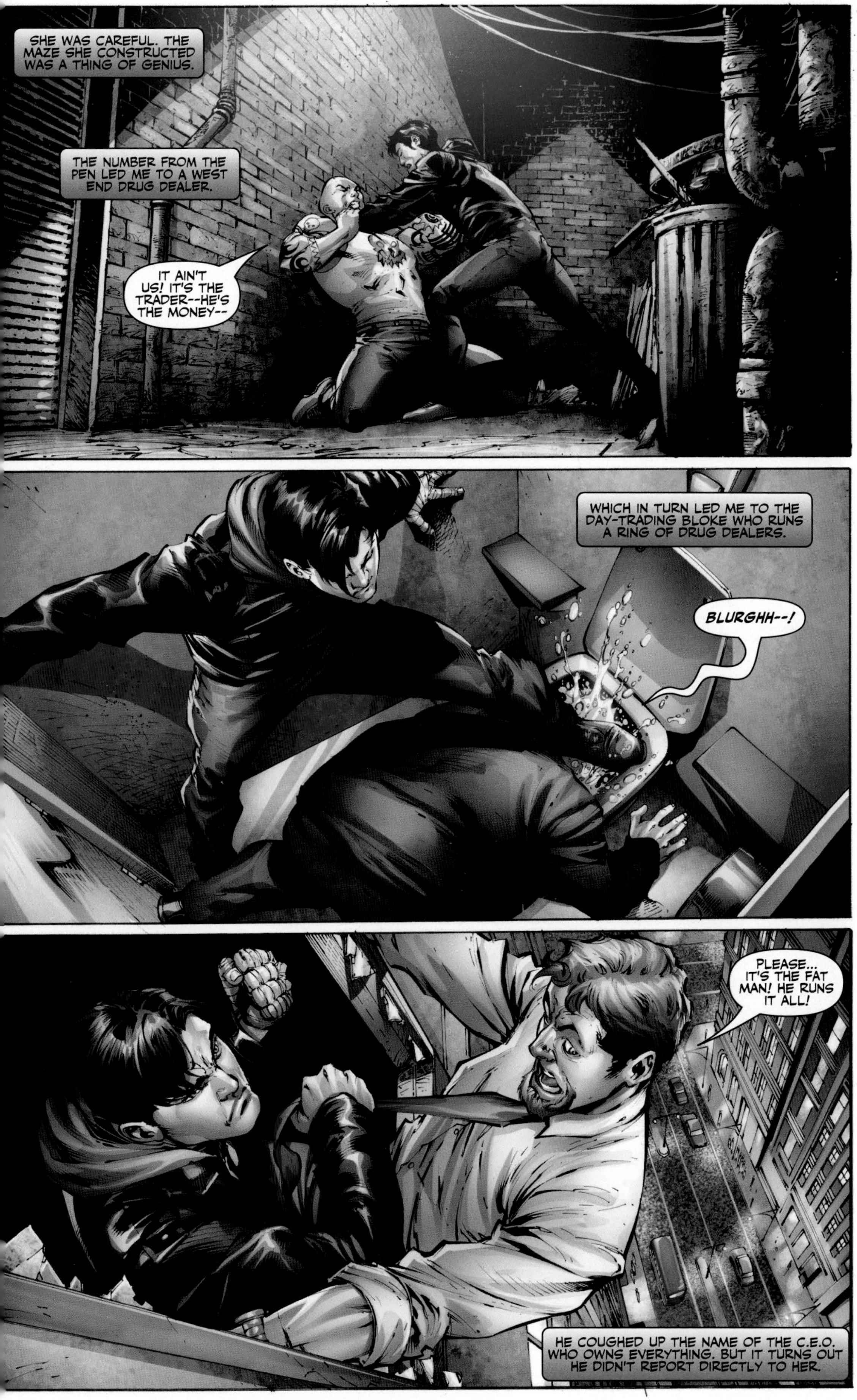
SHE WAS CAREFUL. THE MAZE SHE CONSTRUCTED WAS A THING OF GENIUS.
THE NUMBER FROM THE PEN LED ME TO A WEST END DRUG DEALER.
IT AIN'T US! IT'S THE TRADER--HE'S THE MONEY--
WHICH IN TURN LED ME TO THE DAY-TRADING BLOKE WHO RUNS A RING OF DRUG DEALERS.
BLURGHH--!
PLEASE... IT'S THE FAT MAN! HE RUNS IT ALL!
HE COUGHED UP THE NAME OF THE C.E.O. WHO OWNS EVERYTHING. BUT IT TURNS OUT HE DIDN'T REPORT DIRECTLY TO HER.

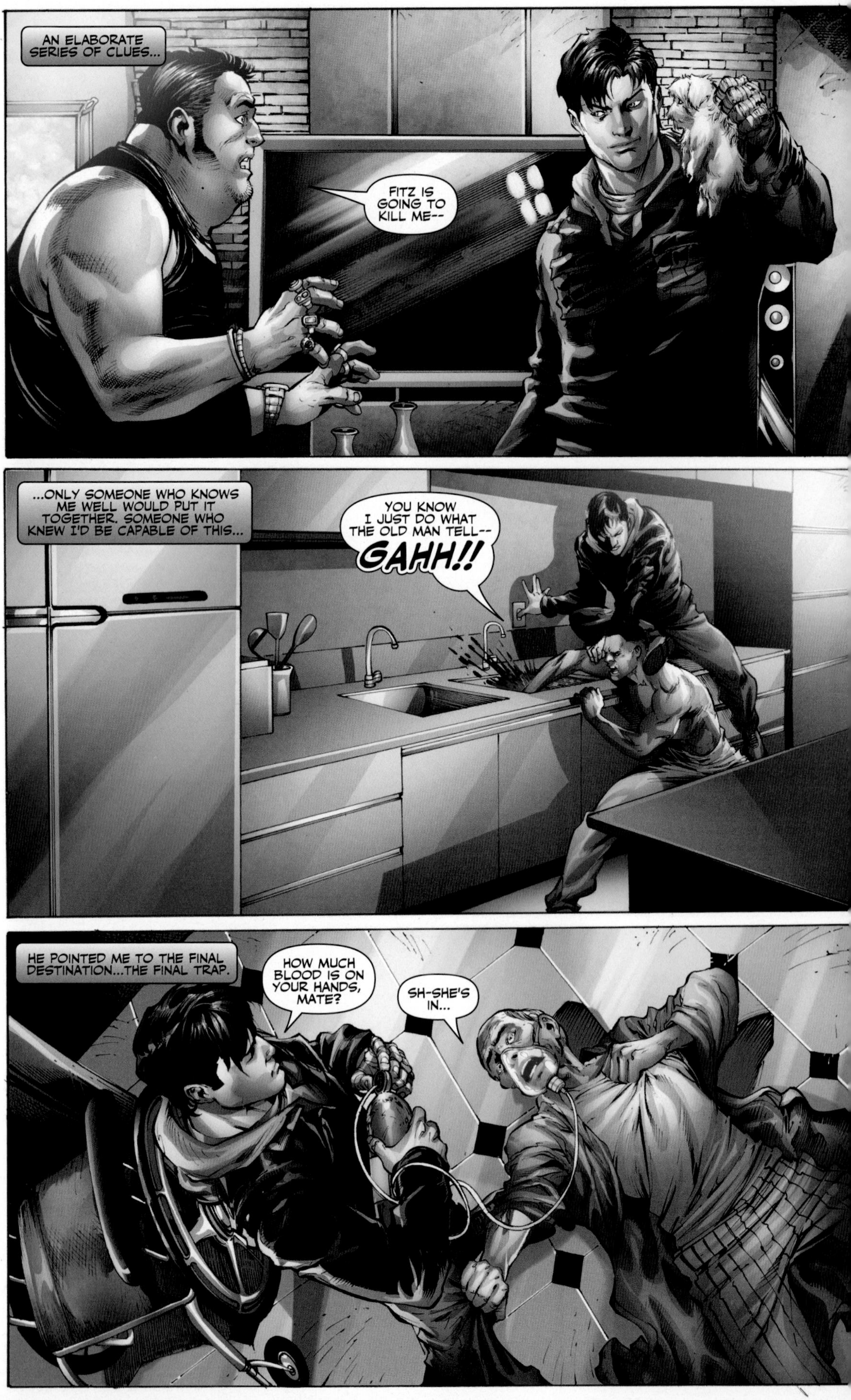
AN ELABORATE SERIES OF CLUES...
FITZ IS GOING TO KILL ME--
...ONLY SOMEONE WHO KNOWS ME WELL WOULD PUT IT TOGETHER. SOMEONE WHO KNEW I'D BE CAPABLE OF THIS...
YOU KNOW I JUST DO WHAT THE OLD MAN TELL-- GAHH!!
HE POINTED ME TO THE FINAL DESTINATION...THE FINAL TRAP.
HOW MUCH BLOOD IS ON YOUR HANDS, MATE?
SH-SHE'S IN...

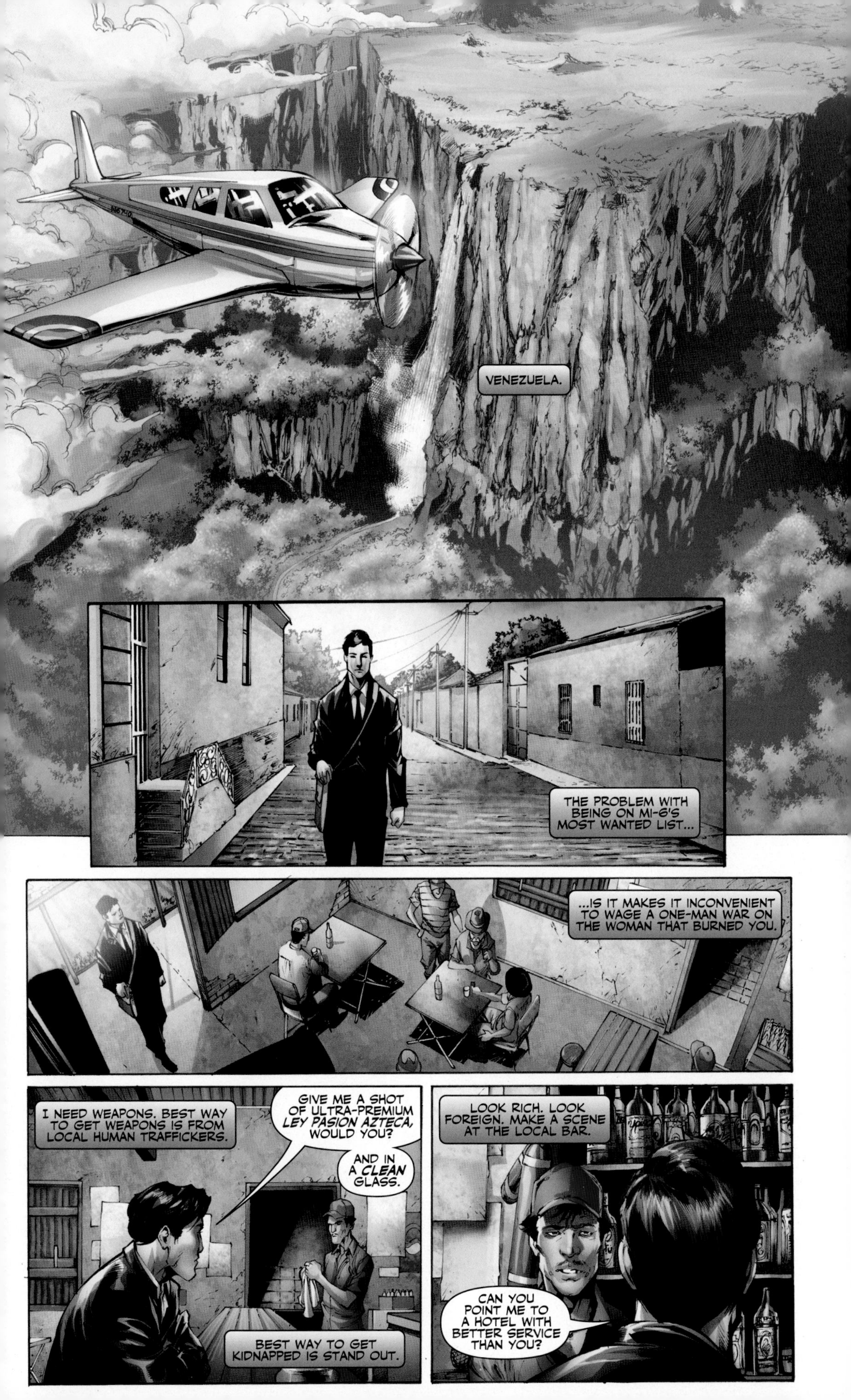
VENEZUELA.
THE PROBLEM WITH BEING ON MI-6'S MOST WANTED LIST...
...IS IT MAKES IT INCONVENIENT TO WAGE A ONE-MAN WAR ON THE WOMAN THAT BURNED YOU.
I NEED WEAPONS. BEST WAY TO GET WEAPONS IS FROM LOCAL HUMAN TRAFFICKERS.
GIVE ME A SHOT OF ULTRA-PREMIUM *LEY PASION AZTECA,* WOULD YOU?
AND IN A *CLEAN* GLASS.
BEST WAY TO GET KIDNAPPED IS STAND OUT.
LOOK RICH. LOOK FOREIGN. MAKE A SCENE AT THE LOCAL BAR.
CAN YOU POINT ME TO A HOTEL WITH BETTER SERVICE THAN YOU?

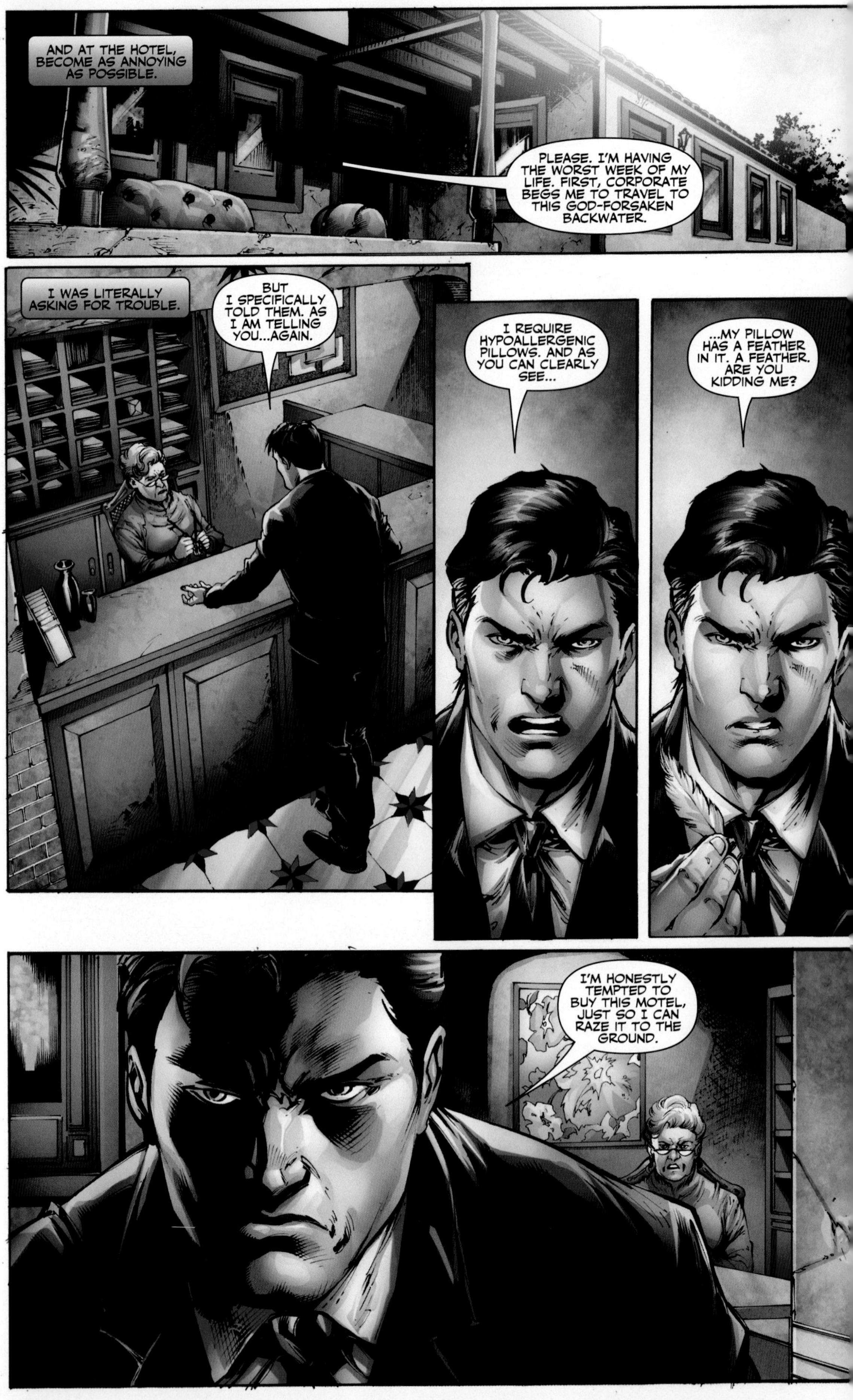
AND AT THE HOTEL, BECOME AS ANNOYING AS POSSIBLE.
PLEASE. I'M HAVING THE WORST WEEK OF MY LIFE. FIRST, CORPORATE BEGS ME TO TRAVEL TO THIS GOD-FORSAKEN BACKWATER.
I WAS LITERALLY ASKING FOR TROUBLE.
BUT I SPECIFICALLY TOLD THEM. AS I AM TELLING YOU...AGAIN.
I REQUIRE HYPOALLERGENIC PILLOWS. AND AS YOU CAN CLEARLY SEE...
...MY PILLOW HAS A FEATHER IN IT. A FEATHER. ARE YOU KIDDING ME?
I'M HONESTLY TEMPTED TO BUY THIS MOTEL, JUST SO I CAN RAZE IT TO THE GROUND.

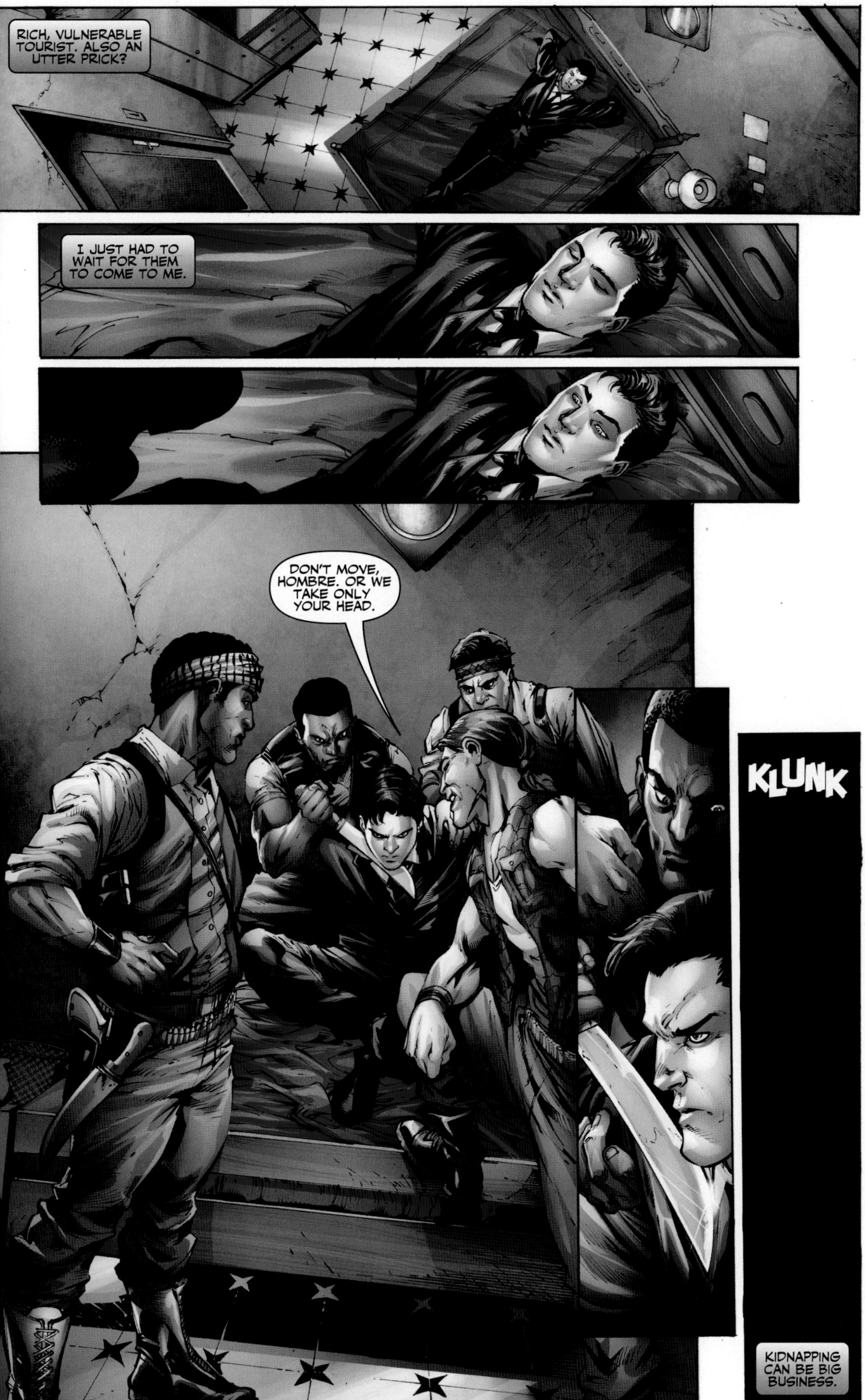
RICH, VULNERABLE TOURIST. ALSO AN UTTER PRICK?
I JUST HAD TO WAIT FOR THEM TO COME TO ME.
DON'T MOVE, HOMBRE. OR WE TAKE ONLY YOUR HEAD.
KLUNK
KIDNAPPING CAN BE BIG BUSINESS.

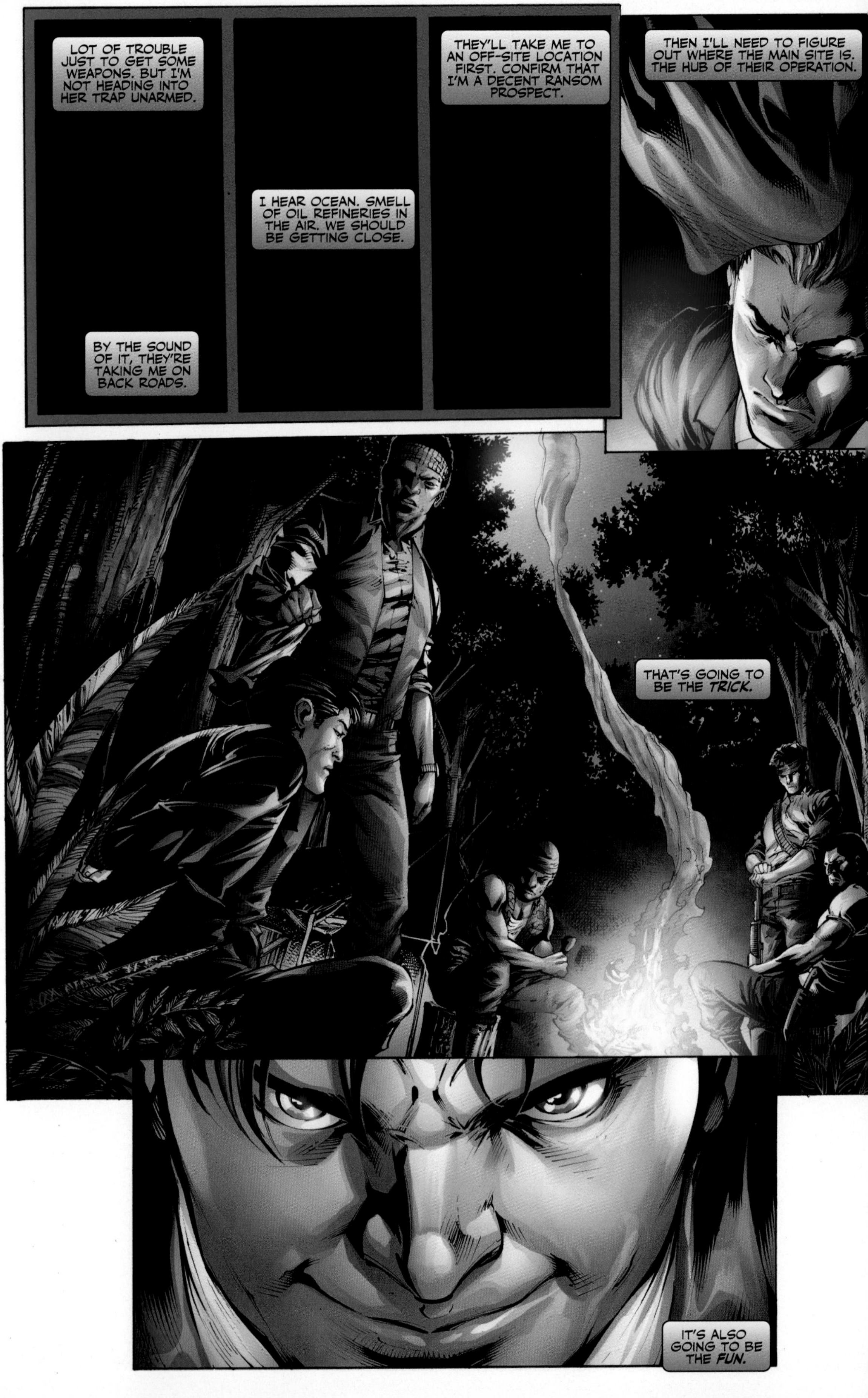
LOT OF TROUBLE JUST TO GET SOME WEAPONS. BUT I'M NOT HEADING INTO HER TRAP UNARMED.
BY THE SOUND OF IT, THEY'RE TAKING ME ON BACK ROADS.
I HEAR OCEAN. SMELL OF OIL REFINERIES IN THE AIR. WE SHOULD BE GETTING CLOSE.
THEY'LL TAKE ME TO AN OFF-SITE LOCATION FIRST. CONFIRM THAT I'M A DECENT RANSOM PROSPECT.
THEN I'LL NEED TO FIGURE OUT WHERE THE MAIN SITE IS. THE HUB OF THEIR OPERATION.
THAT'S GOING TO BE THE *TRICK.*
IT'S ALSO GOING TO BE THE *FUN.*

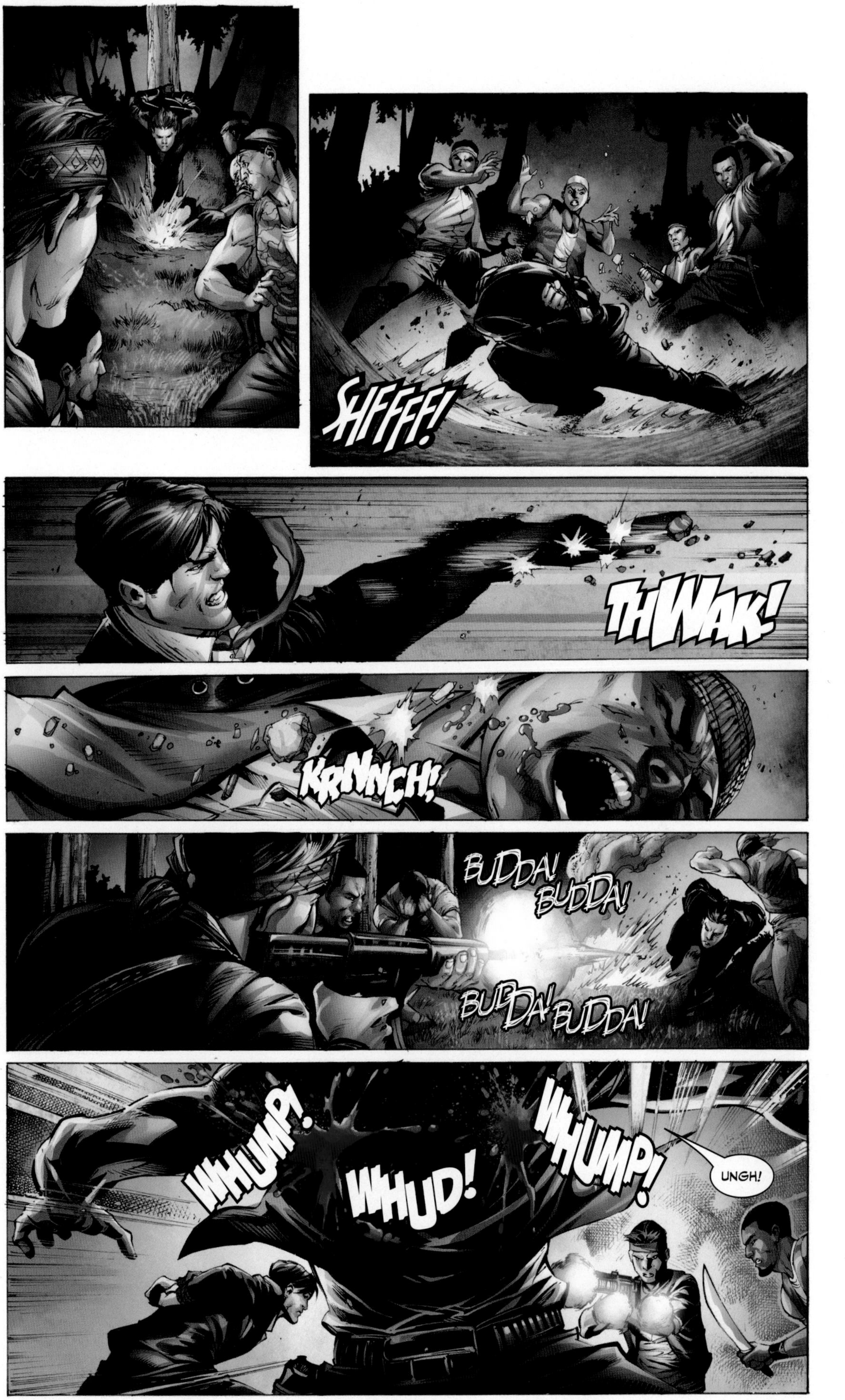
SHFFFF!
THWAK!
KRNNCH!
BUDDA! BUDDA!
BUDDA! BUDDA!
WHUMP!
WHUD!
WHUMP!
UNGH!

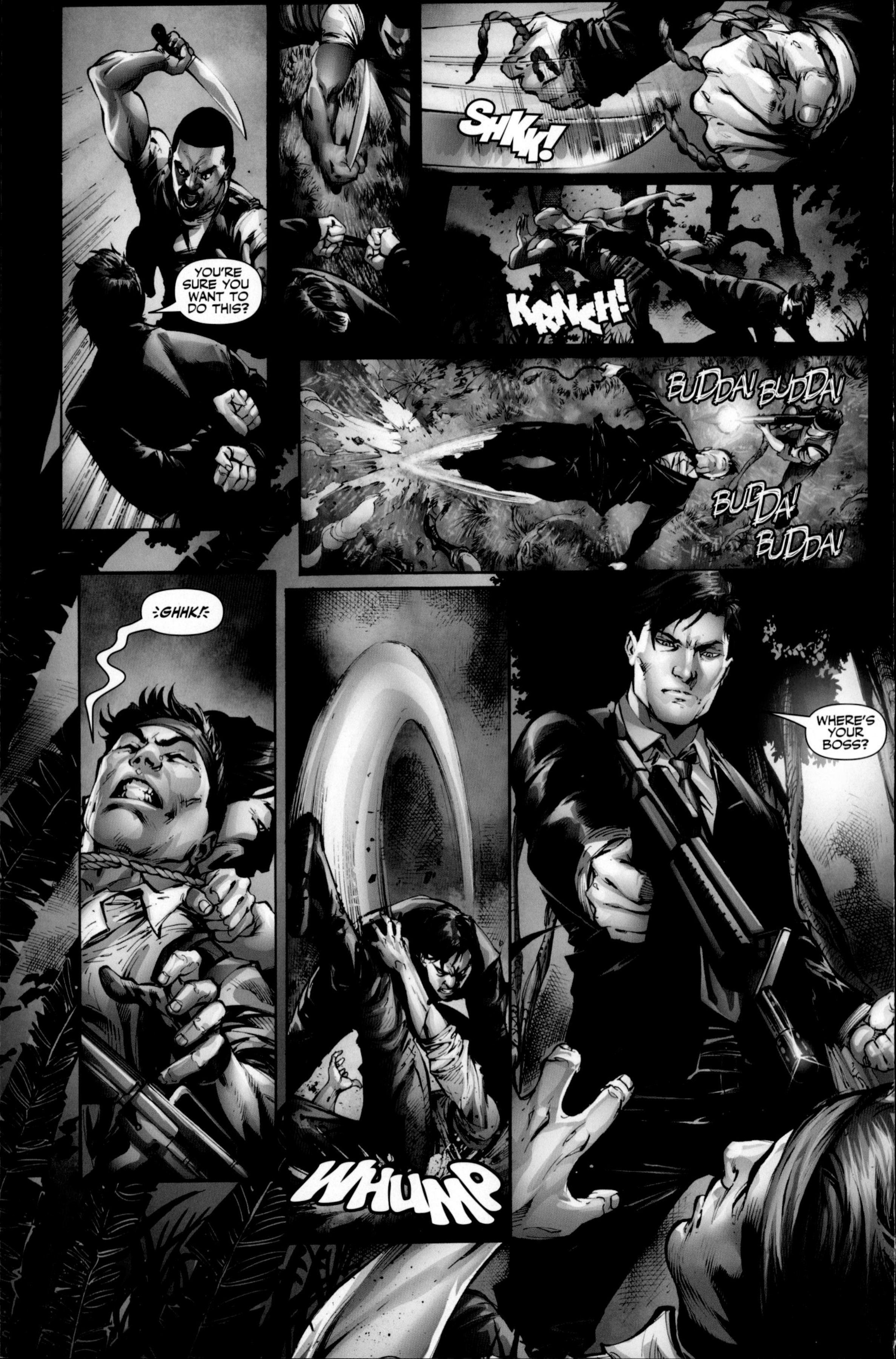

YOU'RE SURE YOU WANT TO DO THIS?
SHKK!
KRNCH!
BUDDA! BUDDA!
BUDDA!
BUDDA!
:GHHK!:
WHUMP
WHERE'S YOUR BOSS?

PETROCHEMICAL FACTORY
OUTSIDE OF CARACAS. PERFECT
COVER FOR HUMAN TRAFFICKING
AND DRUG SMUGGLING.

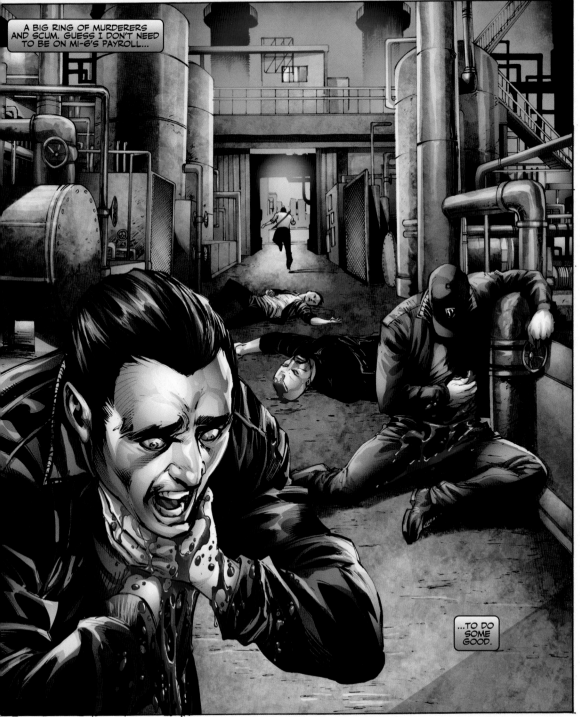

A BIG RING OF MURDERERS
AND SCUM. GUESS I DON'T NEED
TO BE ON MI-6'S PAYROLL...

...TO DO
SOME
GOOD.

I'LL MAKE THIS QUICK. YOU'RE DONE RANSOMING TOURISTS AND HUMAN TRAFFICKING. TELL ME WHERE THE WEAPONS CACHE IS AND I MIGHT LET YOU LIMP OUT OF HERE.

BRILLIANT. NOW TELL ME WHERE YOU KEEP THE REST OF YOUR HOSTAGES.

HURRY! GET OUT OF HERE!

IF THERE'S ANYTHING I'VE LEARNED OVER THE YEARS...

...IT'S HOW TO ACT.

I'VE BEEN ACTING FOR AS LONG AS I CAN REMEMBER. WEARING A MASK. FOR SO LONG IT'S EATEN UP ANYTHING THAT WAS REAL.

YOU KNOW I CAN'T LET YOU WALK AWAY FROM THIS, RIGHT?

Y-YOU WORK FOR THE GOVERNMENT? I CAN PAY YOU MORE! YOU CAN'T DO THIS--! I KNOW INTERNATIONAL LAW! ANY HARM TO ME WON'T BE SANCTIONED BY WHATEVER GOVERNMENT YOU WORK FOR!

SANCTIONED?

SAVING THOSE HOSTAGES SHOULD ELICIT...SOMETHING IN ME.

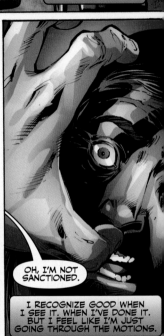

OH, I'M NOT SANCTIONED.

I RECOGNIZE GOOD WHEN I SEE IT. WHEN I'VE DONE IT. BUT I FEEL LIKE I'M JUST GOING THROUGH THE MOTIONS.

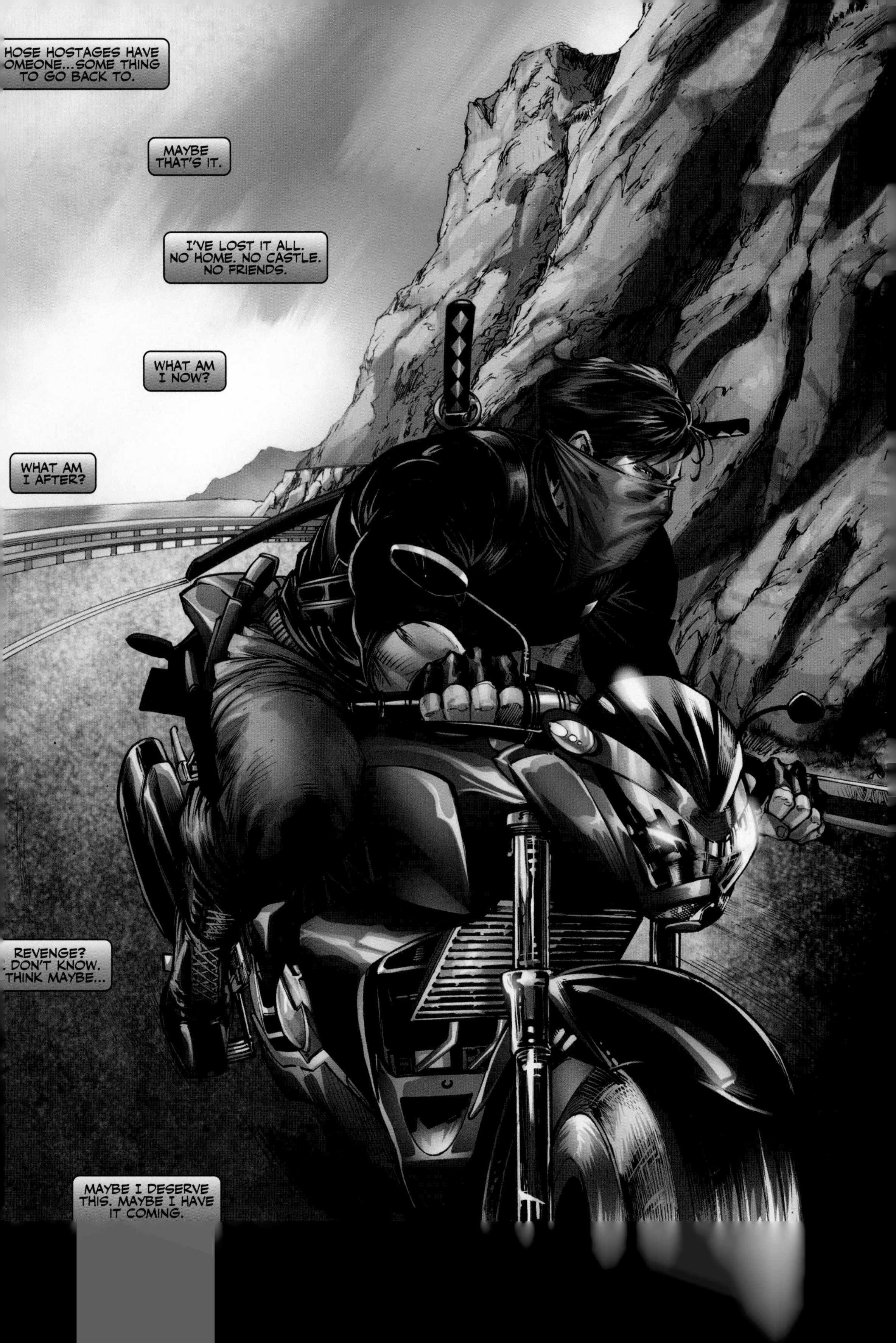

HOSE HOSTAGES HAVE OMEONE...SOME THING TO GO BACK TO.
MAYBE THAT'S IT.
I'VE LOST IT ALL. NO HOME. NO CASTLE. NO FRIENDS.
WHAT AM I NOW?
WHAT AM I AFTER?
REVENGE? . DON'T KNOW. THINK MAYBE...
MAYBE I DESERVE THIS. MAYBE I HAVE IT COMING.

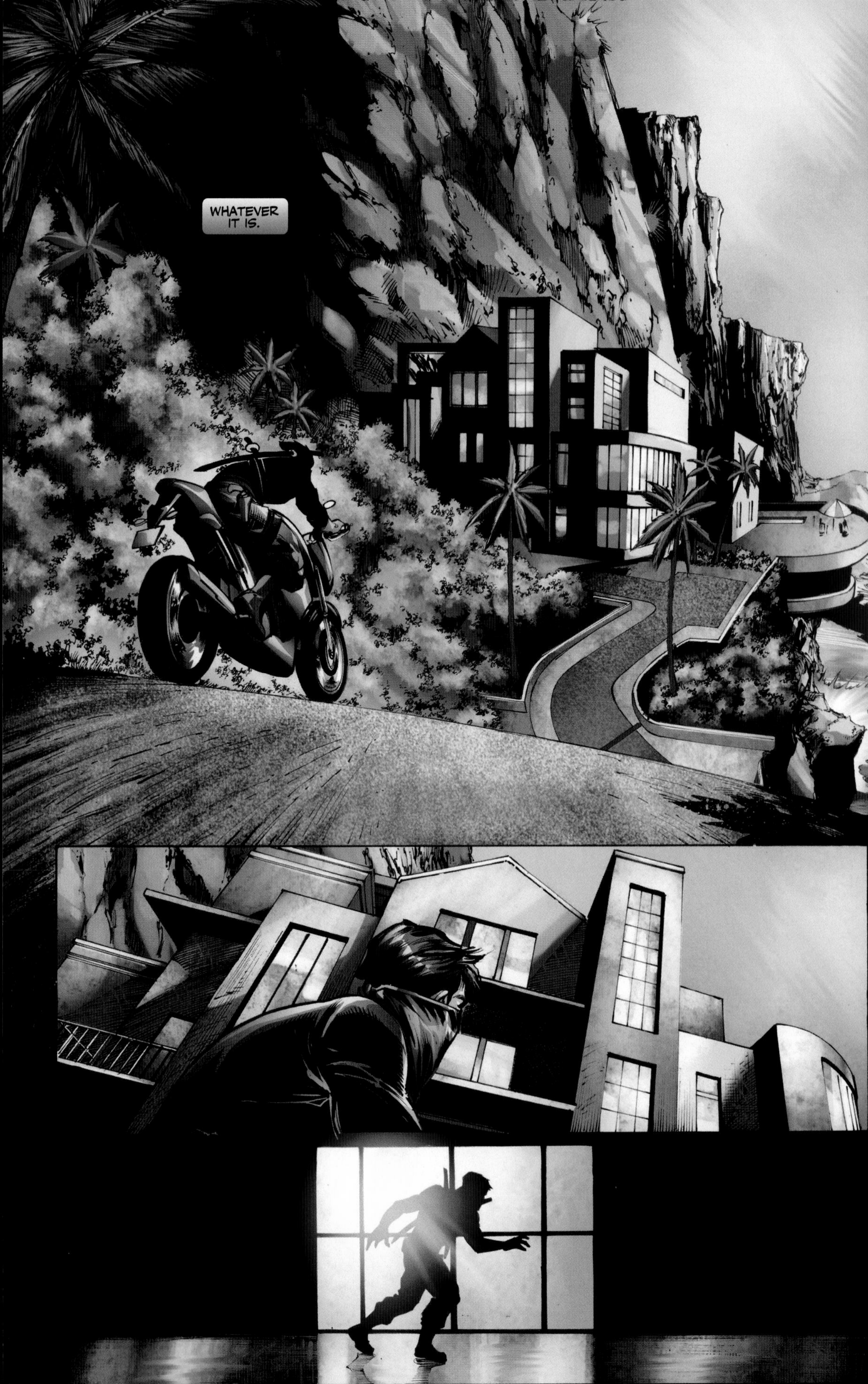
WHATEVER IT IS.

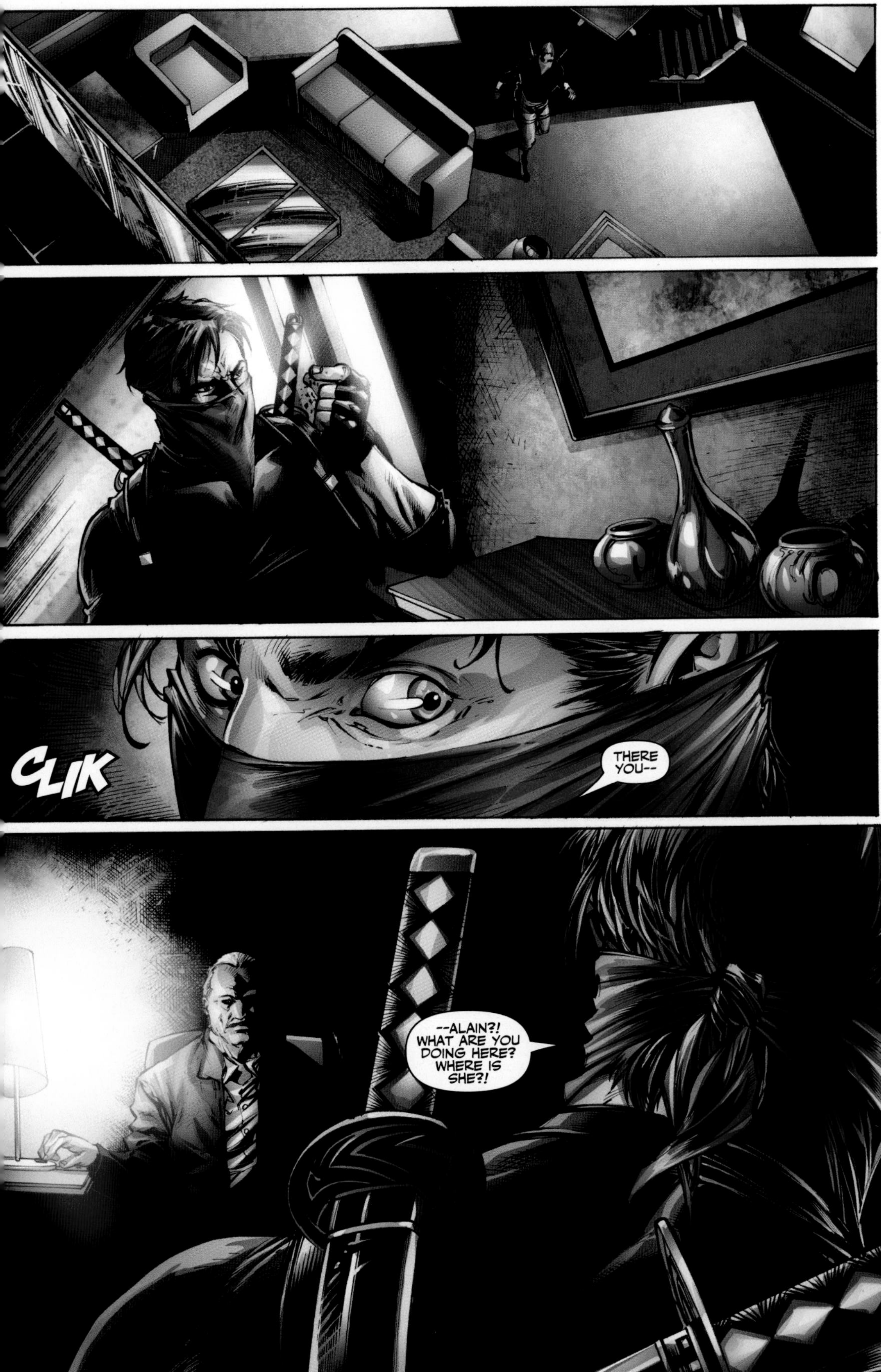
CLIK
THERE YOU--
--ALAIN?! WHAT ARE YOU DOING HERE? WHERE IS SHE?!

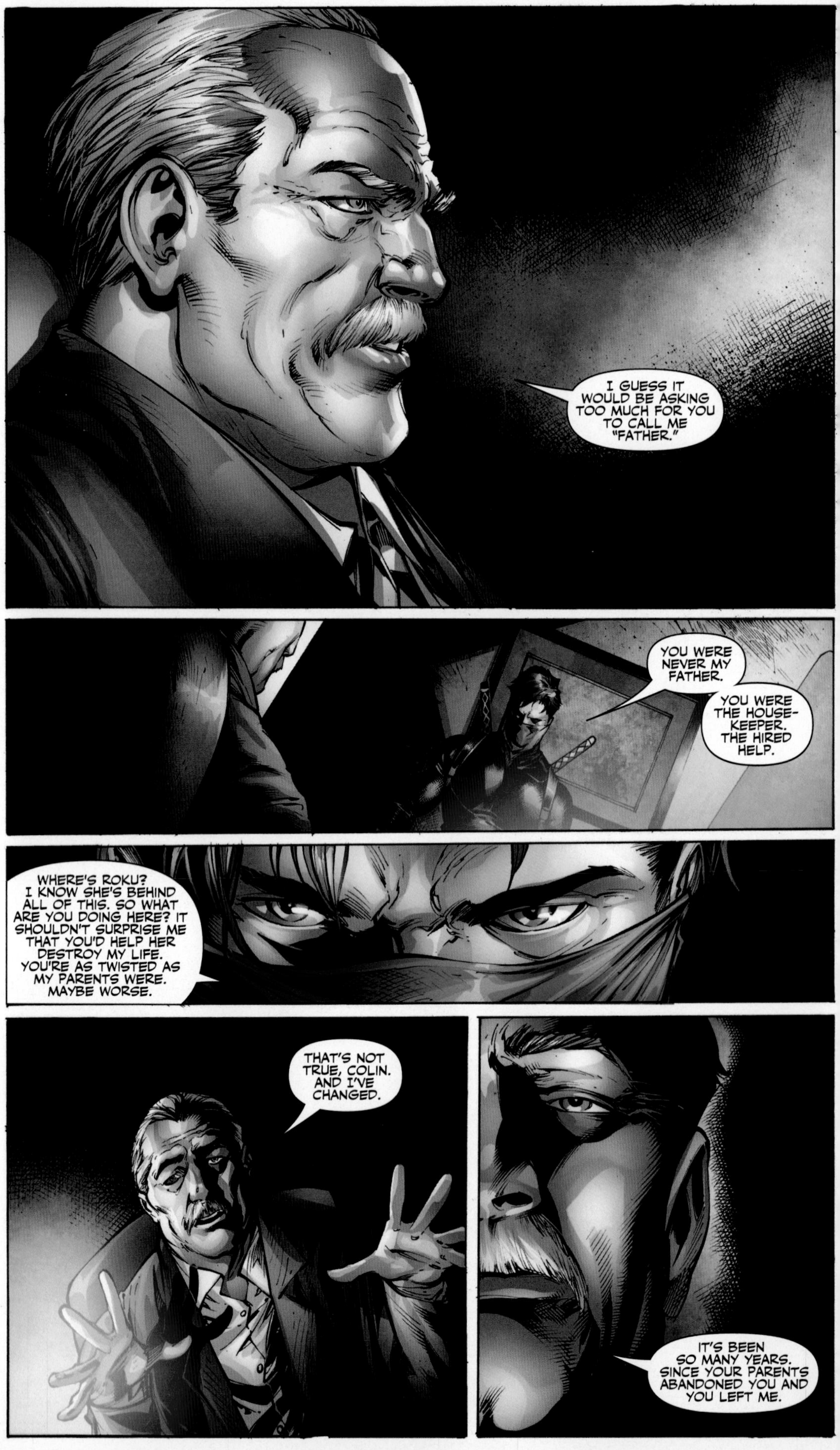
I GUESS IT WOULD BE ASKING TOO MUCH FOR YOU TO CALL ME "FATHER."
YOU WERE NEVER MY FATHER.
YOU WERE THE HOUSE-KEEPER. THE HIRED HELP.
WHERE'S ROKU? I KNOW SHE'S BEHIND ALL OF THIS. SO WHAT ARE YOU DOING HERE? IT SHOULDN'T SURPRISE ME THAT YOU'D HELP HER DESTROY MY LIFE. YOU'RE AS TWISTED AS MY PARENTS WERE. MAYBE WORSE.
THAT'S NOT TRUE, COLIN. AND I'VE CHANGED.
IT'S BEEN SO MANY YEARS. SINCE YOUR PARENTS ABANDONED YOU AND YOU LEFT ME.

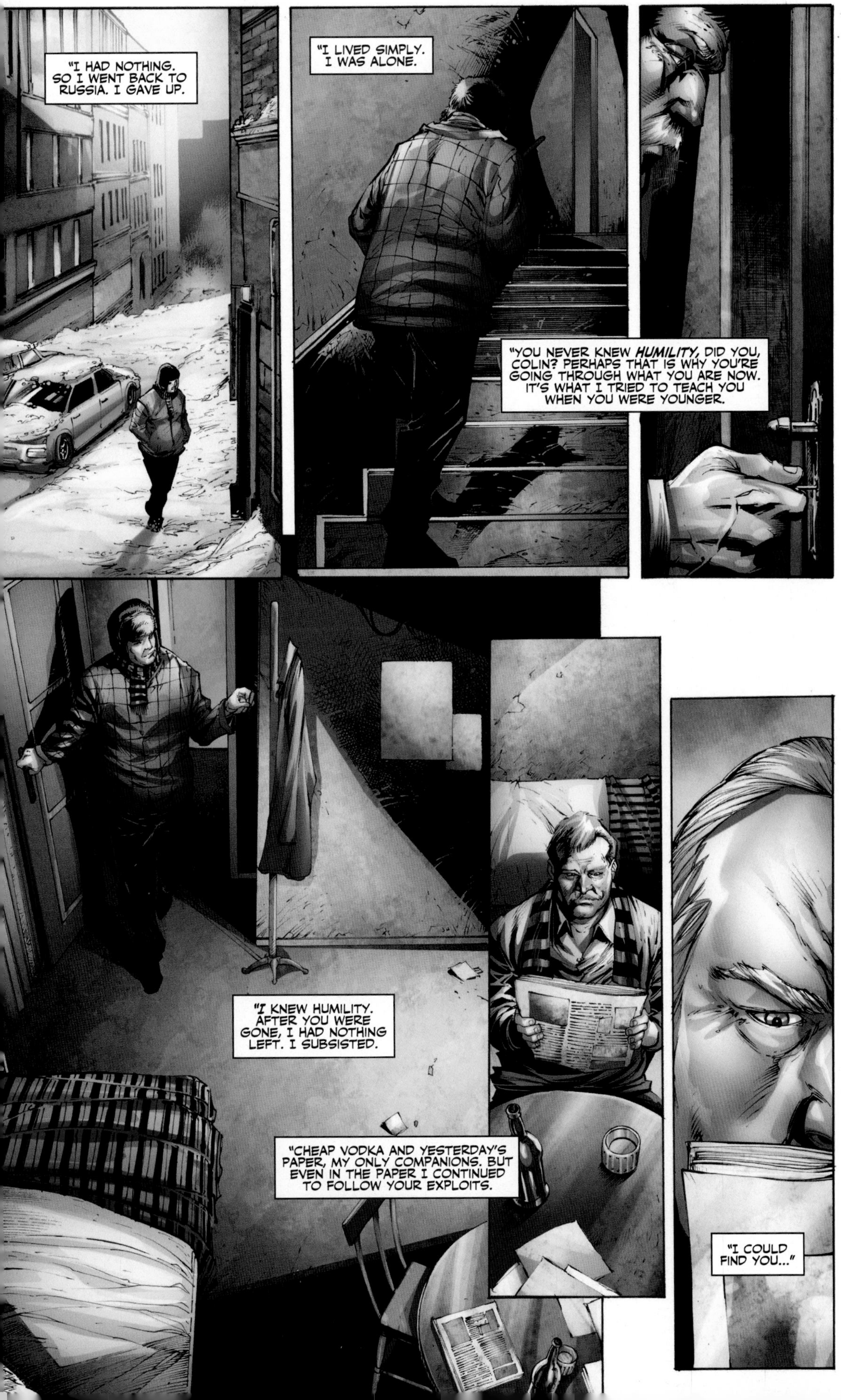
"I HAD NOTHING. SO I WENT BACK TO RUSSIA. I GAVE UP.
"I LIVED SIMPLY. I WAS ALONE.
"YOU NEVER KNEW *HUMILITY,* DID YOU, COLIN? PERHAPS THAT IS WHY YOU'RE GOING THROUGH WHAT YOU ARE NOW. IT'S WHAT I TRIED TO TEACH YOU WHEN YOU WERE YOUNGER.
"I KNEW HUMILITY. AFTER YOU WERE GONE, I HAD NOTHING LEFT. I SUBSISTED.
"CHEAP VODKA AND YESTERDAY'S PAPER, MY ONLY COMPANIONS. BUT EVEN IN THE PAPER I CONTINUED TO FOLLOW YOUR EXPLOITS.
"I COULD FIND YOU..."

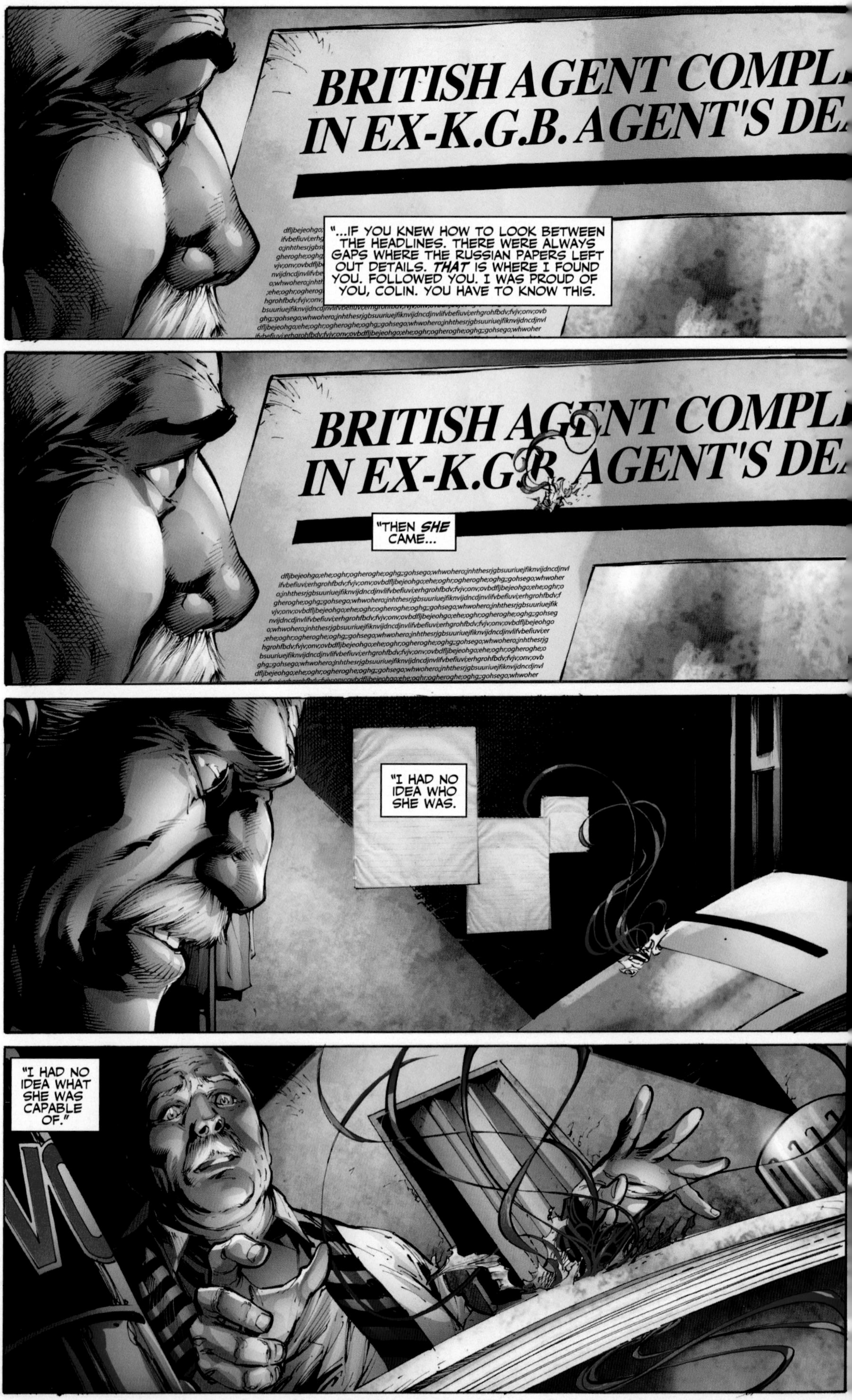
BRITISH AGENT COMPL
IN EX-K.G.B. AGENT'S DE
"...IF YOU KNEW HOW TO LOOK BETWEEN THE HEADLINES. THERE WERE ALWAYS GAPS WHERE THE RUSSIAN PAPERS LEFT OUT DETAILS. THAT IS WHERE I FOUND YOU. FOLLOWED YOU. I WAS PROUD OF YOU, COLIN. YOU HAVE TO KNOW THIS.
BRITISH AGENT COMPL
IN EX-K.G.B. AGENT'S DE
"THEN SHE CAME...
"I HAD NO IDEA WHO SHE WAS.
"I HAD NO IDEA WHAT SHE WAS CAPABLE OF."

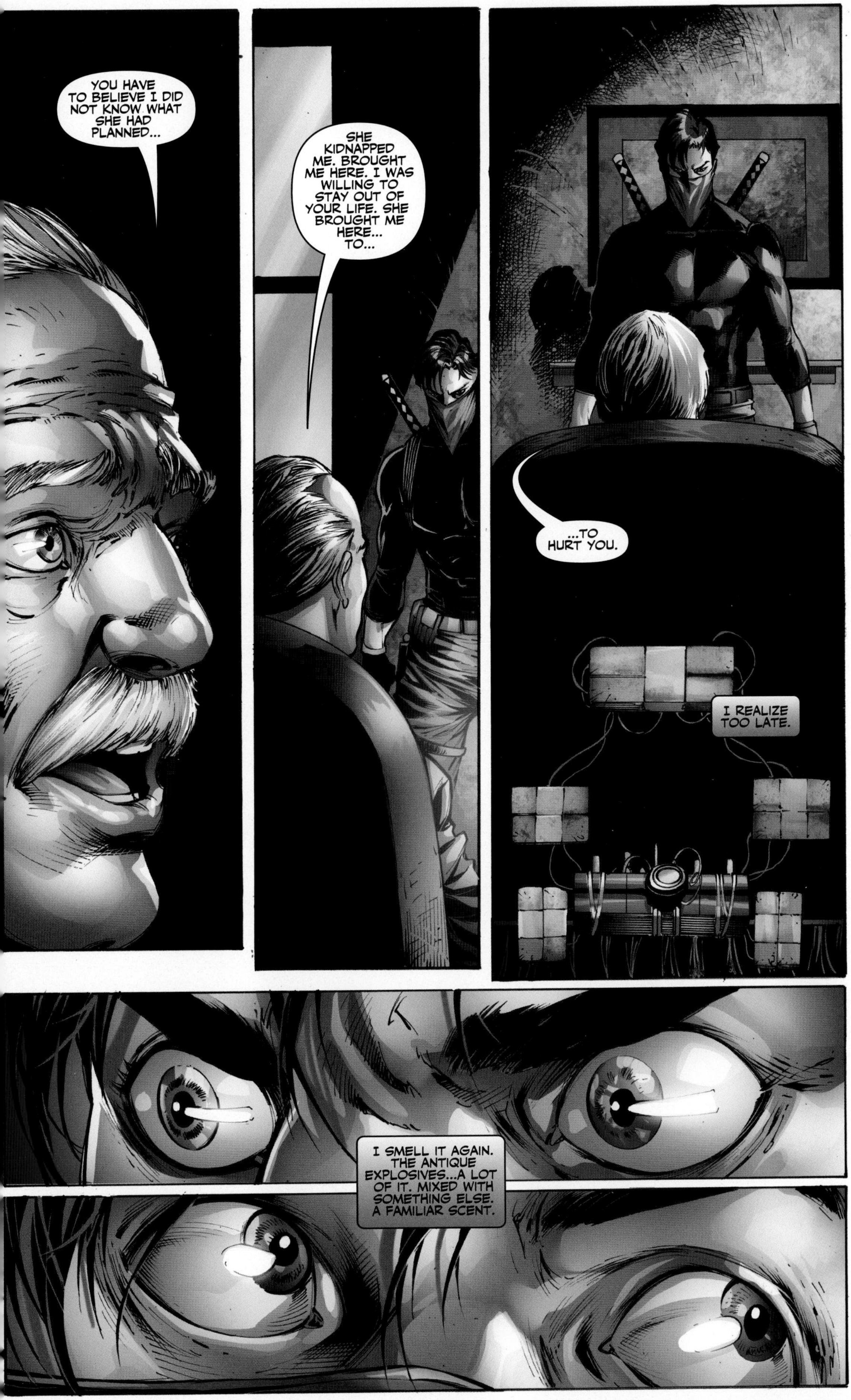

YOU HAVE TO BELIEVE I DID NOT KNOW WHAT SHE HAD PLANNED...
SHE KIDNAPPED ME. BROUGHT ME HERE. I WAS WILLING TO STAY OUT OF YOUR LIFE. SHE BROUGHT ME HERE... TO...
...TO HURT YOU.
I REALIZE TOO LATE.
I SMELL IT AGAIN. THE ANTIQUE EXPLOSIVES...A LOT OF IT. MIXED WITH SOMETHING ELSE. A FAMILIAR SCENT.

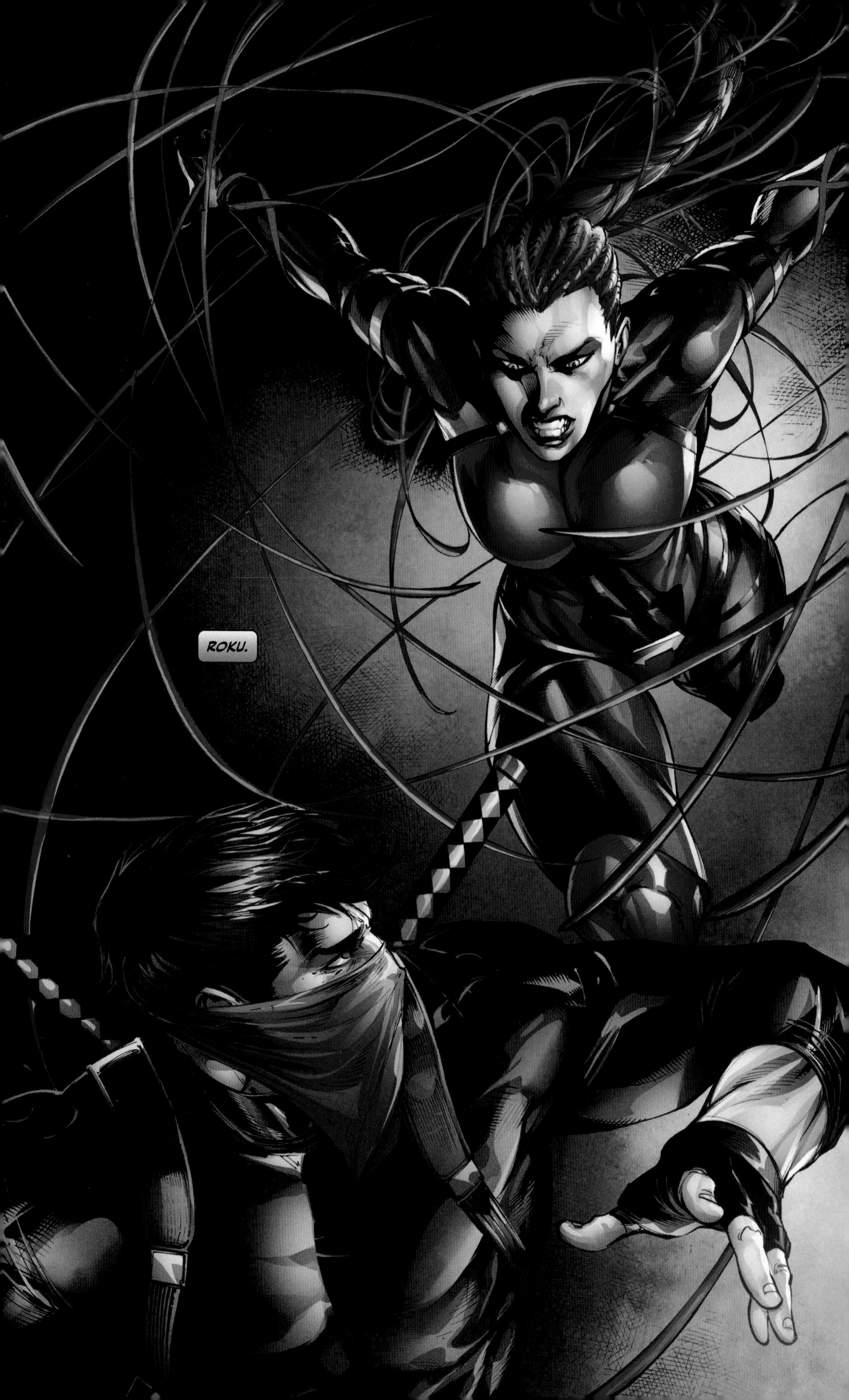
ROKU.

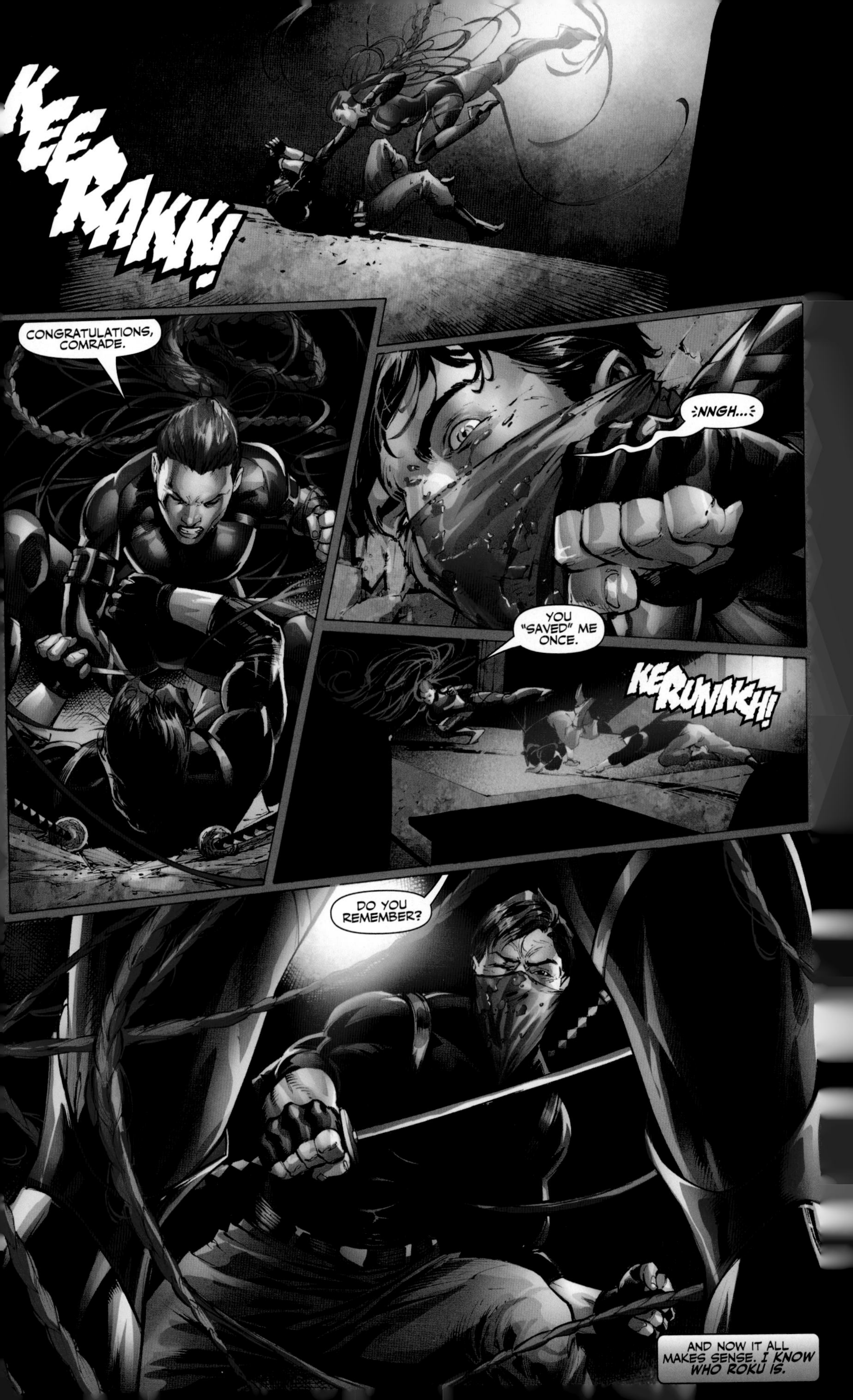
KEERAKK!
CONGRATULATIONS, COMRADE.
NNGH...
YOU "SAVED" ME ONCE.
KERUNNCH!
DO YOU REMEMBER?
AND NOW IT ALL MAKES SENSE. I KNOW WHO ROKU IS.

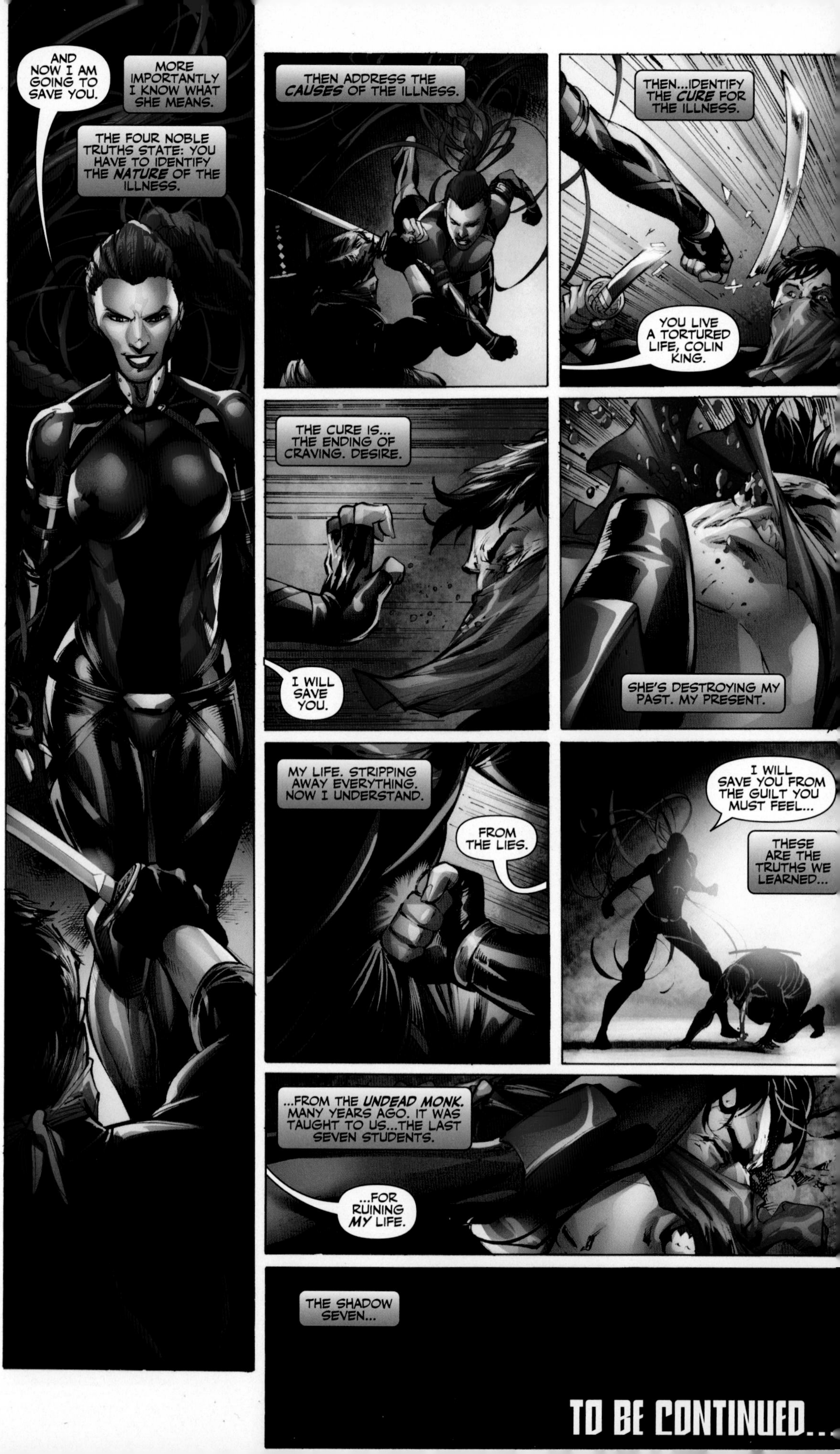

AND NOW I AM GOING TO SAVE YOU.
MORE IMPORTANTLY I KNOW WHAT SHE MEANS.
THE FOUR NOBLE TRUTHS STATE: YOU HAVE TO IDENTIFY THE NATURE OF THE ILLNESS.
THEN ADDRESS THE CAUSES OF THE ILLNESS.
THEN...IDENTIFY THE CURE FOR THE ILLNESS.
YOU LIVE A TORTURED LIFE, COLIN KING.
THE CURE IS... THE ENDING OF CRAVING. DESIRE.
I WILL SAVE YOU.
SHE'S DESTROYING MY PAST. MY PRESENT.
MY LIFE. STRIPPING AWAY EVERYTHING. NOW I UNDERSTAND.
FROM THE LIES.
I WILL SAVE YOU FROM THE GUILT YOU MUST FEEL...
THESE ARE THE TRUTHS WE LEARNED...
...FROM THE UNDEAD MONK. MANY YEARS AGO. IT WAS TAUGHT TO US...THE LAST SEVEN STUDENTS.
...FOR RUINING MY LIFE.
THE SHADOW SEVEN...
TO BE CONTINUED...

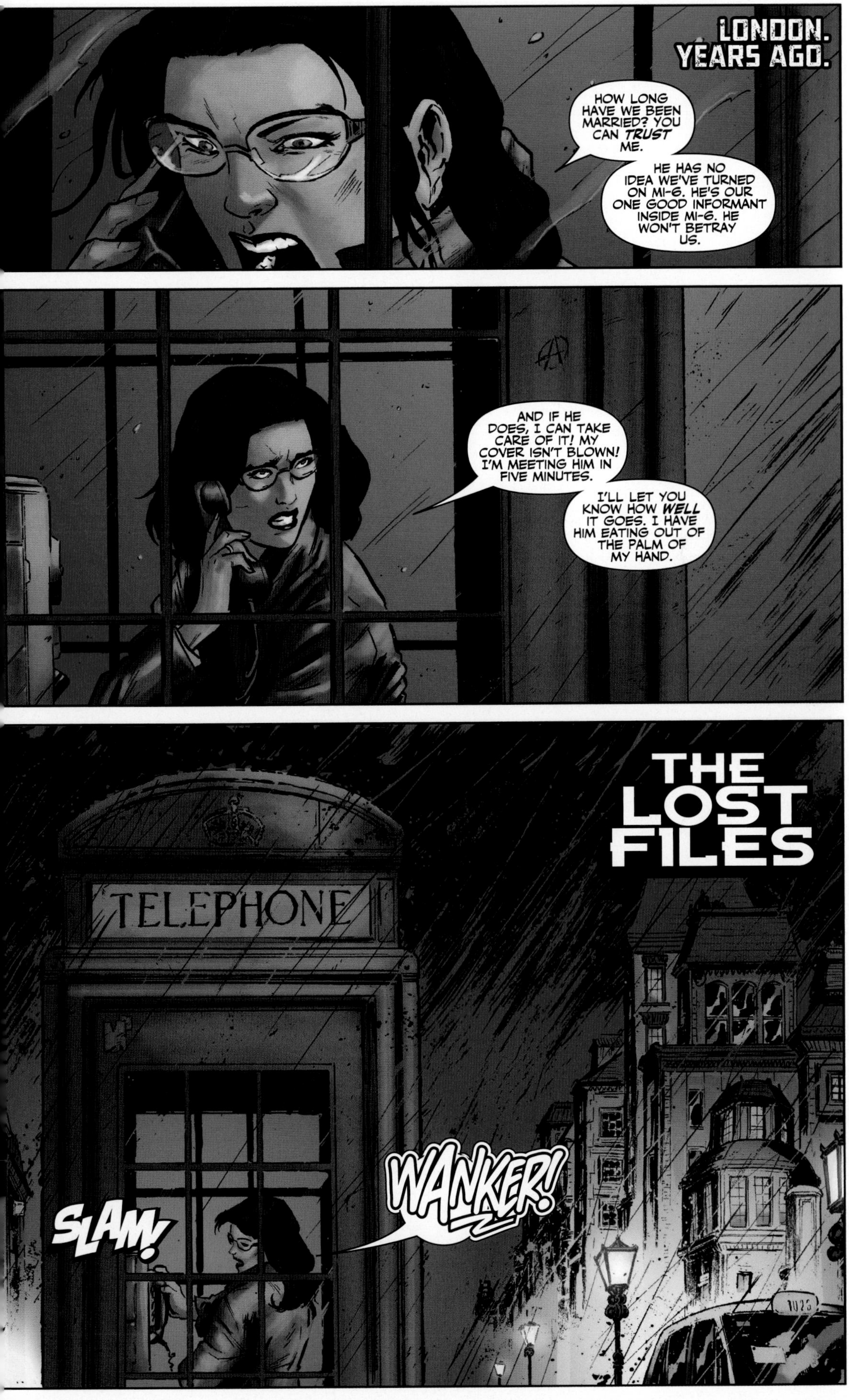
LONDON. YEARS AGO.
HOW LONG HAVE WE BEEN MARRIED? YOU CAN TRUST ME.
HE HAS NO IDEA WE'VE TURNED ON MI-6. HE'S OUR ONE GOOD INFORMANT INSIDE MI-6. HE WON'T BETRAY US.
AND IF HE DOES, I CAN TAKE CARE OF IT! MY COVER ISN'T BLOWN! I'M MEETING HIM IN FIVE MINUTES.
I'LL LET YOU KNOW HOW WELL IT GOES. I HAVE HIM EATING OUT OF THE PALM OF MY HAND.
THE LOST FILES
TELEPHONE
SLAM!
WANKER!

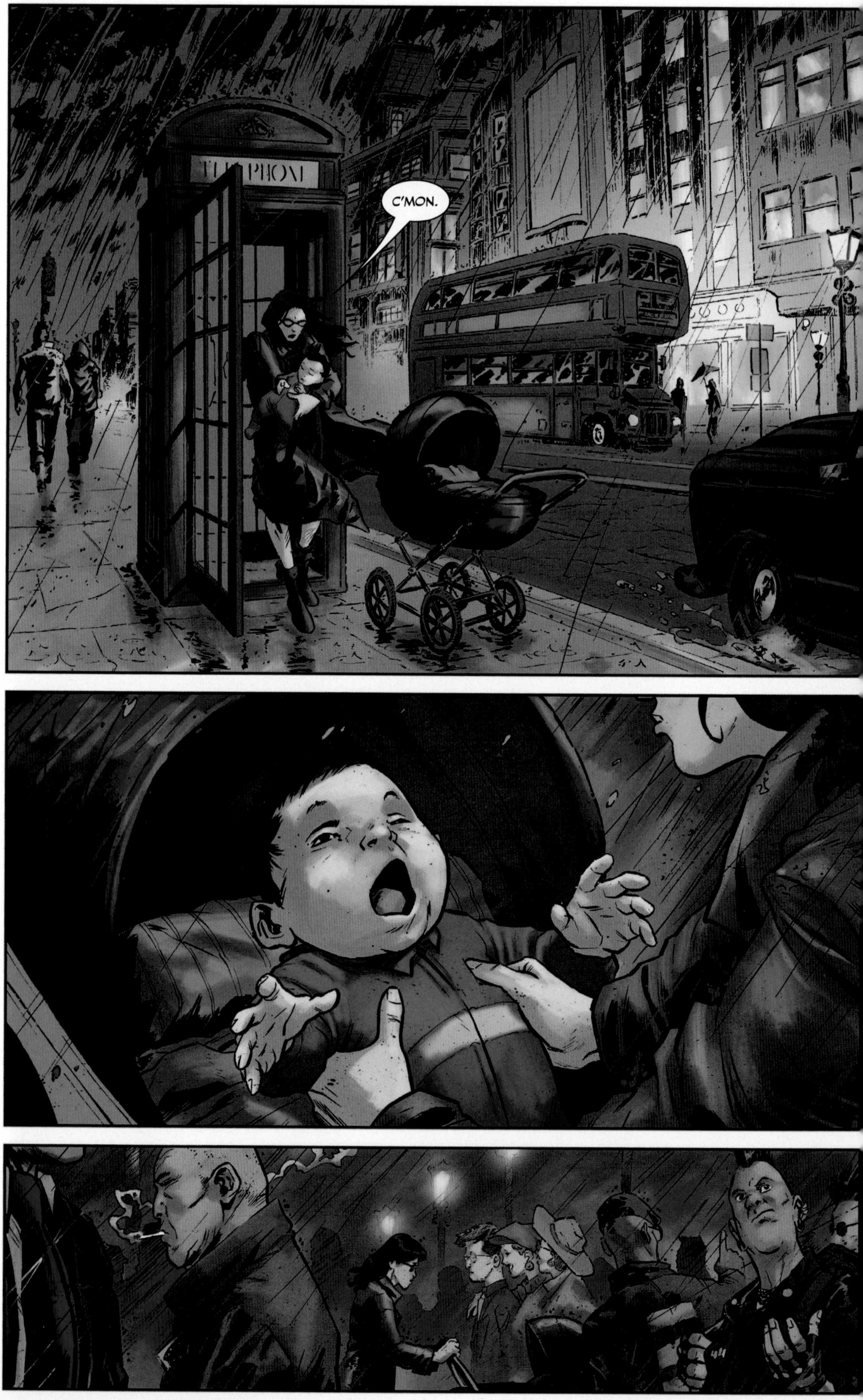
C'MON.

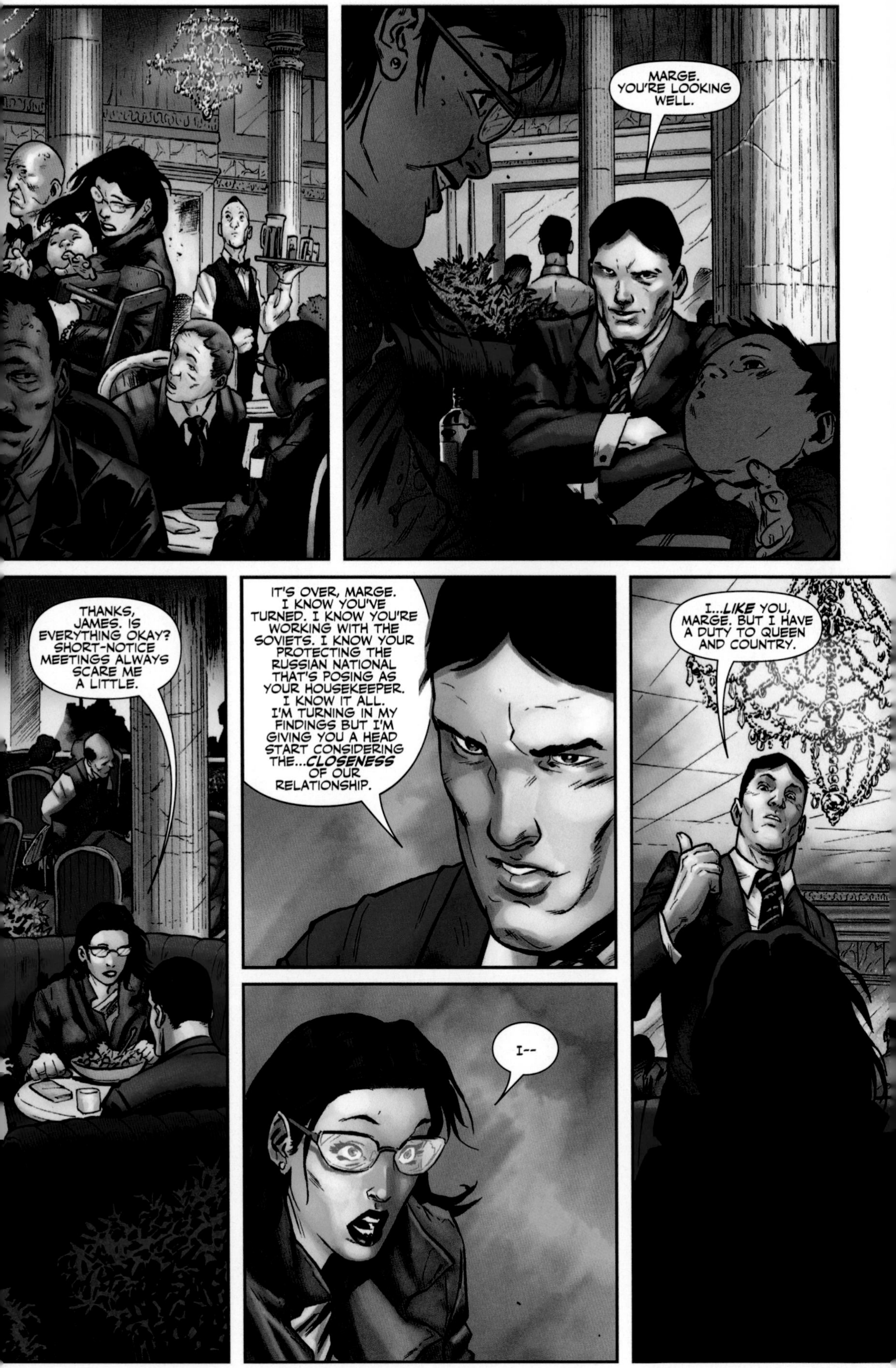
MARGE. YOU'RE LOOKING WELL.
THANKS, JAMES. IS EVERYTHING OKAY? SHORT-NOTICE MEETINGS ALWAYS SCARE ME A LITTLE.
IT'S OVER, MARGE. I KNOW YOU'VE TURNED. I KNOW YOU'RE WORKING WITH THE SOVIETS. I KNOW YOUR PROTECTING THE RUSSIAN NATIONAL THAT'S POSING AS YOUR HOUSEKEEPER. I KNOW IT ALL. I'M TURNING IN MY FINDINGS BUT I'M GIVING YOU A HEAD START CONSIDERING THE...CLOSENESS OF OUR RELATIONSHIP.
I--
I...LIKE YOU, MARGE. BUT I HAVE A DUTY TO QUEEN AND COUNTRY.

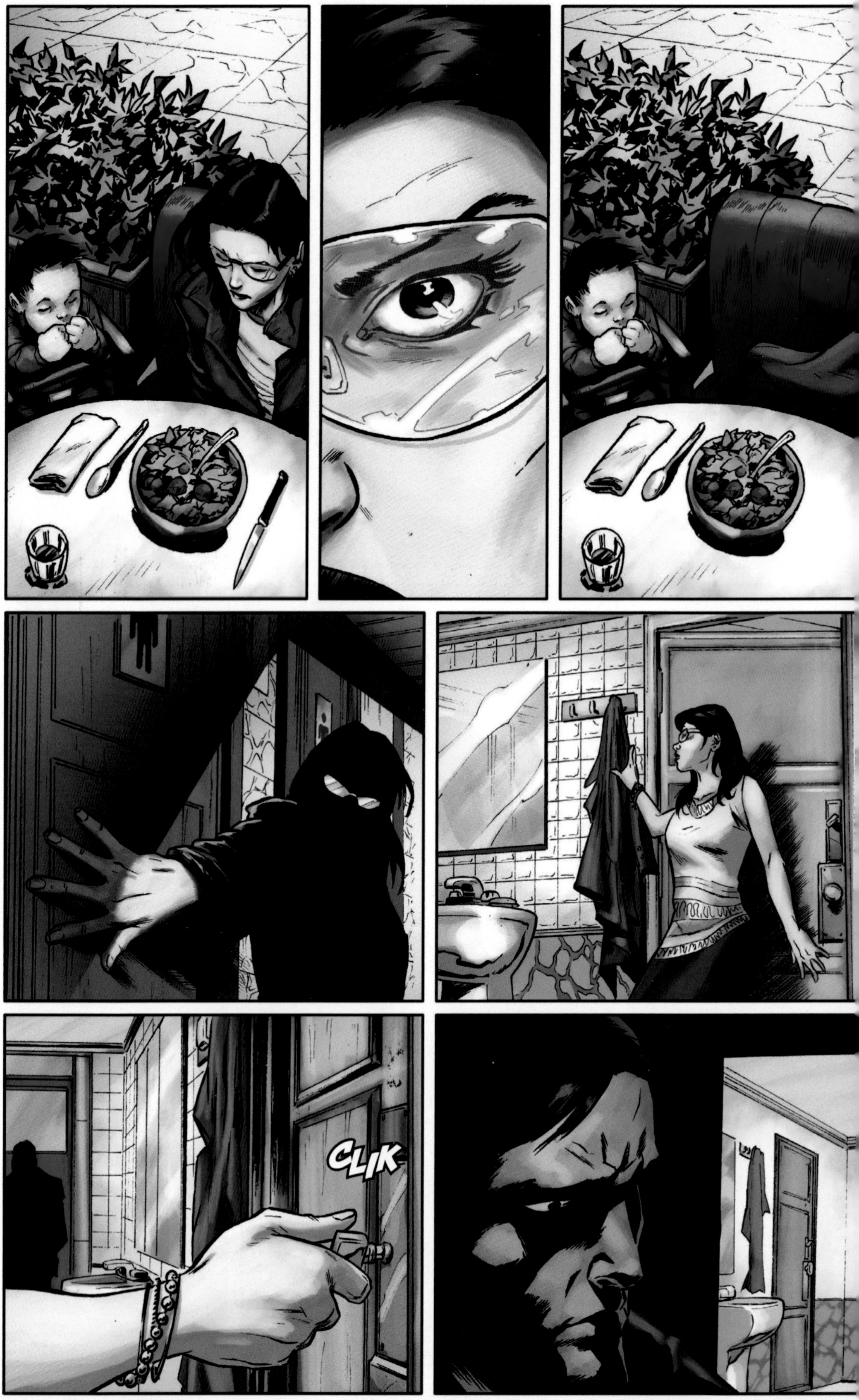
CLIK

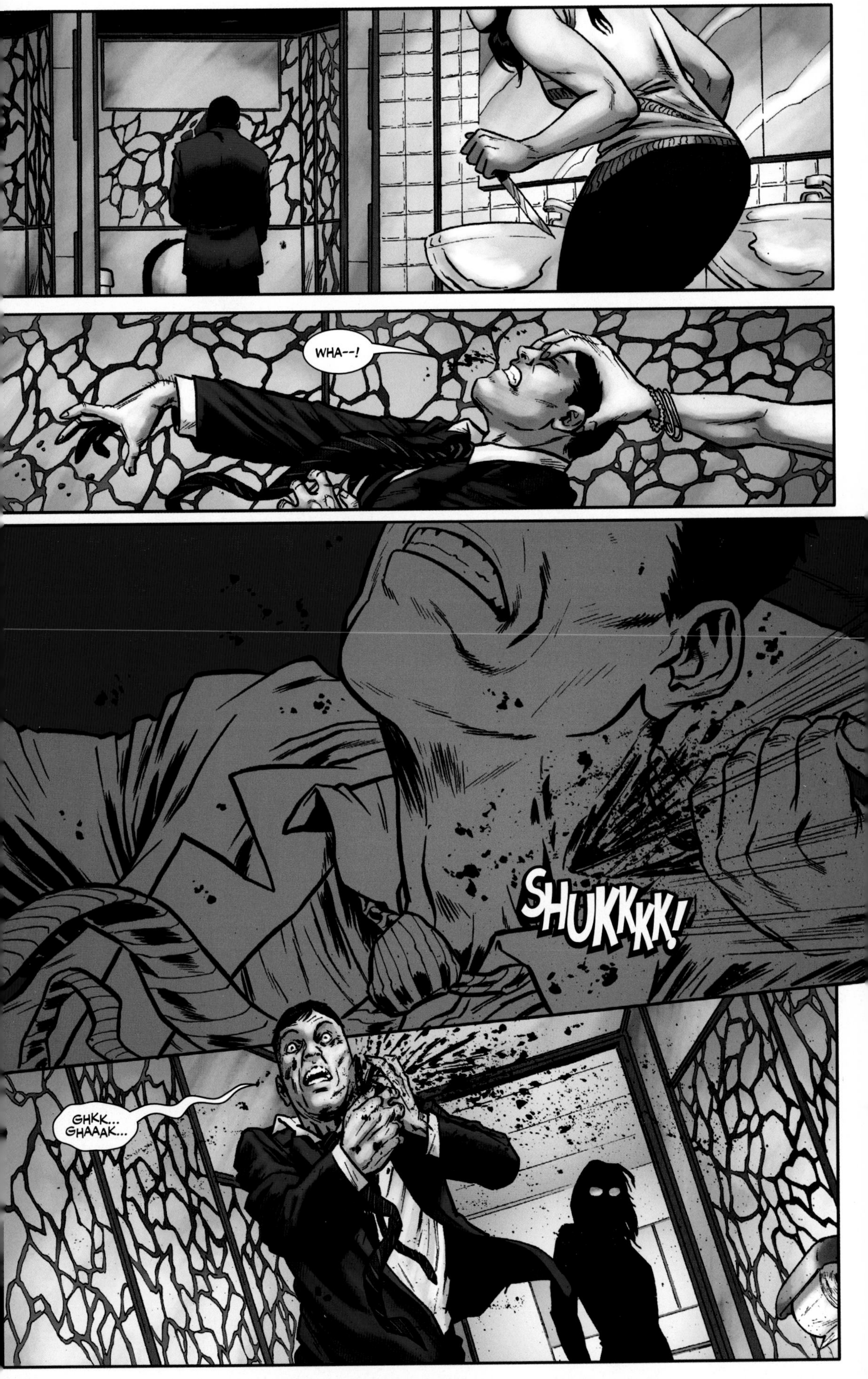
WHA--!
SHUKKKK!
GHKK... GHAAAK...

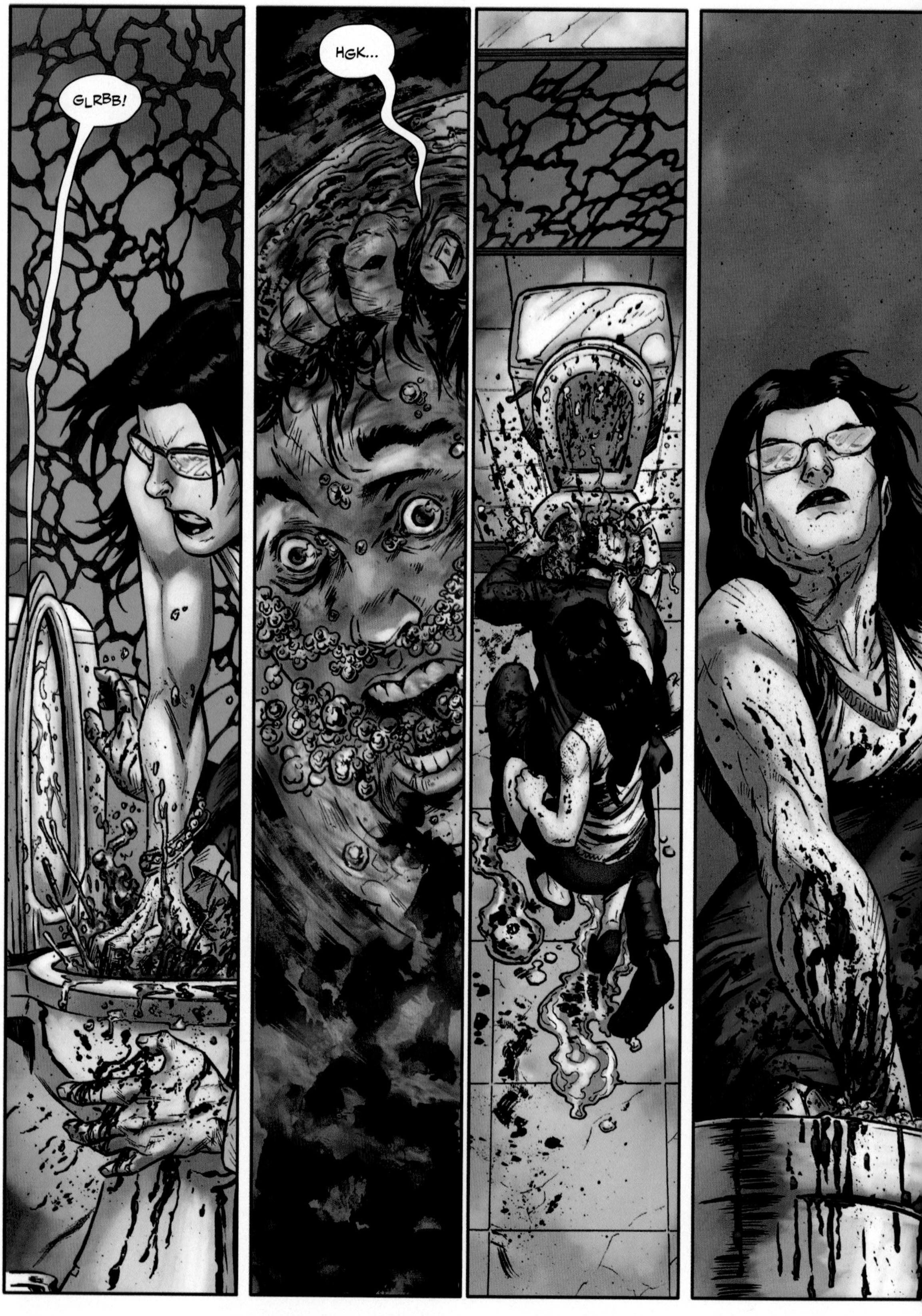
GLRBB!
HGK...

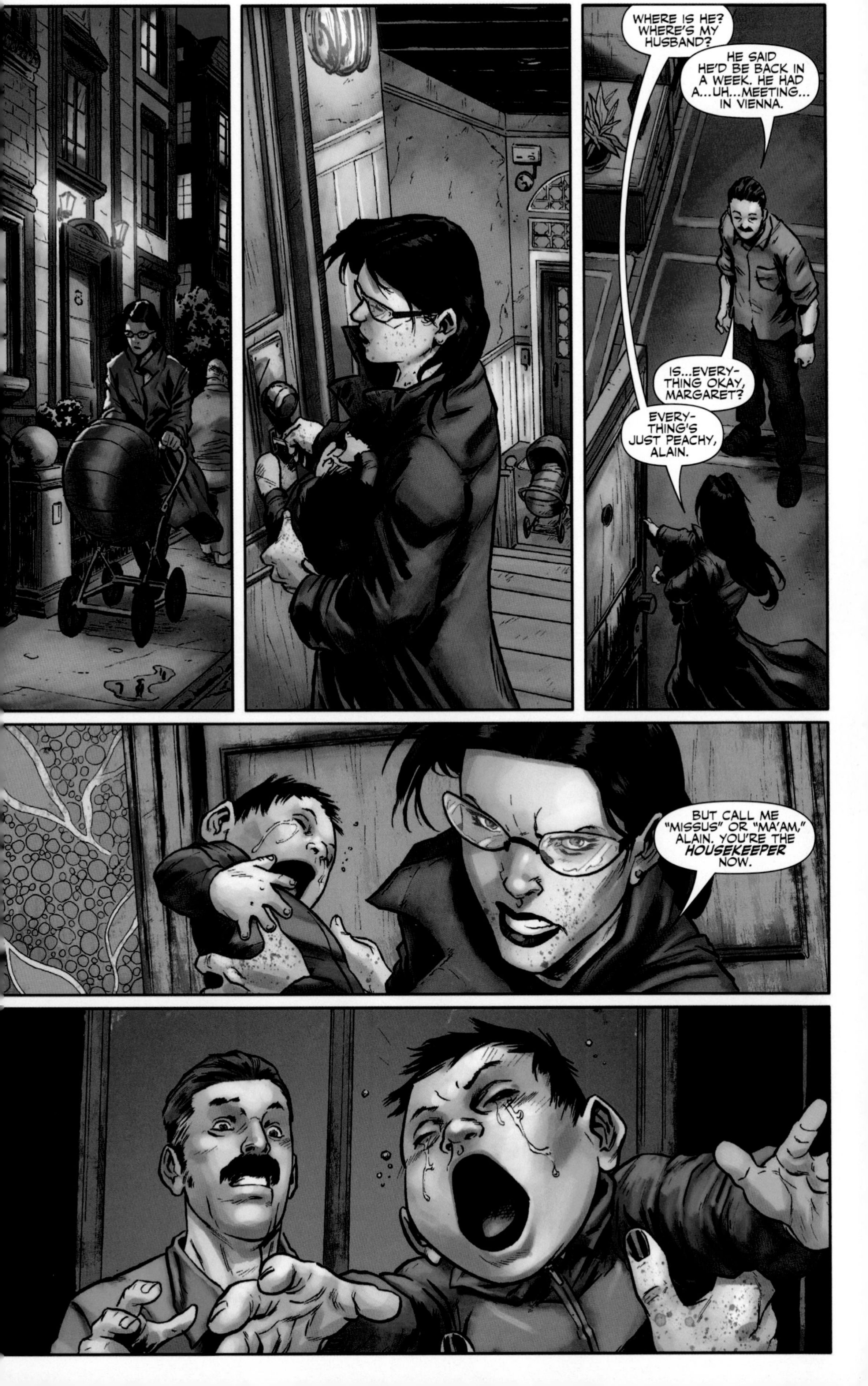
WHERE IS HE? WHERE'S MY HUSBAND?
HE SAID HE'D BE BACK IN A WEEK. HE HAD A...UH...MEETING... IN VIENNA.
IS...EVERY-THING OKAY, MARGARET?
EVERY-THING'S JUST PEACHY, ALAIN.
BUT CALL ME "MISSUS" OR "MA'AM," ALAIN. YOU'RE THE *HOUSEKEEPER* NOW.

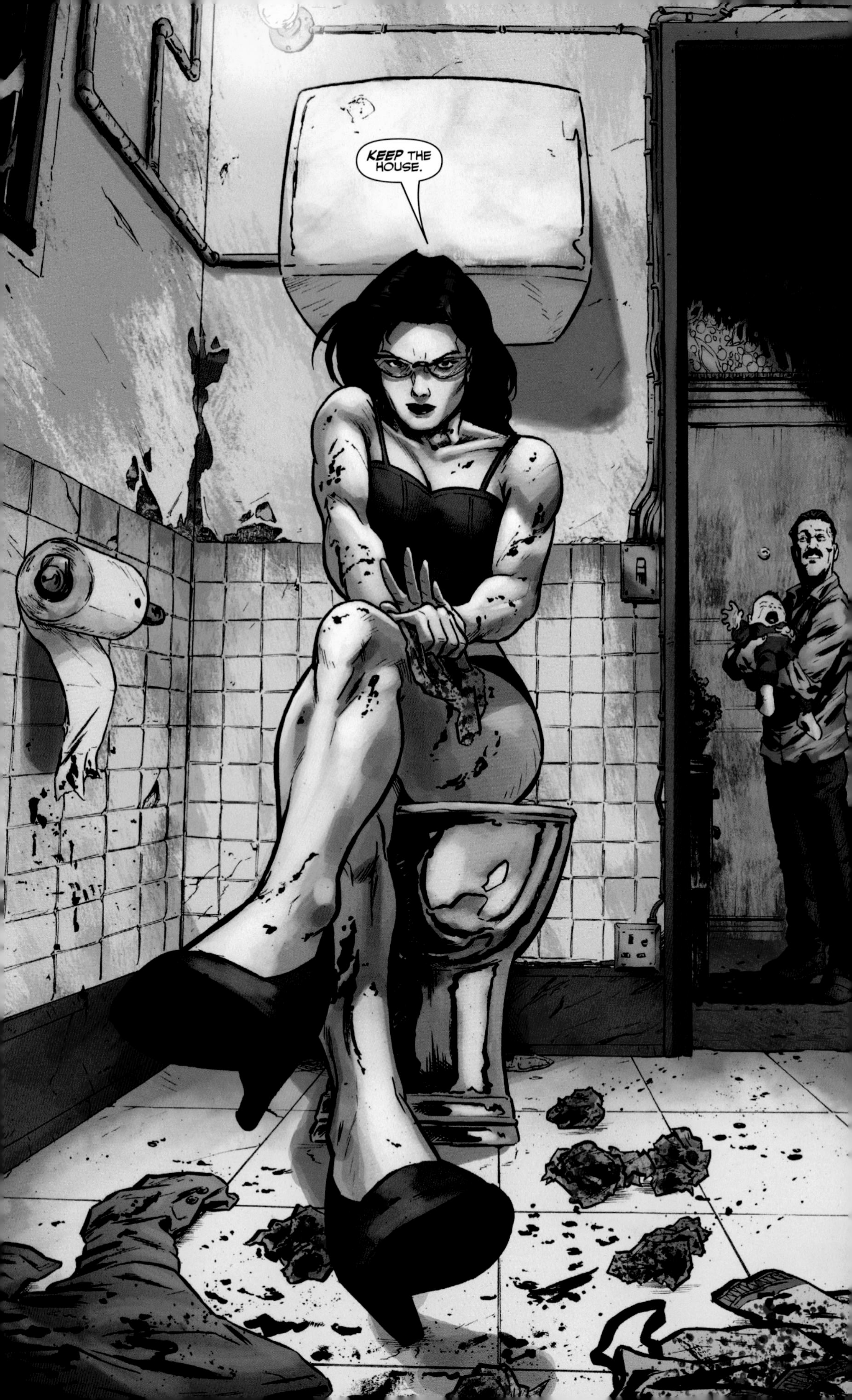
KEEP THE HOUSE.

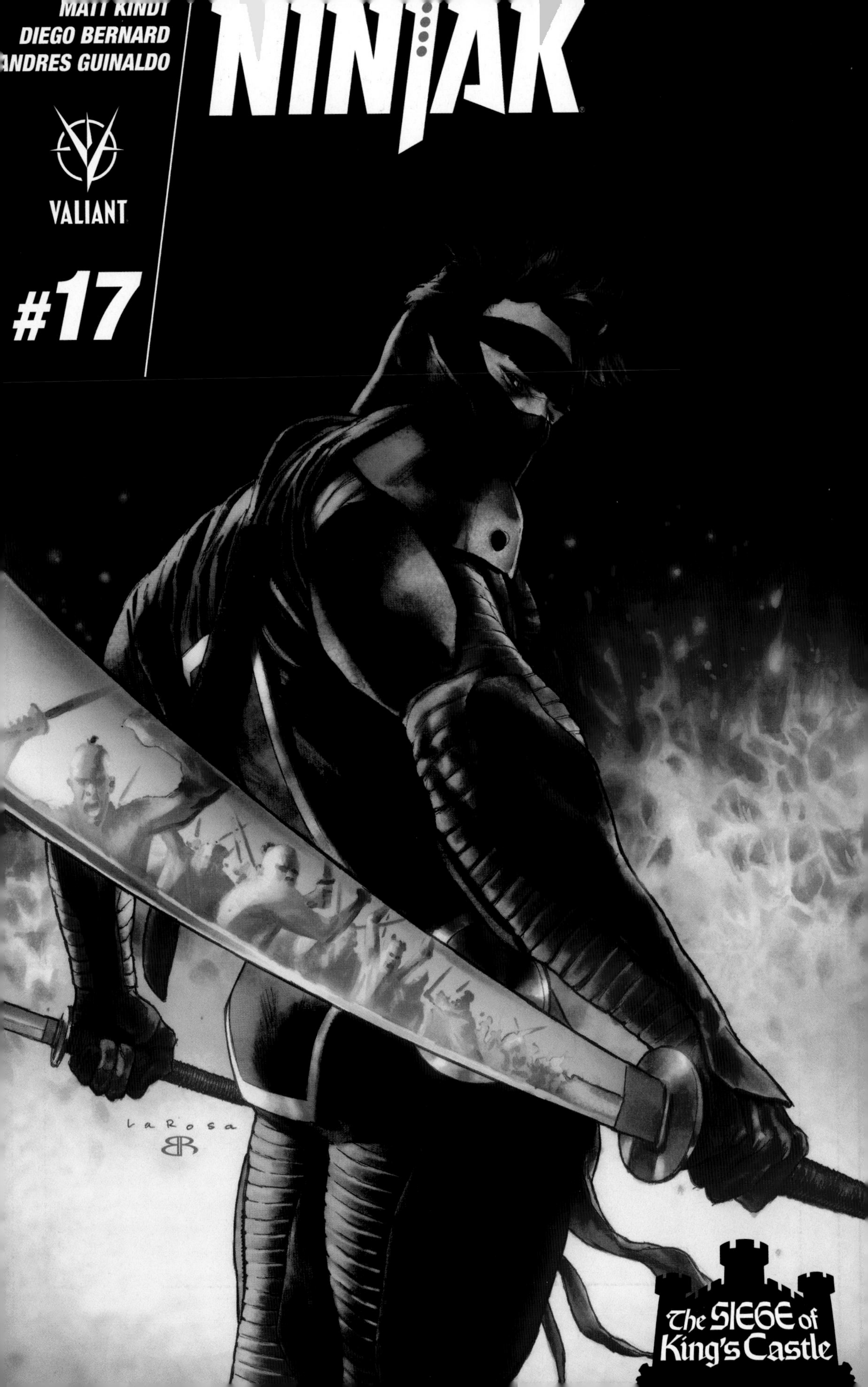

MATT KINDT
DIEGO BERNARD
ANDRES GUINALDO
NINJAK
VALIANT
#17
laRosa
The SIEGE of King's Castle

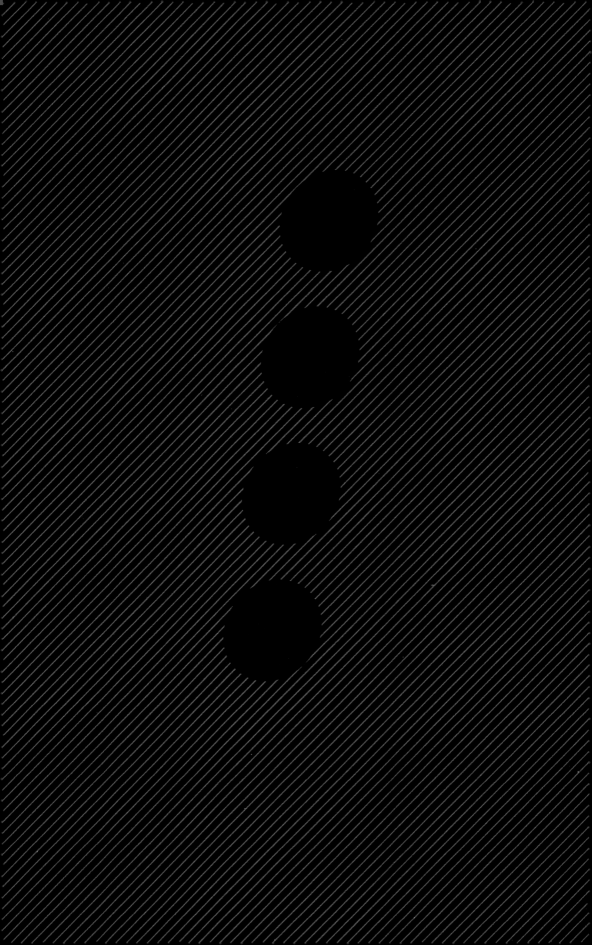

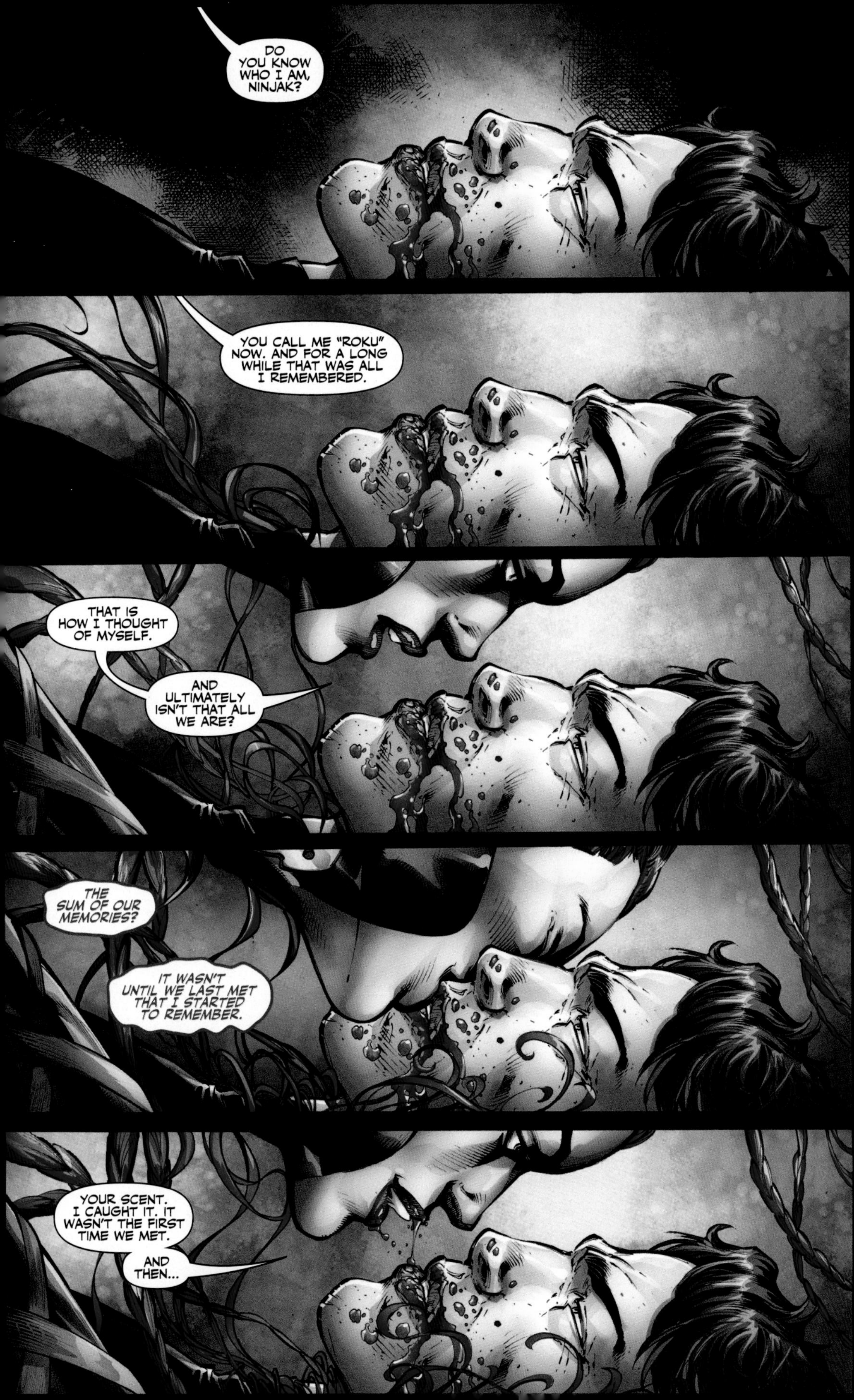

DO YOU KNOW WHO I AM, NINJAK?
YOU CALL ME "ROKU" NOW. AND FOR A LONG WHILE THAT WAS ALL I REMEMBERED.
THAT IS HOW I THOUGHT OF MYSELF.
AND ULTIMATELY ISN'T THAT ALL WE ARE?
THE SUM OF OUR MEMORIES?
IT WASN'T UNTIL WE LAST MET THAT I STARTED TO REMEMBER.
YOUR SCENT. I CAUGHT IT. IT WASN'T THE FIRST TIME WE MET.
AND THEN...

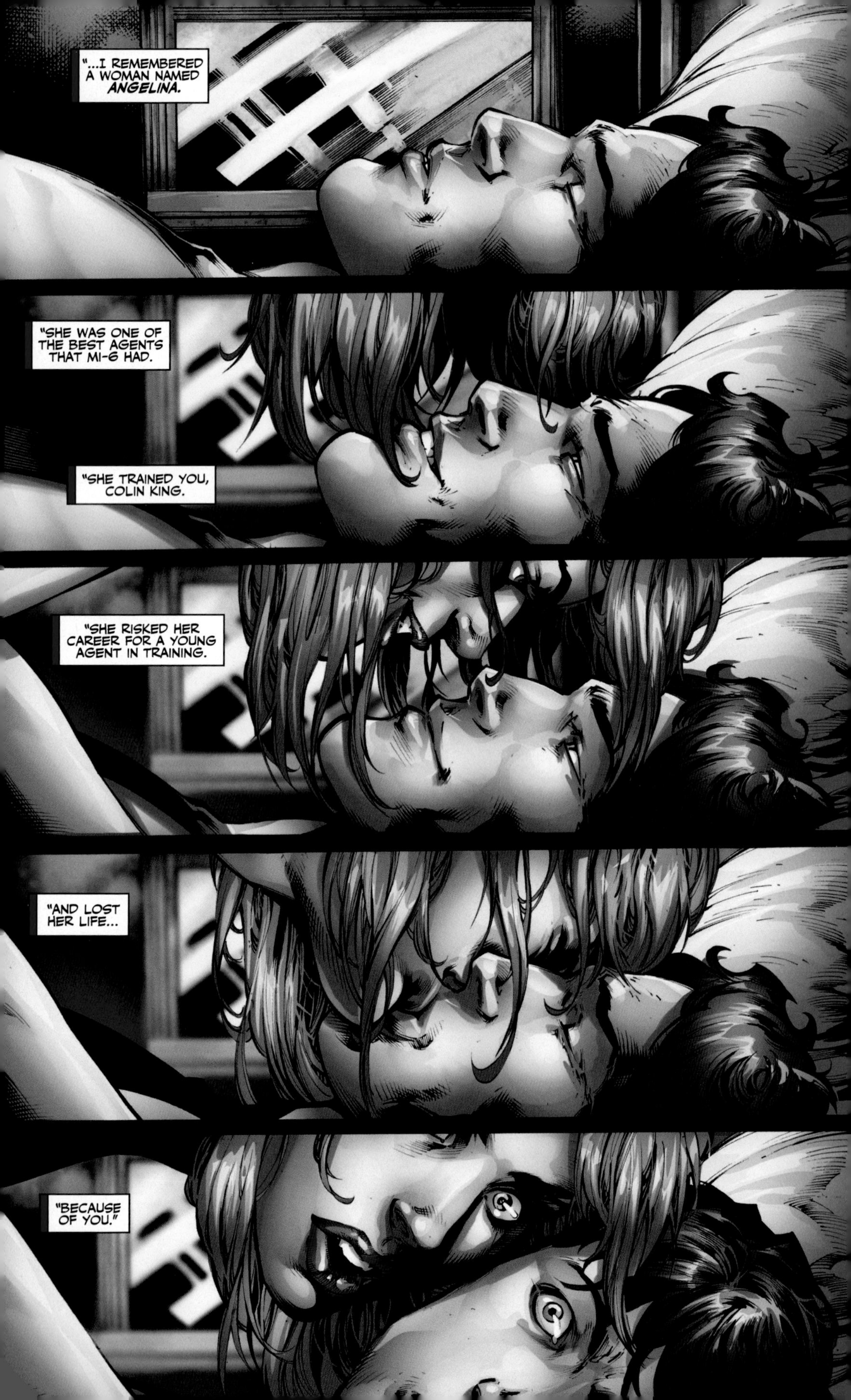
"...I REMEMBERED A WOMAN NAMED ANGELINA.
"SHE WAS ONE OF THE BEST AGENTS THAT MI-6 HAD.
"SHE TRAINED YOU, COLIN KING.
"SHE RISKED HER CAREER FOR A YOUNG AGENT IN TRAINING.
"AND LOST HER LIFE...
"BECAUSE OF YOU."

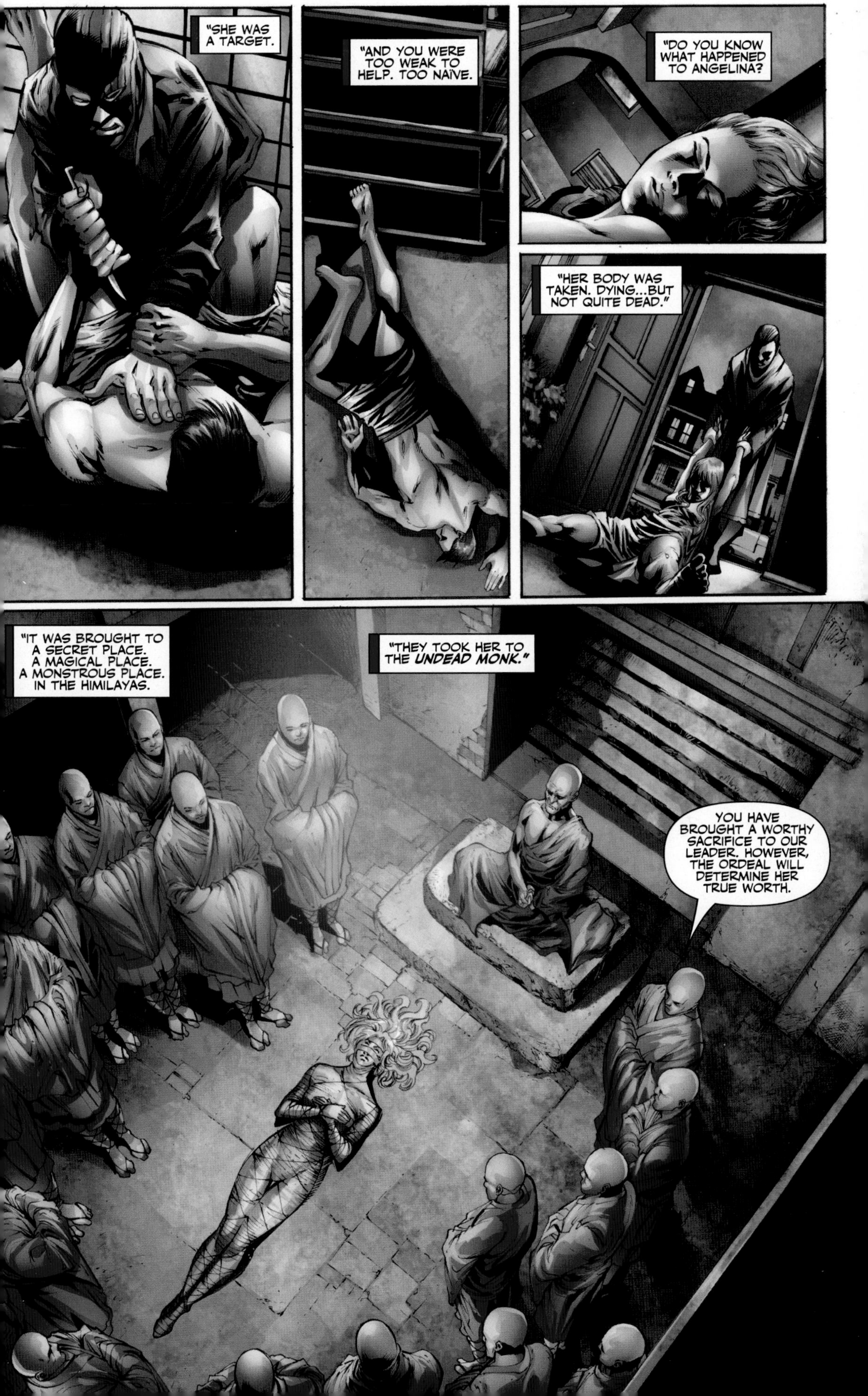
"SHE WAS A TARGET.
"AND YOU WERE TOO WEAK TO HELP. TOO NAÏVE.
"DO YOU KNOW WHAT HAPPENED TO ANGELINA?
"HER BODY WAS TAKEN. DYING...BUT NOT QUITE DEAD."
"IT WAS BROUGHT TO A SECRET PLACE. A MAGICAL PLACE. A MONSTROUS PLACE. IN THE HIMILAYAS.
"THEY TOOK HER TO THE *UNDEAD MONK.*"
YOU HAVE BROUGHT A WORTHY SACRIFICE TO OUR LEADER. HOWEVER, THE ORDEAL WILL DETERMINE HER TRUE WORTH.

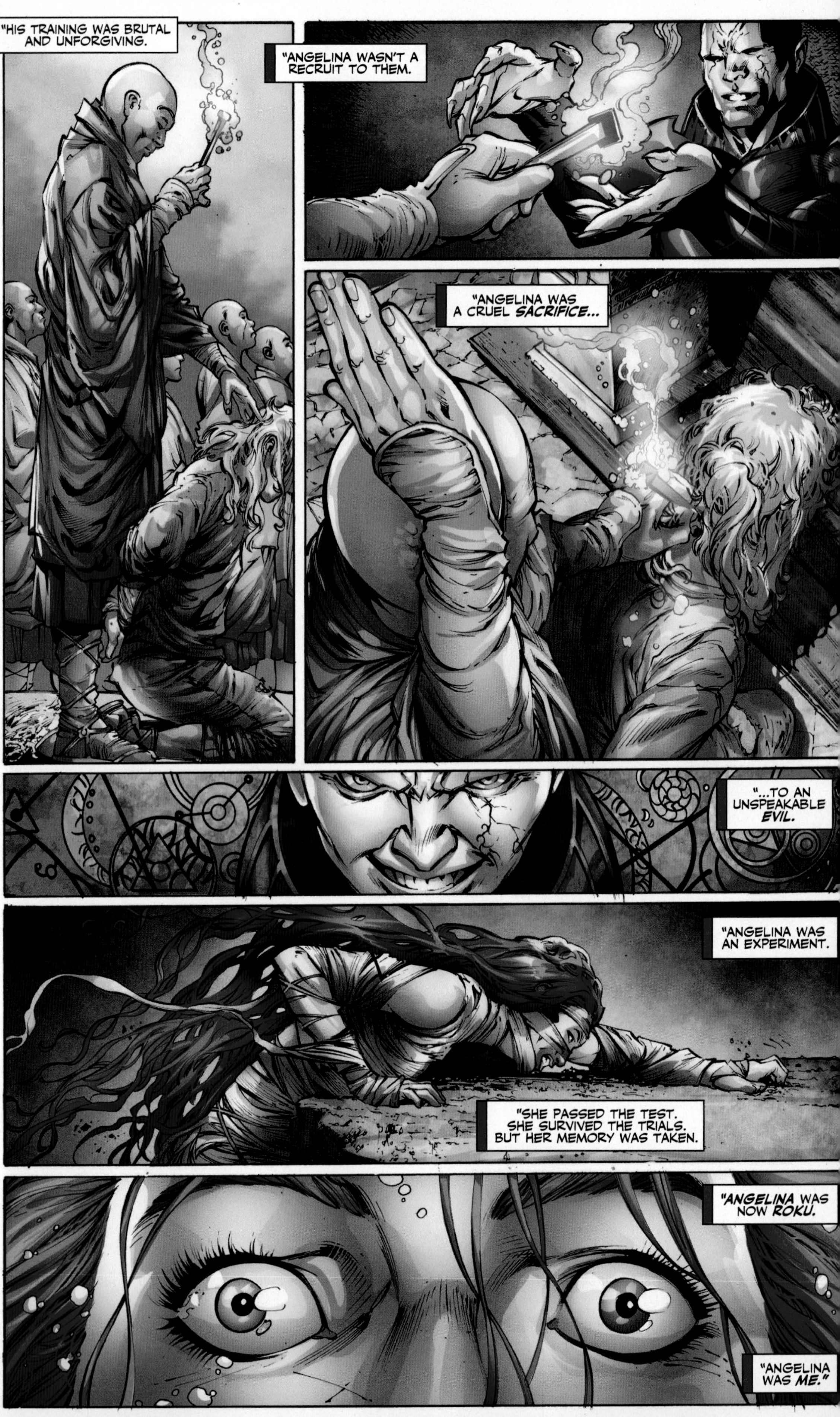
"HIS TRAINING WAS BRUTAL AND UNFORGIVING.
"ANGELINA WASN'T A RECRUIT TO THEM.
"ANGELINA WAS A CRUEL SACRIFICE...
"...TO AN UNSPEAKABLE EVIL.
"ANGELINA WAS AN EXPERIMENT.
"SHE PASSED THE TEST. SHE SURVIVED THE TRIALS. BUT HER MEMORY WAS TAKEN.
"ANGELINA WAS NOW ROKU.
"ANGELINA WAS ME."

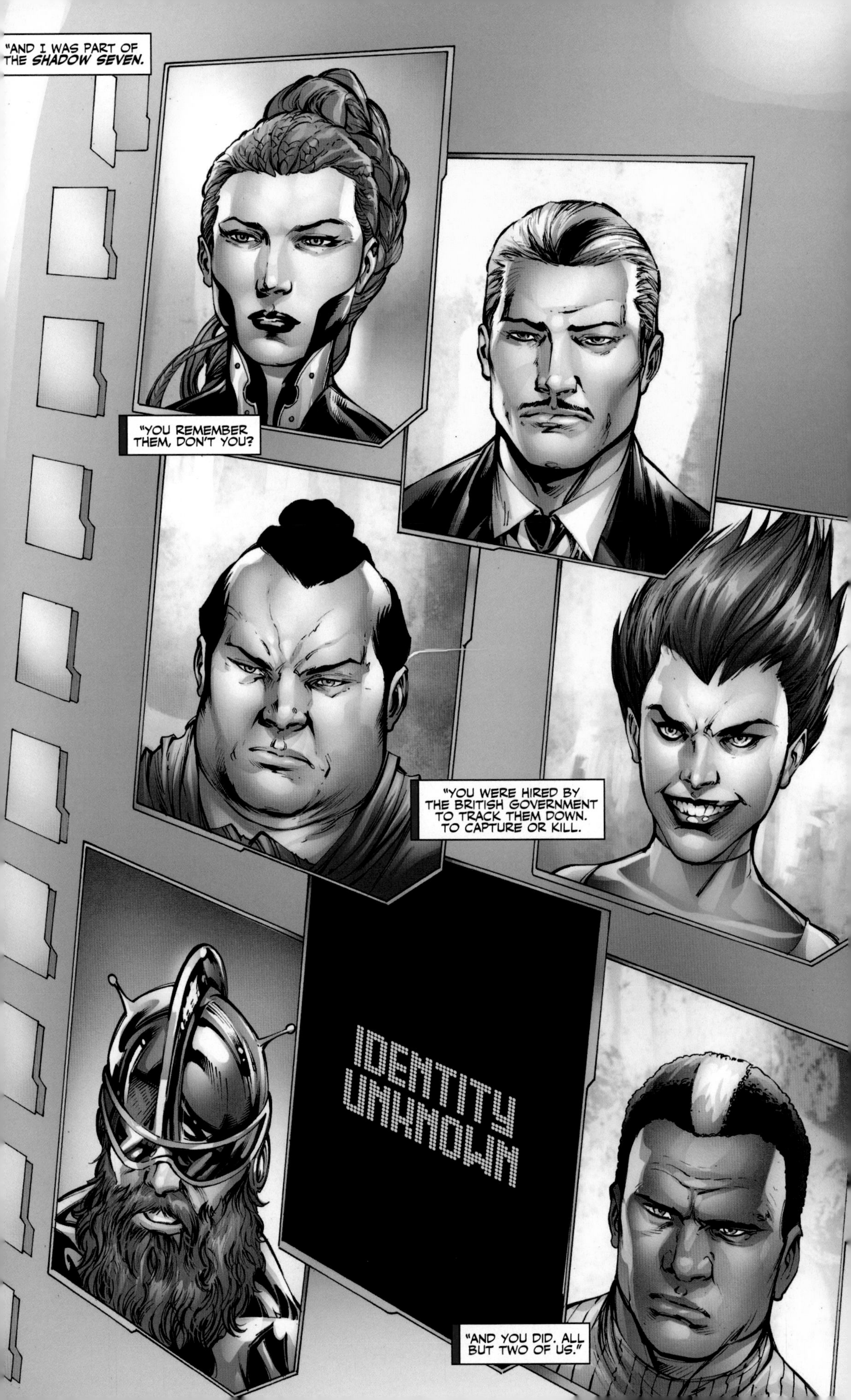
"AND I WAS PART OF THE SHADOW SEVEN.
"YOU REMEMBER THEM, DON'T YOU?
"YOU WERE HIRED BY THE BRITISH GOVERNMENT TO TRACK THEM DOWN. TO CAPTURE OR KILL.
IDENTITY UNKNOWN
"AND YOU DID. ALL BUT TWO OF US."

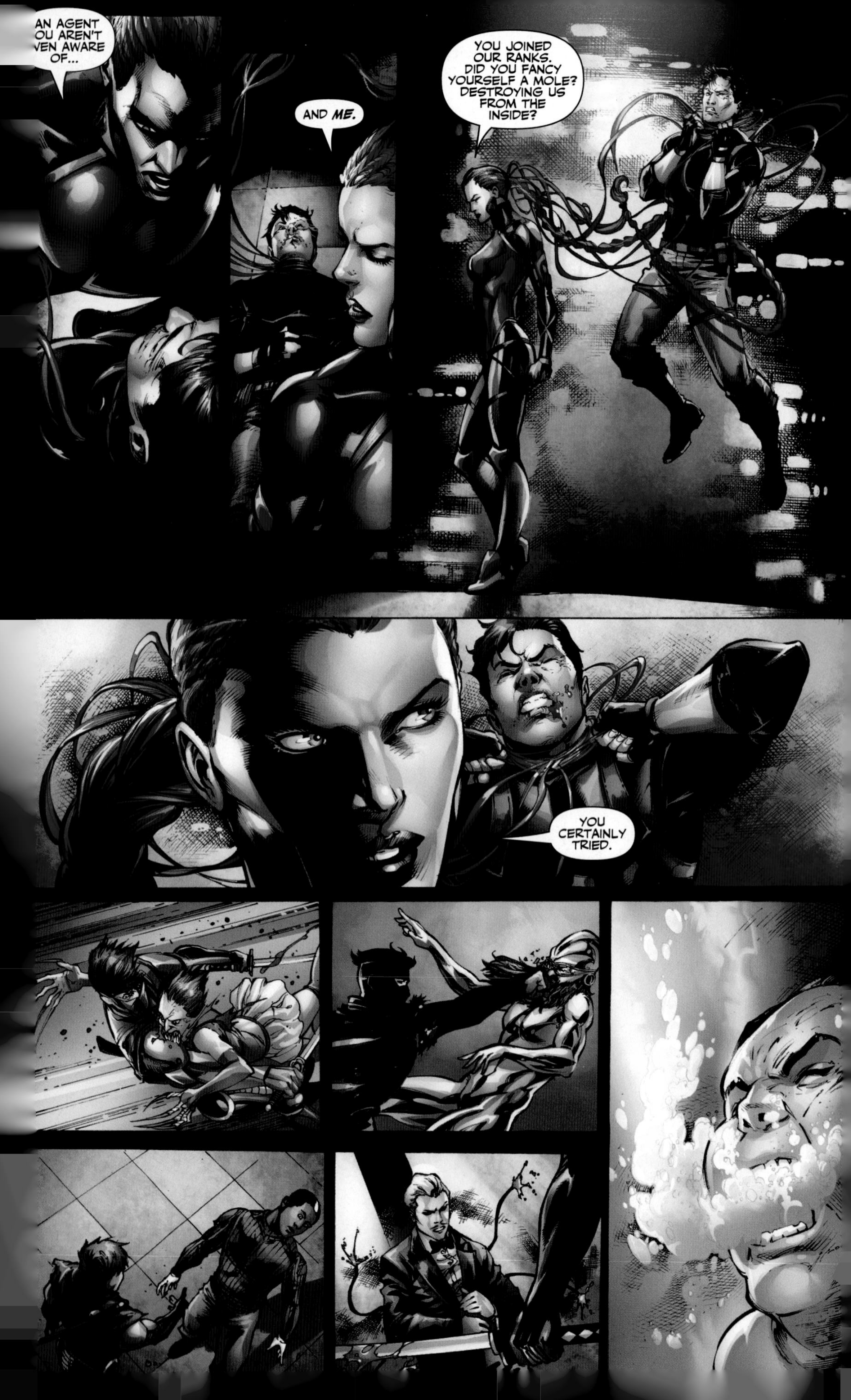
AN AGENT
OU AREN'T
VEN AWARE
OF...
AND ME.
YOU JOINED OUR RANKS. DID YOU FANCY YOURSELF A MOLE? DESTROYING US FROM THE INSIDE?
YOU CERTAINLY TRIED.

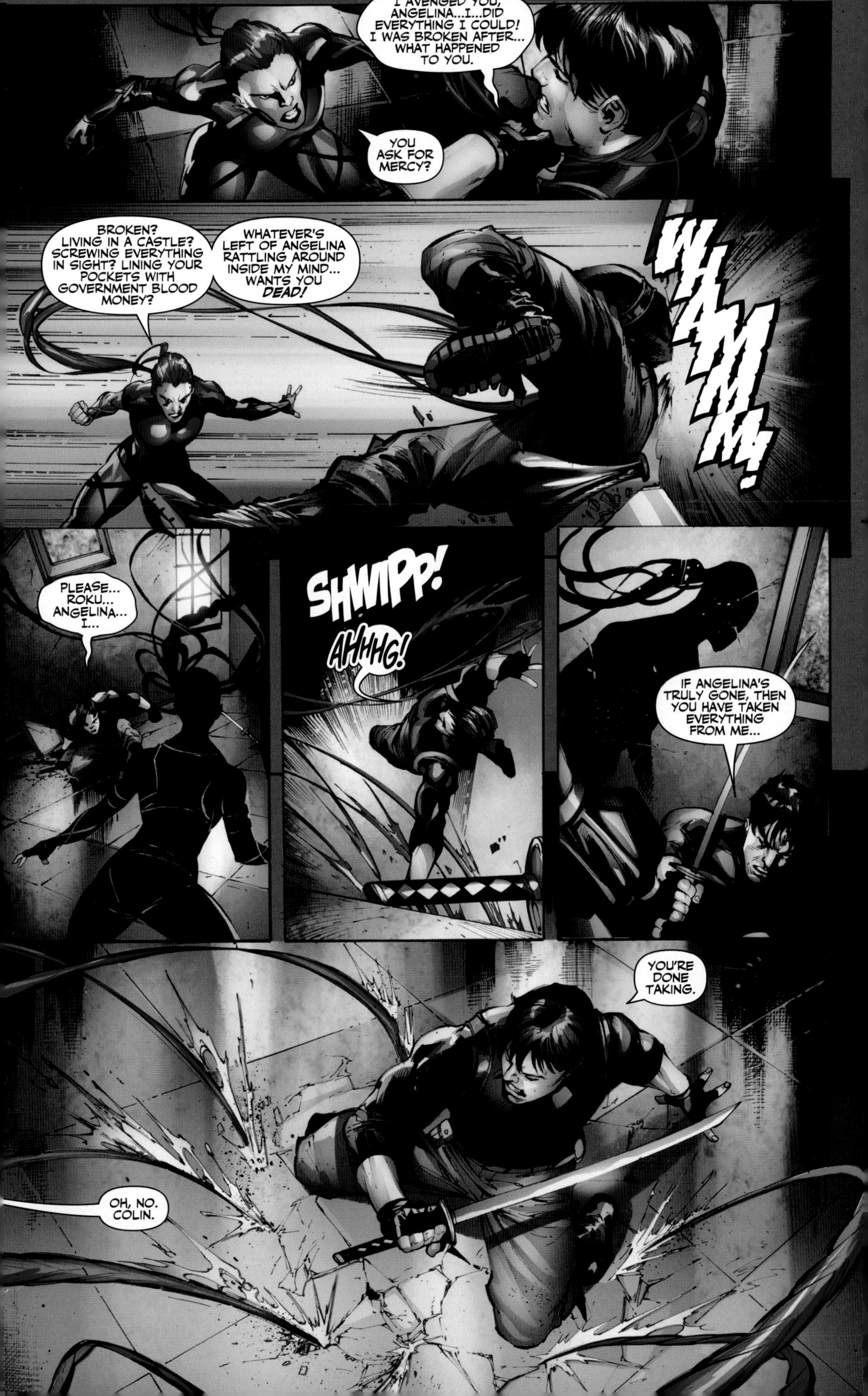
I AVENGED YOU, ANGELINA...I...DID EVERYTHING I COULD! I WAS BROKEN AFTER... WHAT HAPPENED TO YOU.
YOU ASK FOR MERCY?
BROKEN? LIVING IN A CASTLE? SCREWING EVERYTHING IN SIGHT? LINING YOUR POCKETS WITH GOVERNMENT BLOOD MONEY?
WHATEVER'S LEFT OF ANGELINA RATTLING AROUND INSIDE MY MIND... WANTS YOU DEAD!
WHAMM!
PLEASE... ROKU... ANGELINA... I...
SHWIPP!
AHHHG!
IF ANGELINA'S TRULY GONE, THEN YOU HAVE TAKEN EVERYTHING FROM ME...
YOU'RE DONE TAKING.
OH, NO. COLIN.

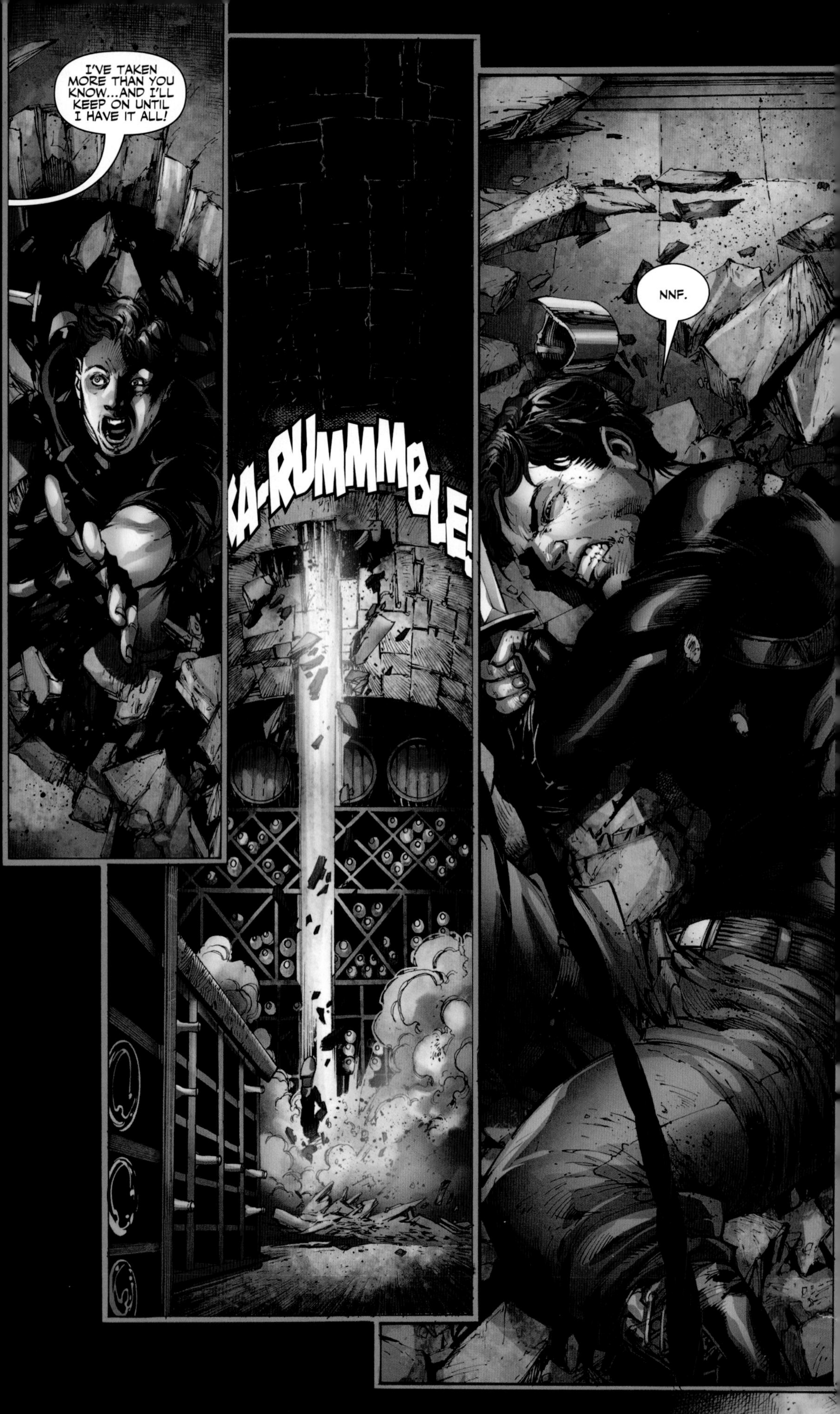
I'VE TAKEN MORE THAN YOU KNOW...AND I'LL KEEP ON UNTIL I HAVE IT ALL!
KA-RUMMMBLE!
NNF.

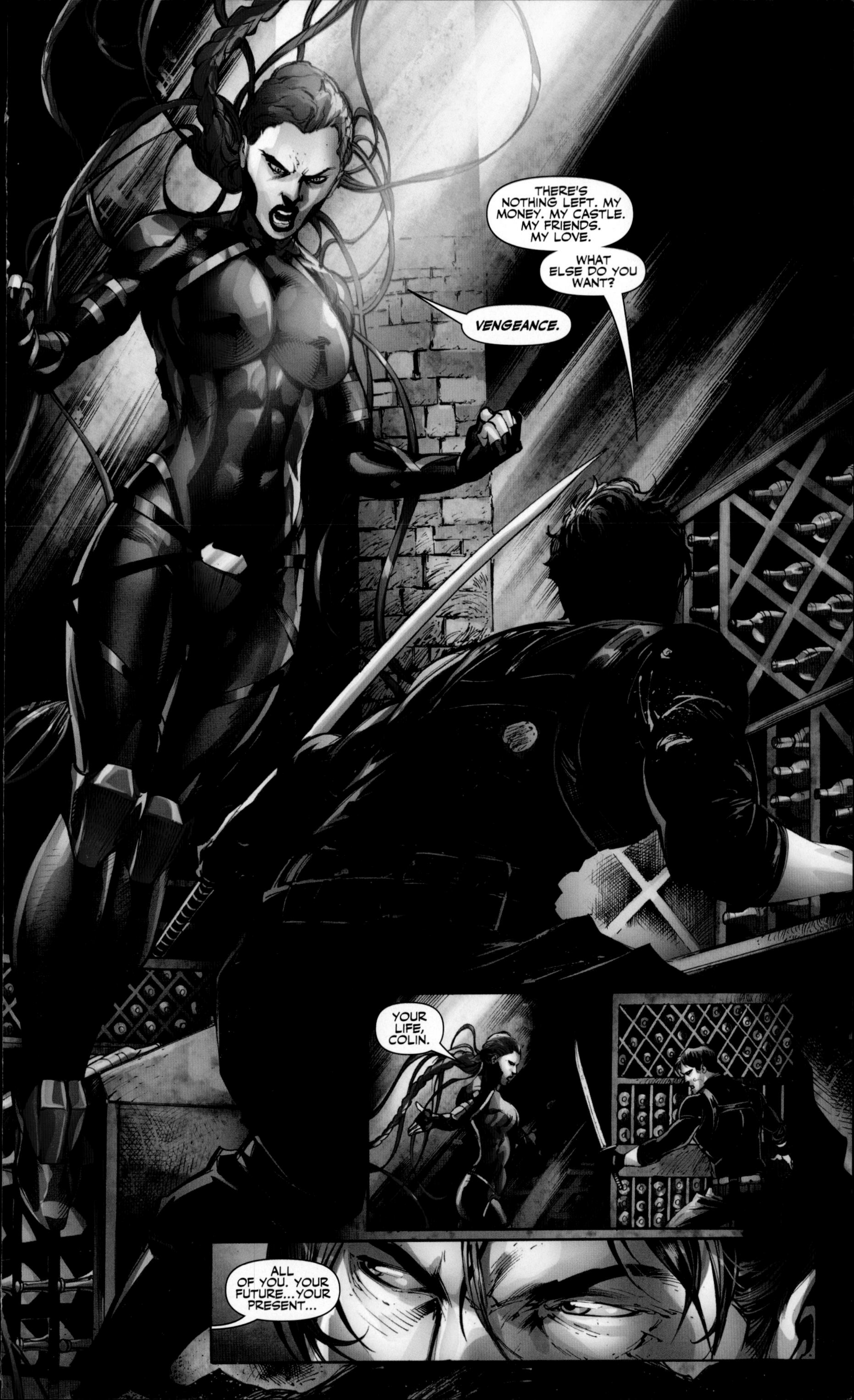
THERE'S NOTHING LEFT. MY MONEY. MY CASTLE. MY FRIENDS. MY LOVE.
WHAT ELSE DO YOU WANT?
VENGEANCE.
YOUR LIFE, COLIN.
ALL OF YOU. YOUR FUTURE...YOUR PRESENT...

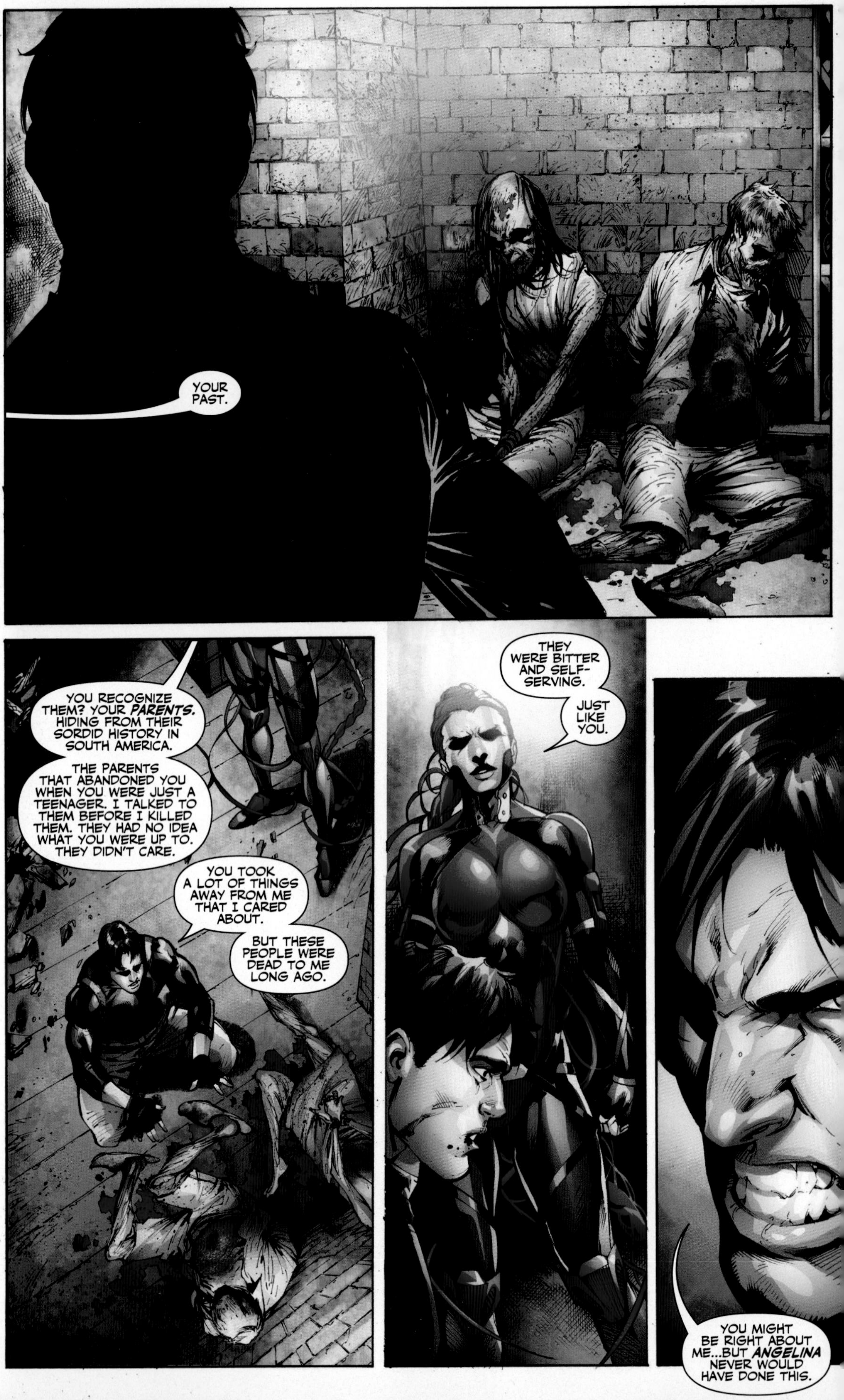
YOUR PAST.
YOU RECOGNIZE THEM? YOUR PARENTS. HIDING FROM THEIR SORDID HISTORY IN SOUTH AMERICA.
THE PARENTS THAT ABANDONED YOU WHEN YOU WERE JUST A TEENAGER. I TALKED TO THEM BEFORE I KILLED THEM. THEY HAD NO IDEA WHAT YOU WERE UP TO. THEY DIDN'T CARE.
YOU TOOK A LOT OF THINGS AWAY FROM ME THAT I CARED ABOUT.
BUT THESE PEOPLE WERE DEAD TO ME LONG AGO.
THEY WERE BITTER AND SELF-SERVING.
JUST LIKE YOU.
YOU MIGHT BE RIGHT ABOUT ME...BUT ANGELINA NEVER WOULD HAVE DONE THIS.

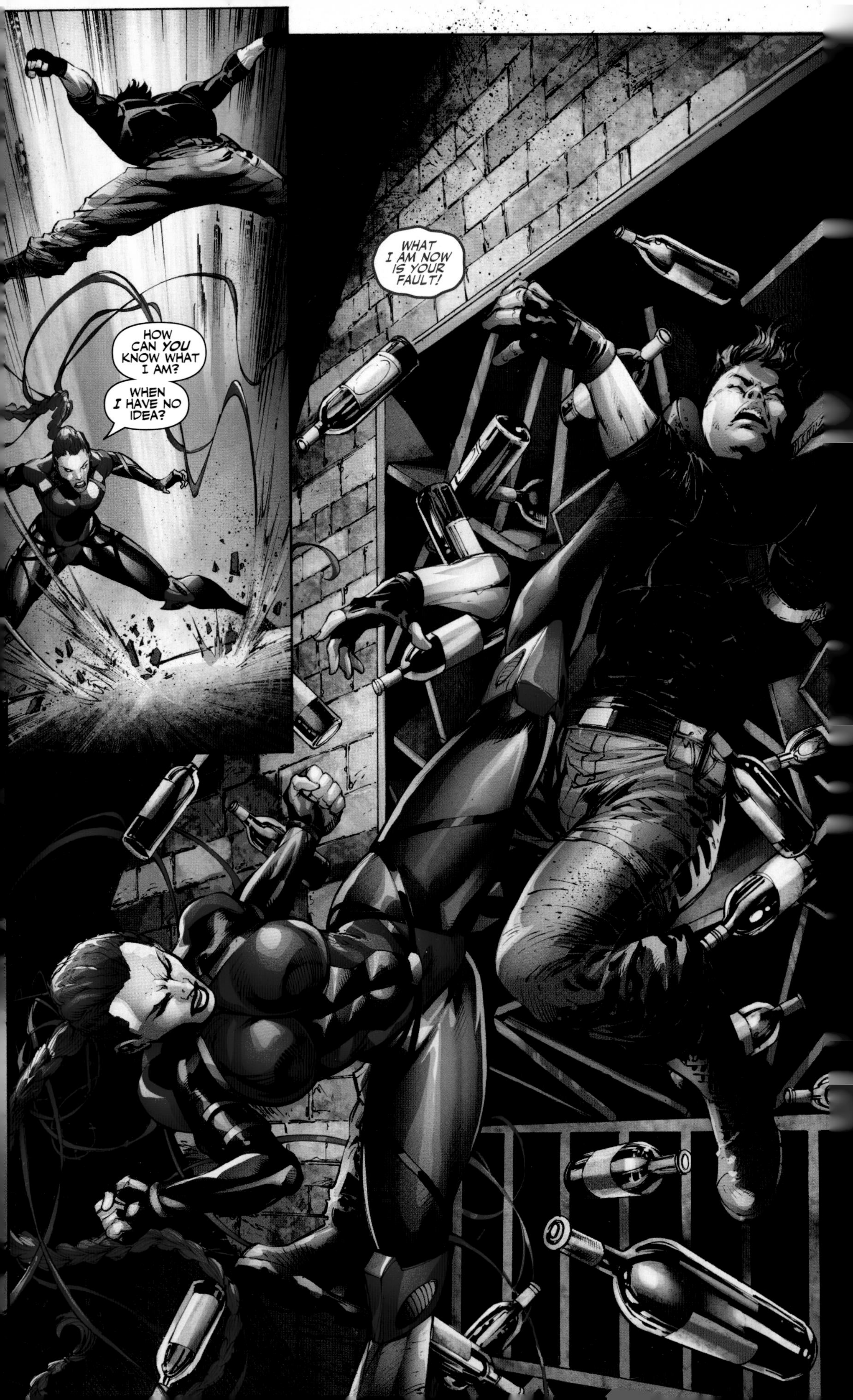
HOW CAN YOU KNOW WHAT I AM?
WHEN I HAVE NO IDEA?
WHAT I AM NOW IS YOUR FAULT!

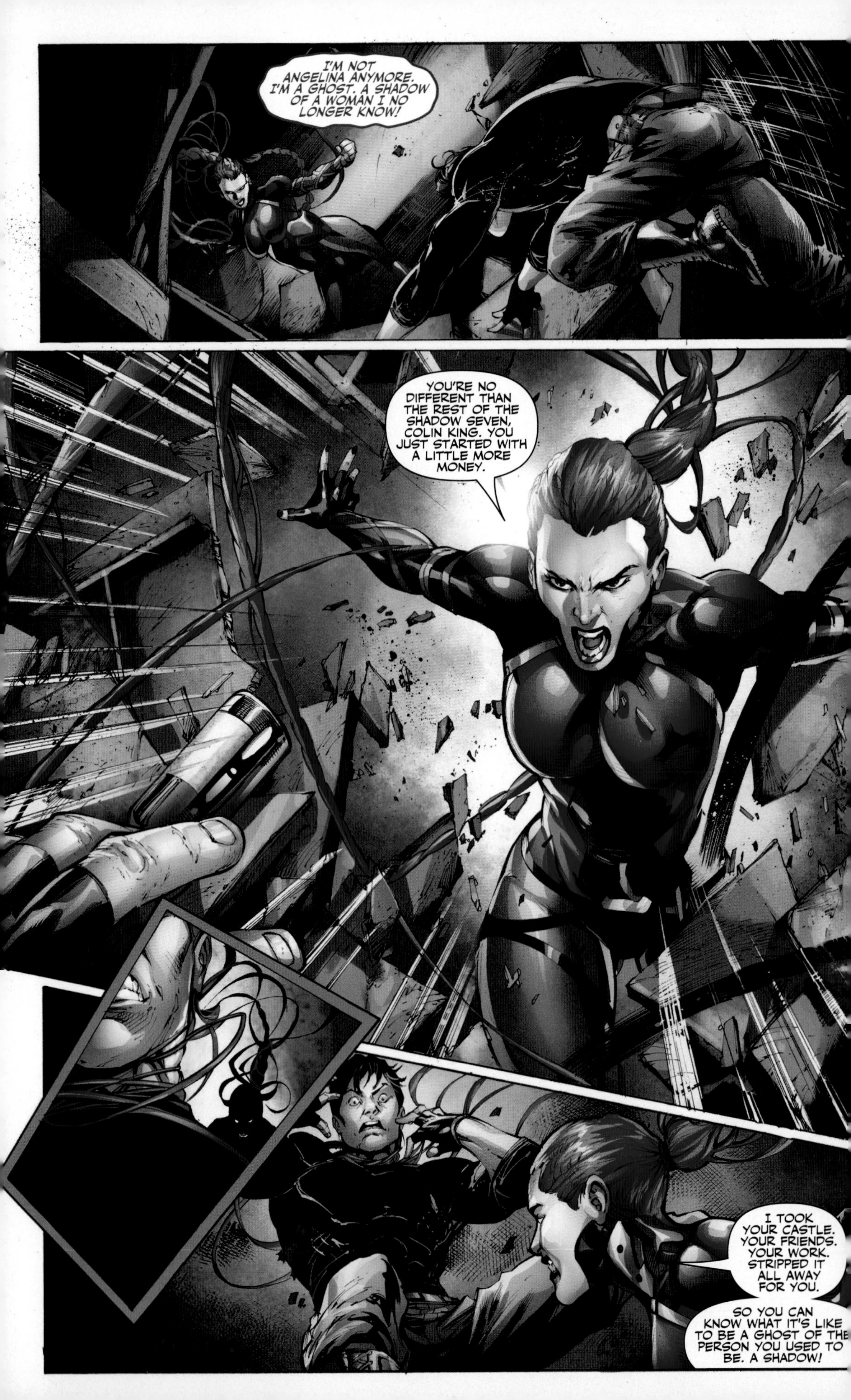
I'M NOT ANGELINA ANYMORE. I'M A GHOST. A SHADOW OF A WOMAN I NO LONGER KNOW!
YOU'RE NO DIFFERENT THAN THE REST OF THE SHADOW SEVEN, COLIN KING. YOU JUST STARTED WITH A LITTLE MORE MONEY.
I TOOK YOUR CASTLE. YOUR FRIENDS. YOUR WORK. STRIPPED IT ALL AWAY FOR YOU.
SO YOU CAN KNOW WHAT IT'S LIKE TO BE A GHOST OF THE PERSON YOU USED TO BE. A SHADOW!

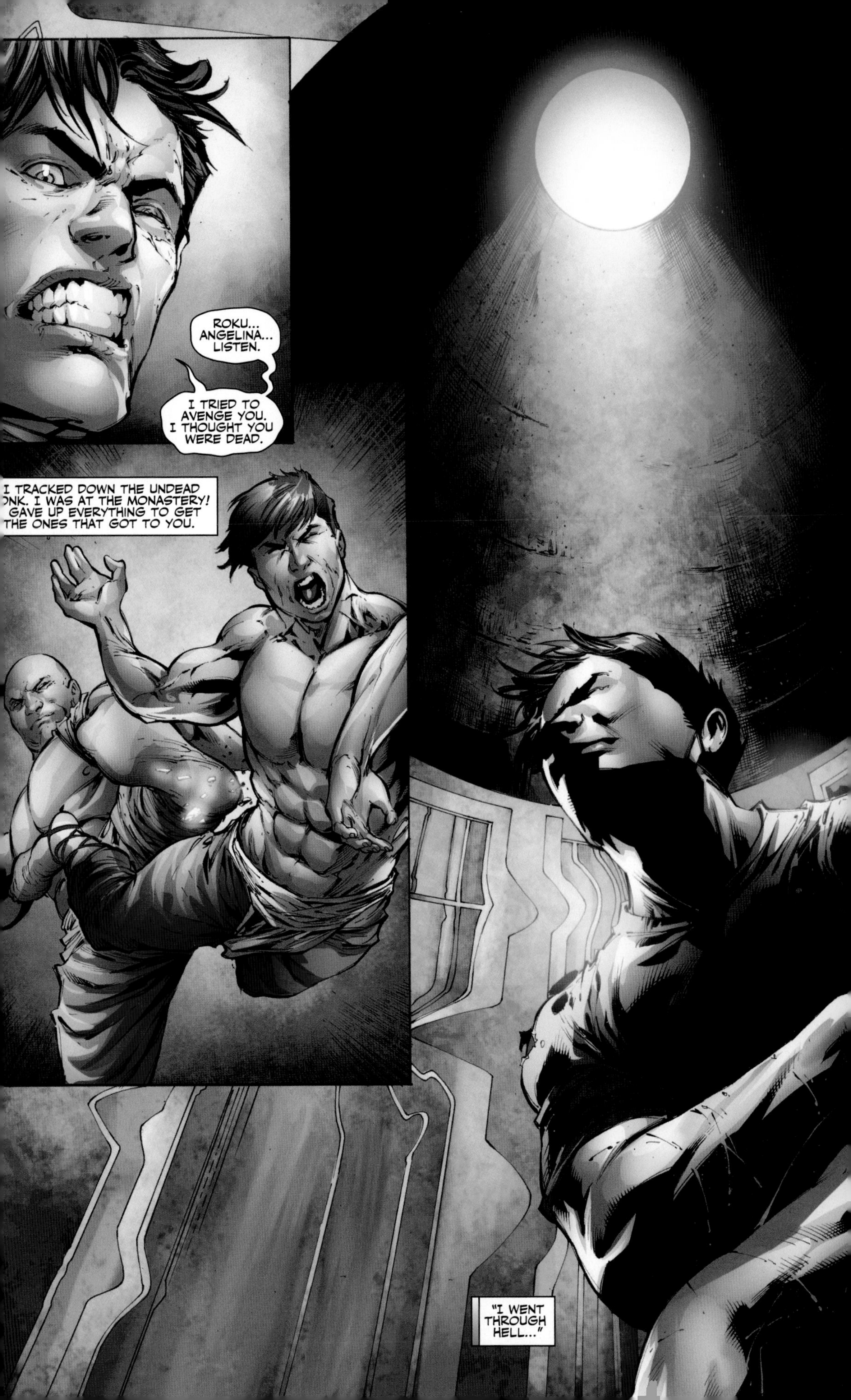
ROKU... ANGELINA... LISTEN.
I TRIED TO AVENGE YOU. I THOUGHT YOU WERE DEAD.
I TRACKED DOWN THE UNDEAD
ONK. I WAS AT THE MONASTERY!
GAVE UP EVERYTHING TO GET
THE ONES THAT GOT TO YOU.
"I WENT THROUGH HELL..."

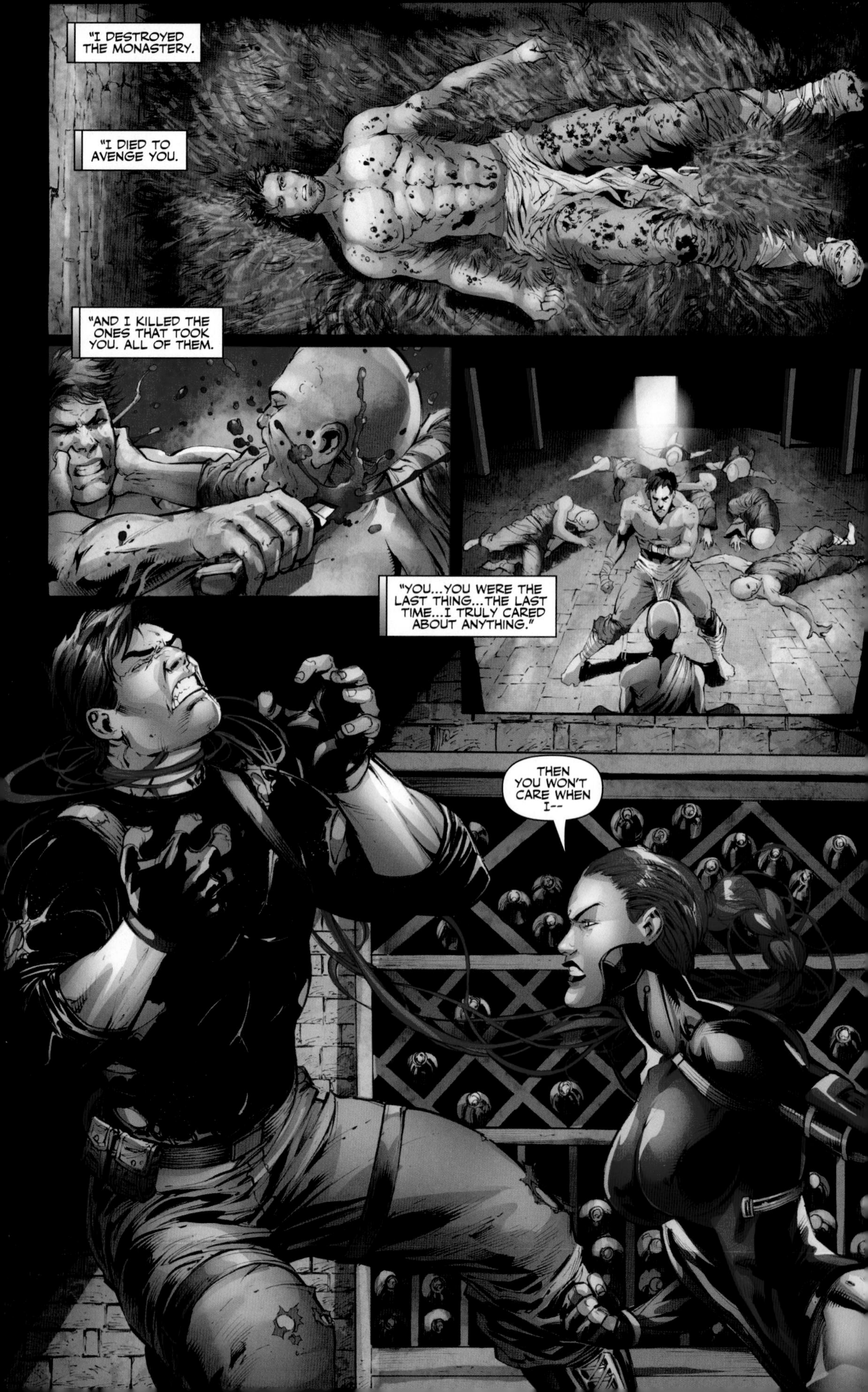
"I DESTROYED THE MONASTERY.
"I DIED TO AVENGE YOU.
"AND I KILLED THE ONES THAT TOOK YOU. ALL OF THEM.
"YOU...YOU WERE THE LAST THING...THE LAST TIME...I TRULY CARED ABOUT ANYTHING."
THEN YOU WON'T CARE WHEN I--

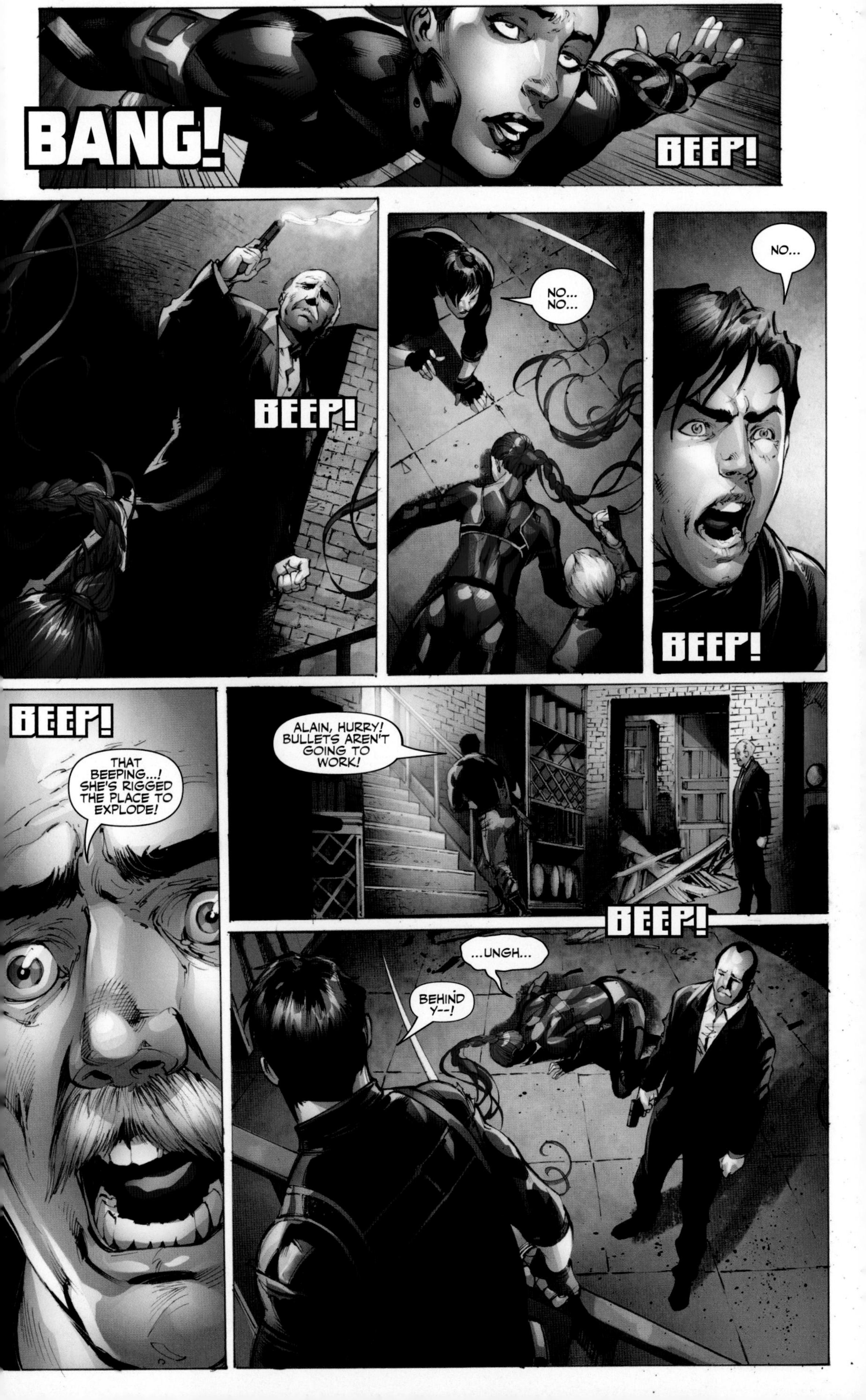
BANG!
BEEP!
BEEP!
NO... NO...
NO...
BEEP!
BEEP!
THAT BEEPING...! SHE'S RIGGED THE PLACE TO EXPLODE!
ALAIN, HURRY! BULLETS AREN'T GOING TO WORK!
BEEP!
...UNGH...
BEHIND Y--!

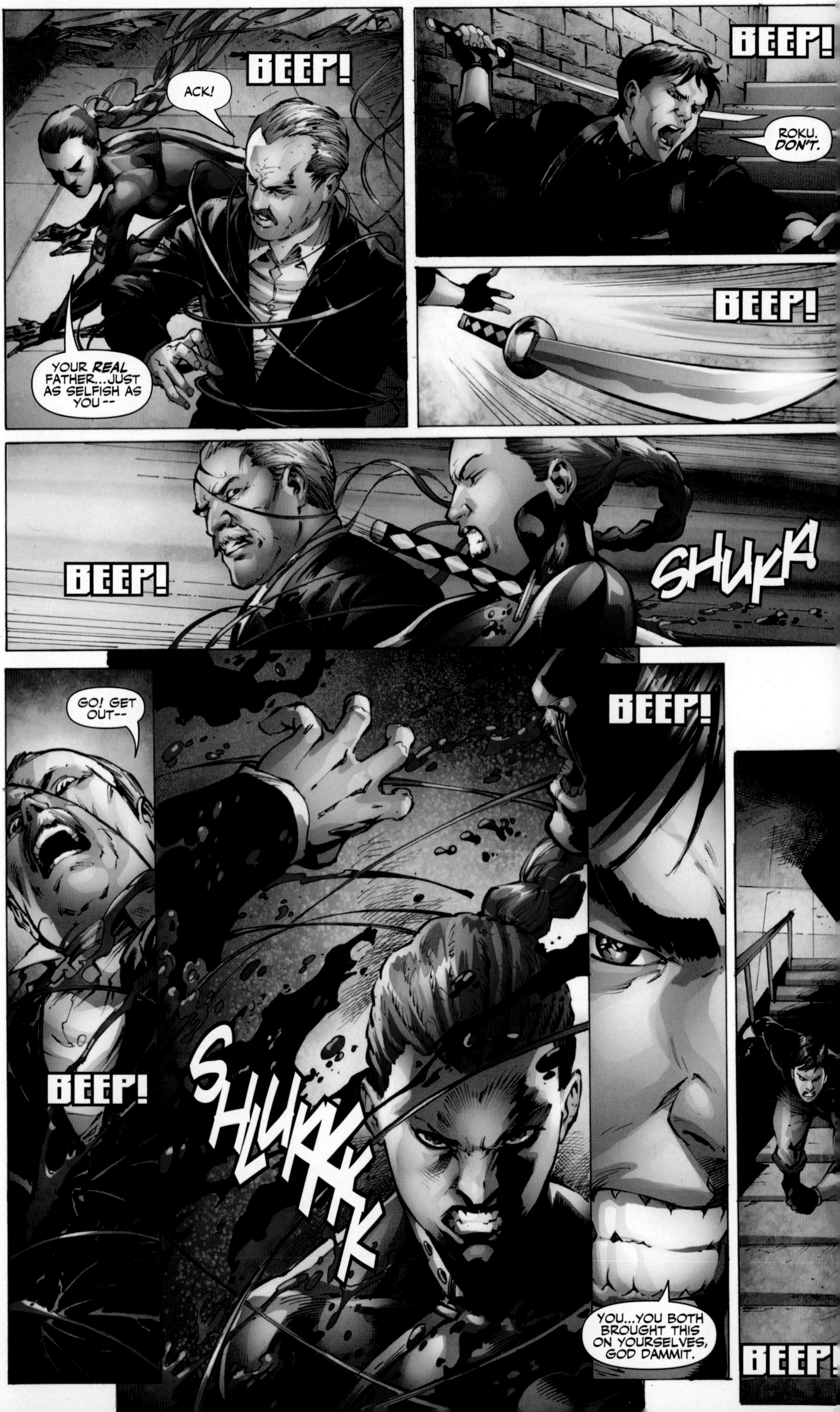
BEEP!
ACK!
YOUR REAL FATHER...JUST AS SELFISH AS YOU--
BEEP!
ROKU. DON'T.
BEEP!
BEEP!
SHUKK!
GO! GET OUT--
BEEP!
SHLUKKK
BEEP!
YOU...YOU BOTH BROUGHT THIS ON YOURSELVES, GOD DAMMIT.
BEEP!

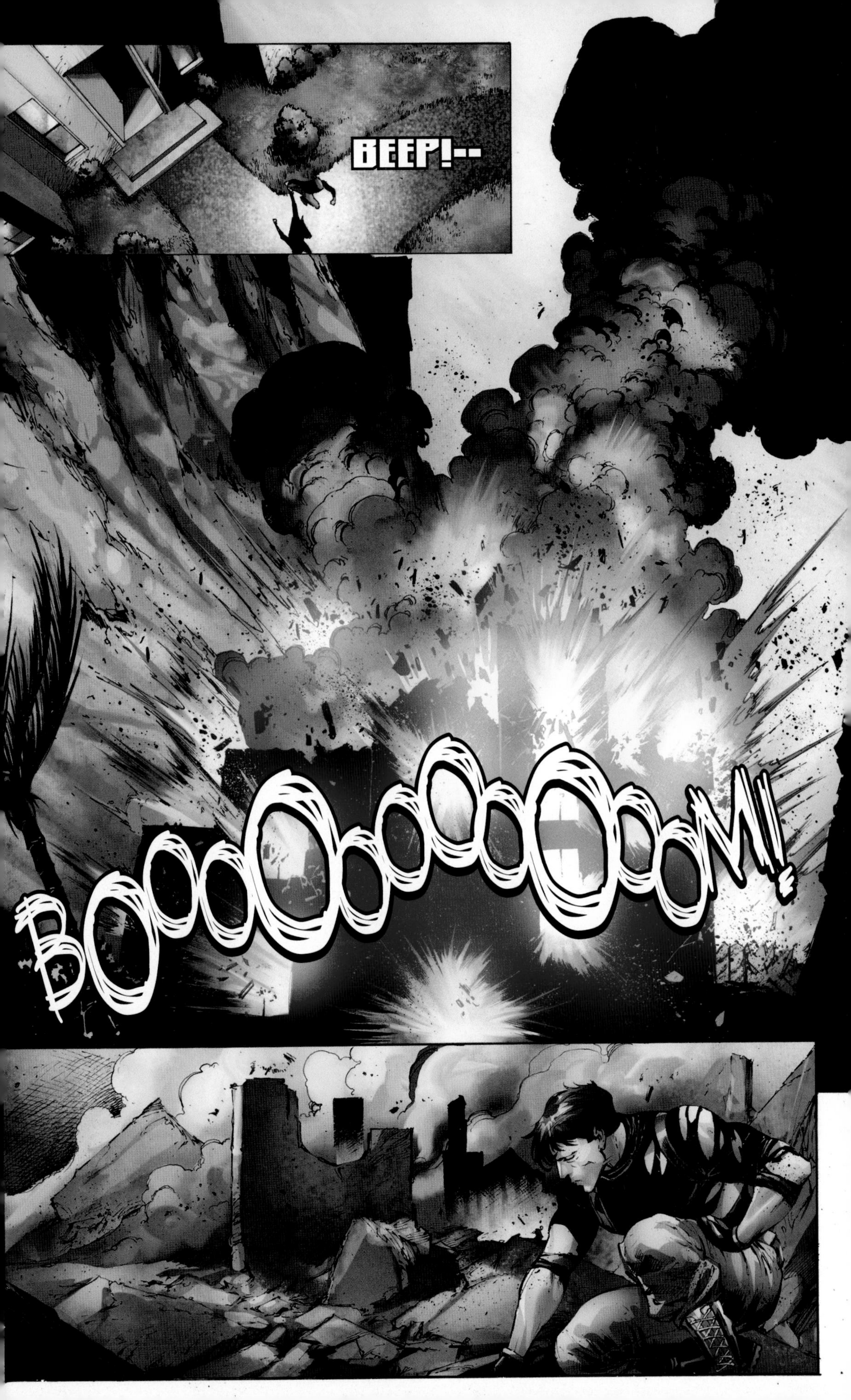
BEEP!--
BOOOOOOOOOOOM!!

I HIRED A LOCAL CONSTRUCTION CREW TO SEARCH THE RUBBLE. THEY FOUND ALAIN. BUT NO ROKU.

I'M NOT SURE HOW TO PROCESS ALL OF IT. USUALLY I JUST... I JUST PUT IT IN A BOX AND FILE IT AWAY. BUT THAT'S NOT REALLY WORKING THIS TIME.

I CAN'T THANK YOU ENOUGH FOR GETTING ME SOME MONEY. FAKE I.D.S. HELPING ME GET TO VENEZUELA.

YOU DID A LOT. PUT YOUR NECK OUT FOR ME.

RISKED BETRAYING YOUR FRIENDS. LOSING YOUR JOB.

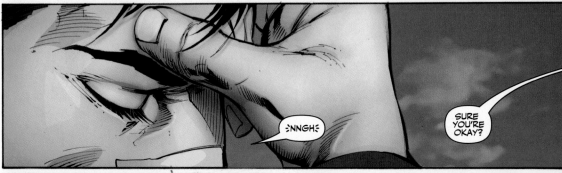

ƎNNGHƎ

SURE YOU'RE OKAY?

YEAH. SORRY. IT'S BEEN...IT'S BEEN A BLOODY MISERABLE COUPLE OF WEEKS.

COLIN. IT'S OKAY. THIS IS WHAT...WHAT FRIENDS DO.

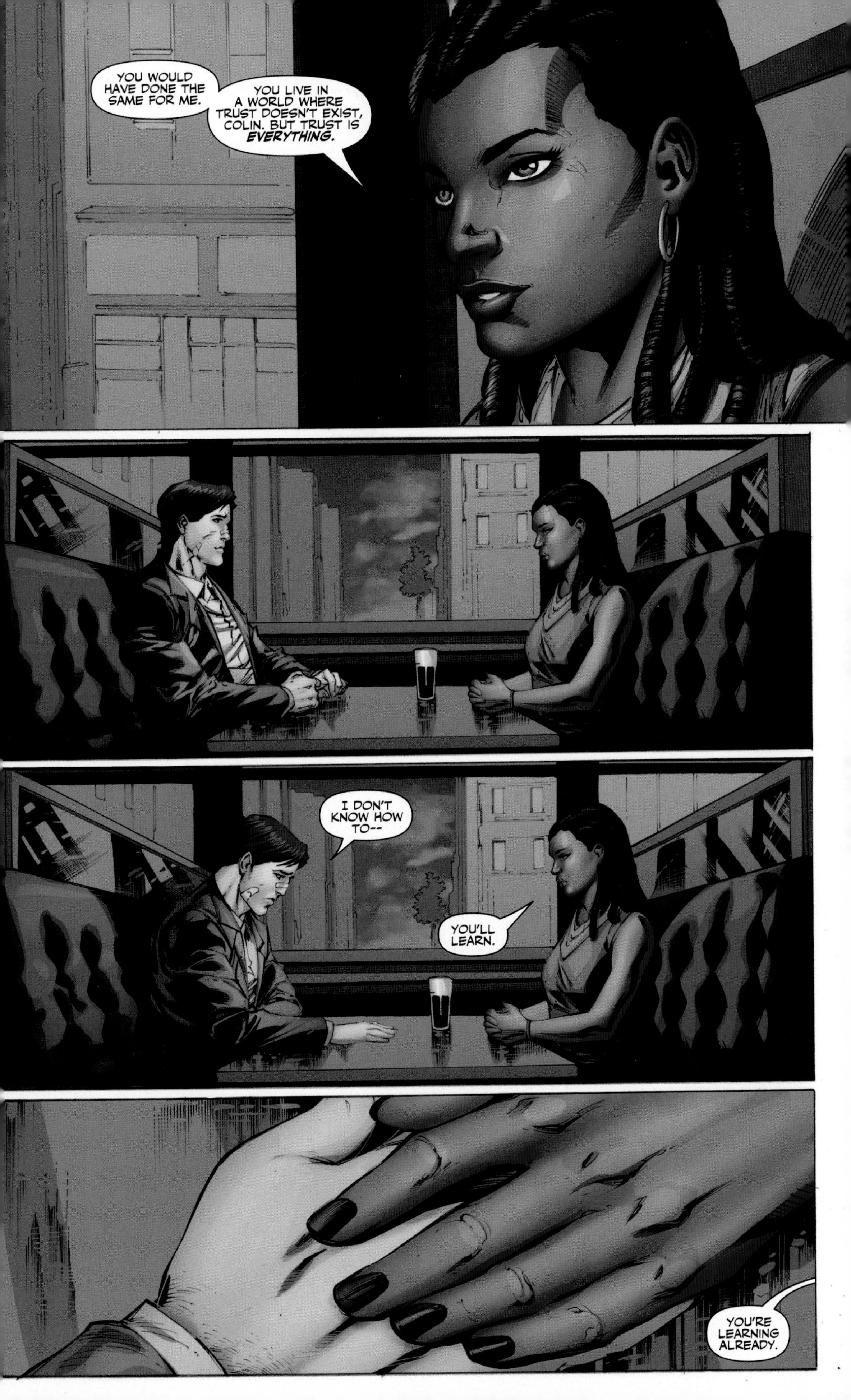
YOU WOULD HAVE DONE THE SAME FOR ME.
YOU LIVE IN A WORLD WHERE TRUST DOESN'T EXIST, COLIN. BUT TRUST IS *EVERYTHING*.
I DON'T KNOW HOW TO--
YOU'LL LEARN.
YOU'RE LEARNING ALREADY.

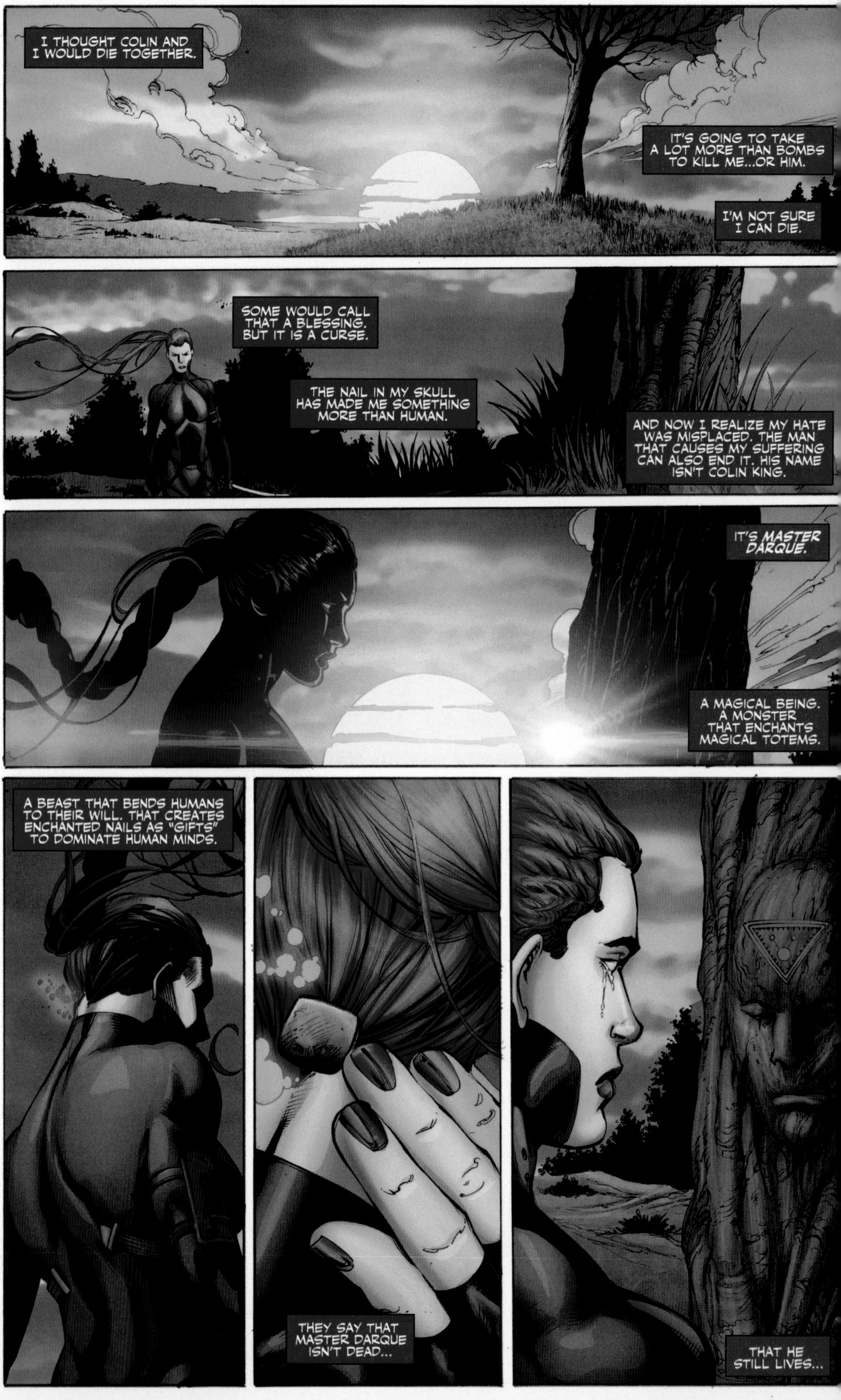
I THOUGHT COLIN AND I WOULD DIE TOGETHER.
IT'S GOING TO TAKE A LOT MORE THAN BOMBS TO KILL ME...OR HIM.
I'M NOT SURE I CAN DIE.
SOME WOULD CALL THAT A BLESSING. BUT IT IS A CURSE.
THE NAIL IN MY SKULL HAS MADE ME SOMETHING MORE THAN HUMAN.
AND NOW I REALIZE MY HATE WAS MISPLACED. THE MAN THAT CAUSES MY SUFFERING CAN ALSO END IT. HIS NAME ISN'T COLIN KING.
IT'S MASTER DARQUE.
A MAGICAL BEING. A MONSTER THAT ENCHANTS MAGICAL TOTEMS.
A BEAST THAT BENDS HUMANS TO THEIR WILL. THAT CREATES ENCHANTED NAILS AS "GIFTS" TO DOMINATE HUMAN MINDS.
THEY SAY THAT MASTER DARQUE ISN'T DEAD...
THAT HE STILL LIVES...

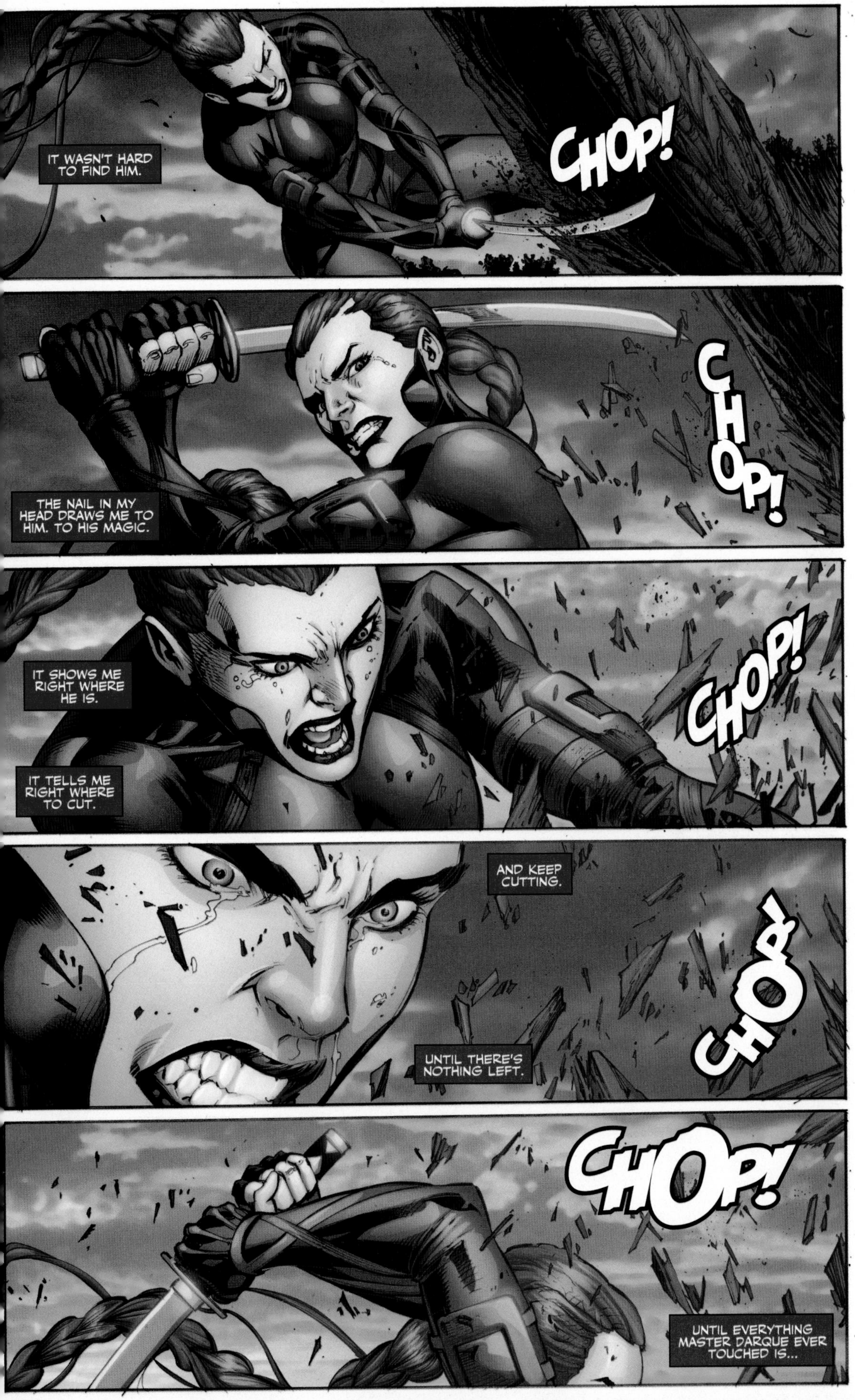
IT WASN'T HARD TO FIND HIM.
CHOP!
THE NAIL IN MY HEAD DRAWS ME TO HIM. TO HIS MAGIC.
CHOP!
IT SHOWS ME RIGHT WHERE HE IS.
IT TELLS ME RIGHT WHERE TO CUT.
CHOP!
AND KEEP CUTTING.
UNTIL THERE'S NOTHING LEFT.
CHOP!
CHOP!
UNTIL EVERYTHING MASTER DARQUE EVER TOUCHED IS...

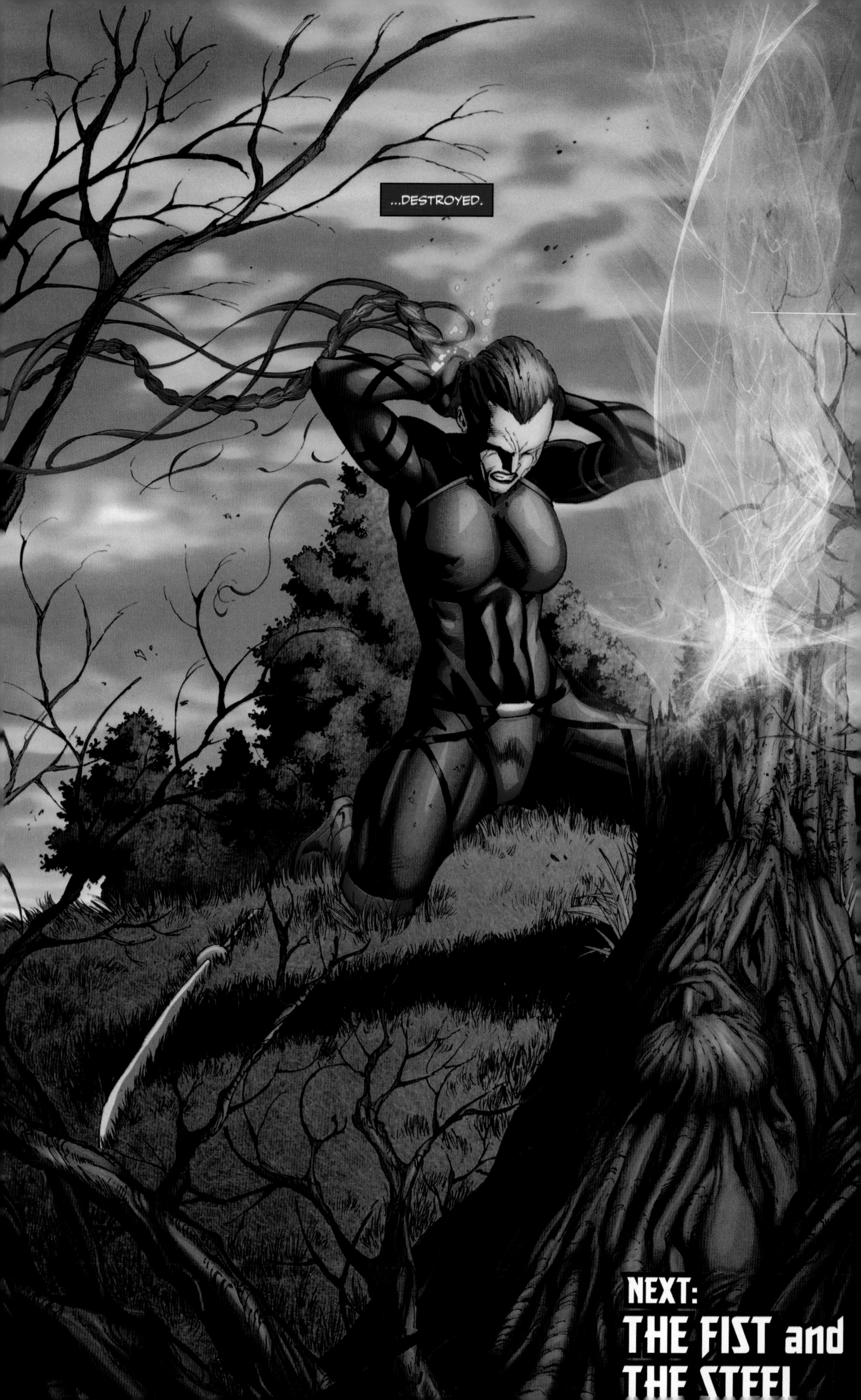
...DESTROYED.
NEXT:
THE FIST and
THE STEEL

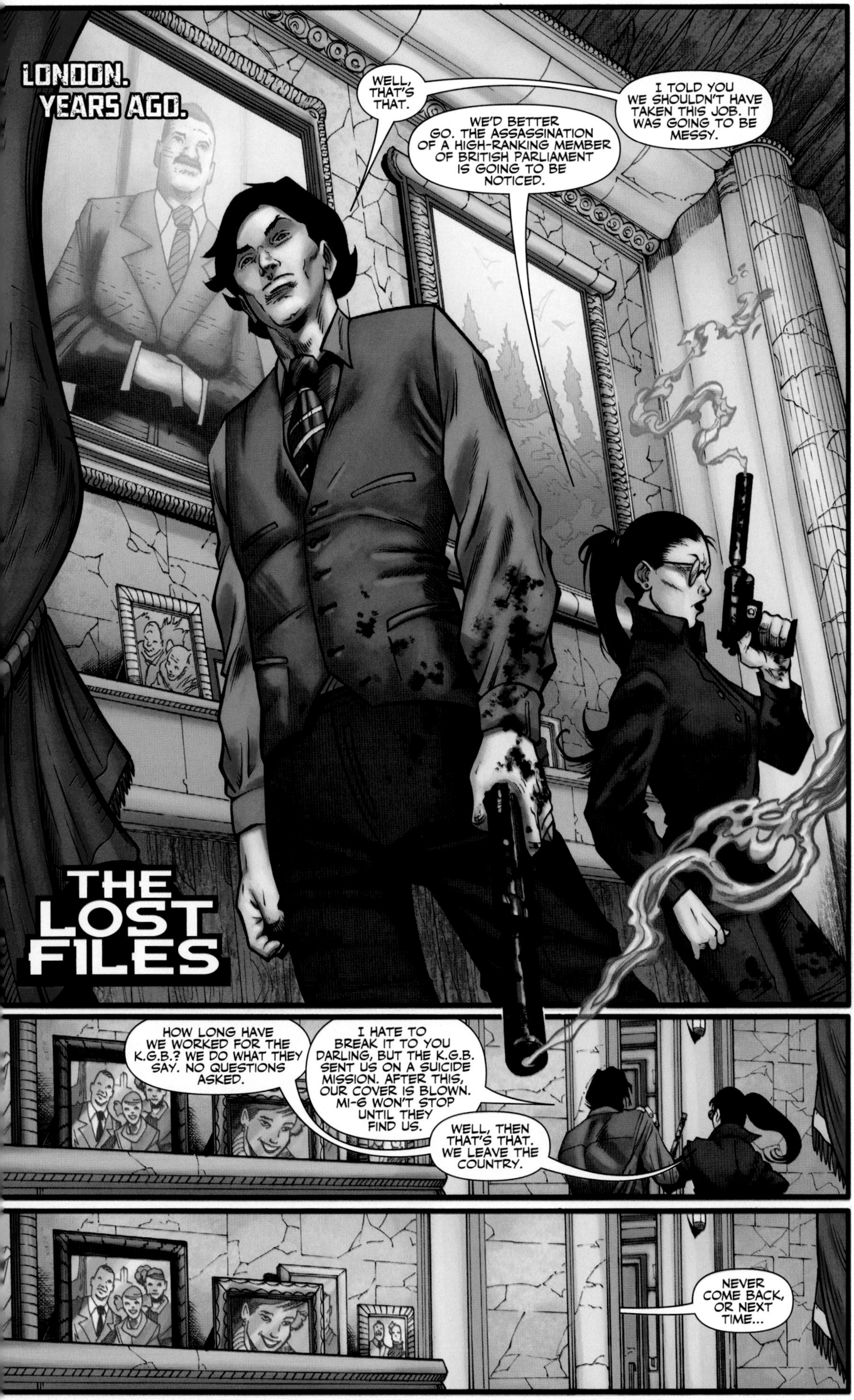
LONDON.
YEARS AGO.
WELL, THAT'S THAT.
WE'D BETTER GO. THE ASSASSINATION OF A HIGH-RANKING MEMBER OF BRITISH PARLIAMENT IS GOING TO BE NOTICED.
I TOLD YOU WE SHOULDN'T HAVE TAKEN THIS JOB. IT WAS GOING TO BE MESSY.
THE LOST FILES
HOW LONG HAVE WE WORKED FOR THE K.G.B.? WE DO WHAT THEY SAY. NO QUESTIONS ASKED.
I HATE TO BREAK IT TO YOU DARLING, BUT THE K.G.B. SENT US ON A SUICIDE MISSION. AFTER THIS, OUR COVER IS BLOWN. MI-6 WON'T STOP UNTIL THEY FIND US.
WELL, THEN THAT'S THAT. WE LEAVE THE COUNTRY.
NEVER COME BACK, OR NEXT TIME...

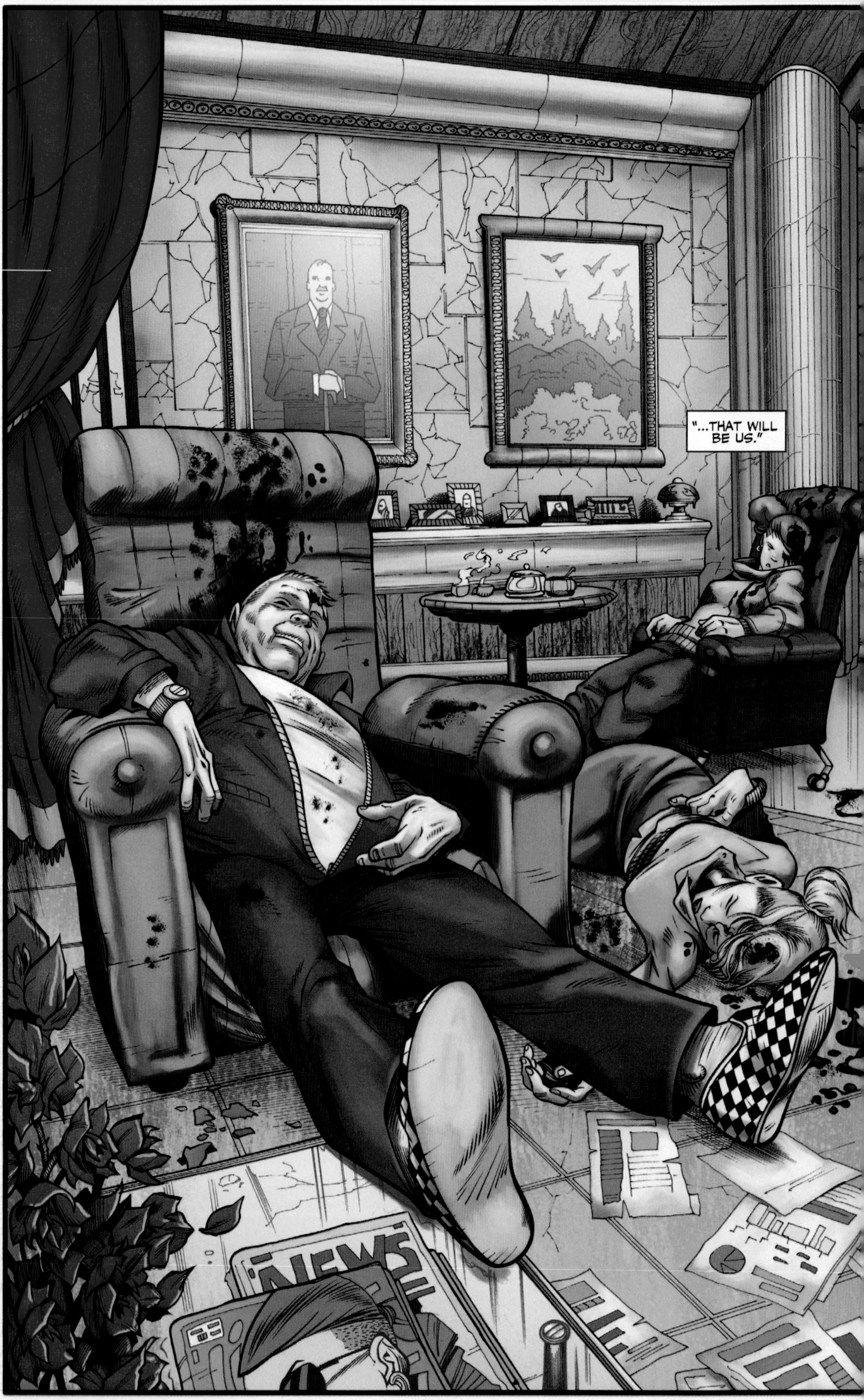
"...THAT WILL BE US."
NEWS

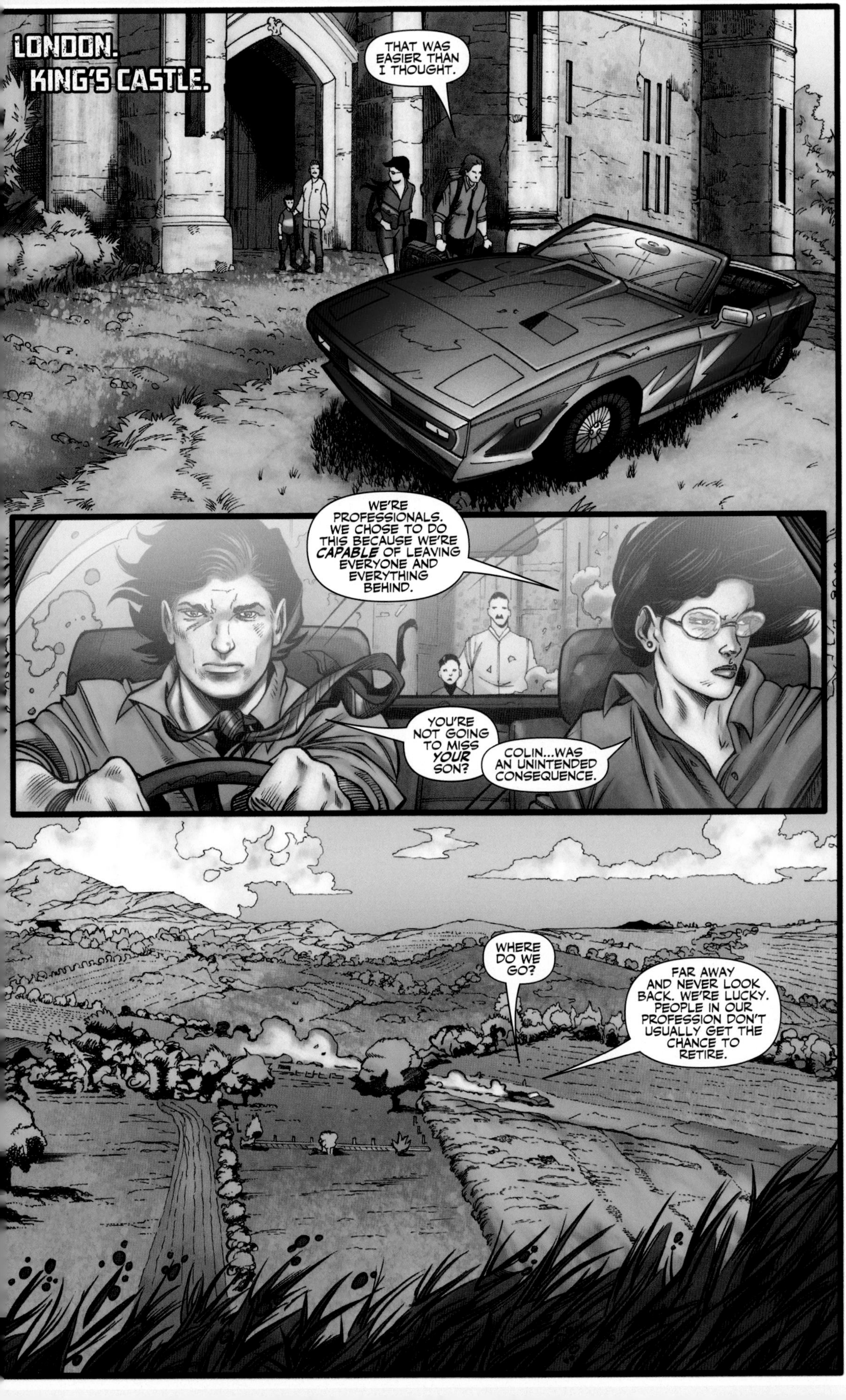
LONDON.
KING'S CASTLE.
THAT WAS EASIER THAN I THOUGHT.
WE'RE PROFESSIONALS. WE CHOSE TO DO THIS BECAUSE WE'RE *CAPABLE* OF LEAVING EVERYONE AND EVERYTHING BEHIND.
YOU'RE NOT GOING TO MISS *YOUR* SON?
COLIN...WAS AN UNINTENDED CONSEQUENCE.
WHERE DO WE GO?
FAR AWAY AND NEVER LOOK BACK. WE'RE LUCKY. PEOPLE IN OUR PROFESSION DON'T USUALLY GET THE CHANCE TO RETIRE.

VENEZUELA.

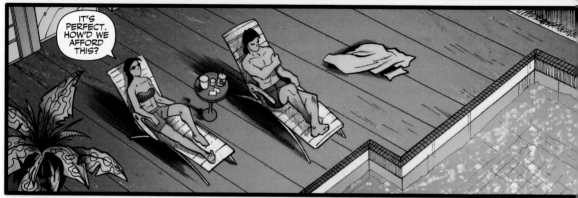

IT'S PERFECT. HOW'D WE AFFORD THIS?

I'D BEEN SKIMMING K.G.B. MONEY FOR YEARS. HAVING IT SHUTTLED TO OFFSHORE ACCOUNTS ALL OVER SOUTH AMERICA.

WE'RE SET FOR LIFE.

YOU FEEL AS GOOD AS I DO?

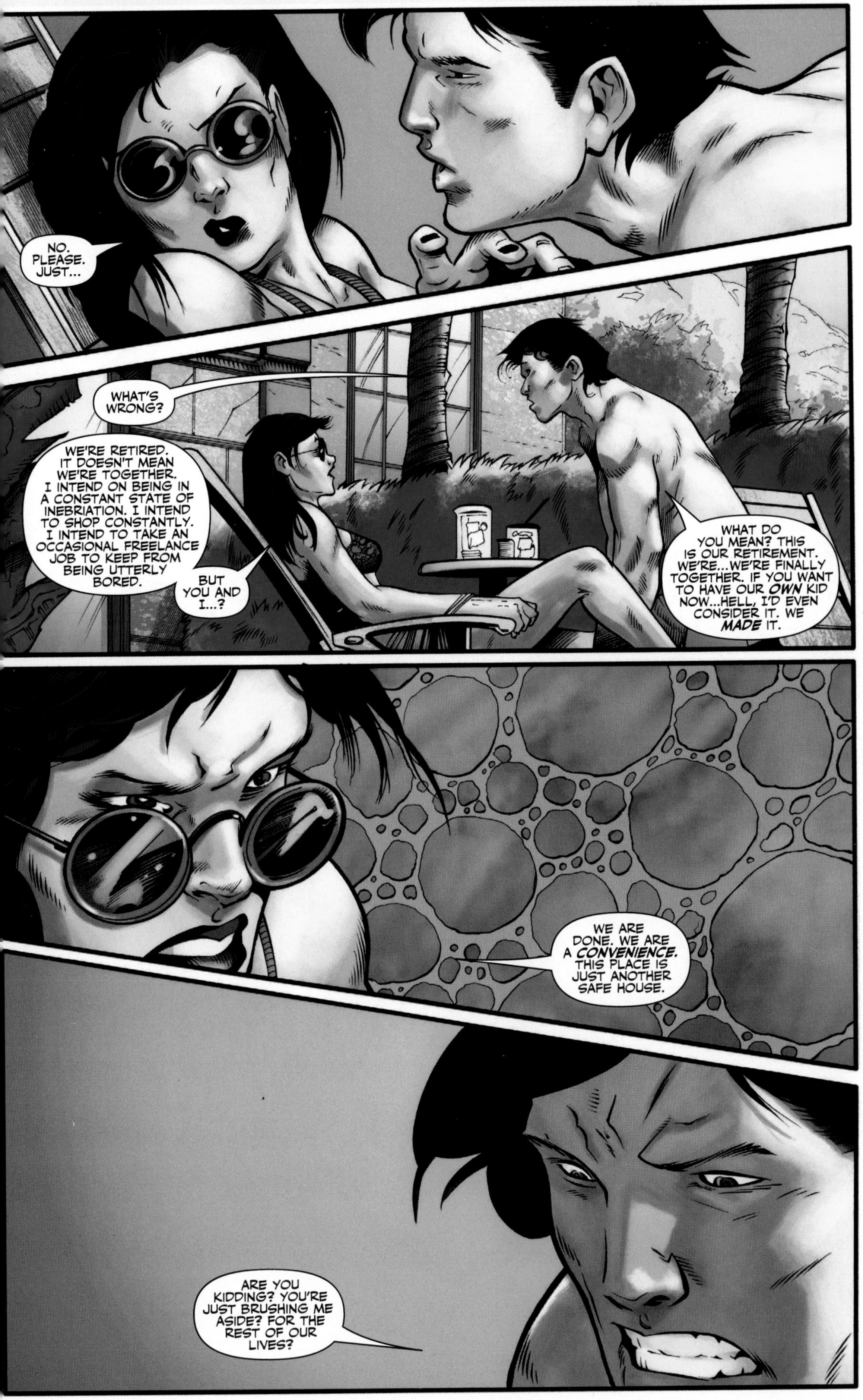
NO. PLEASE. JUST...
WHAT'S WRONG?
WHAT DO YOU MEAN? THIS IS OUR RETIREMENT. WE'RE...WE'RE FINALLY TOGETHER. IF YOU WANT TO HAVE OUR OWN KID NOW...HELL, I'D EVEN CONSIDER IT. WE MADE IT.
WE'RE RETIRED. IT DOESN'T MEAN WE'RE TOGETHER. I INTEND ON BEING IN A CONSTANT STATE OF INEBRIATION. I INTEND TO SHOP CONSTANTLY. I INTEND TO TAKE AN OCCASIONAL FREELANCE JOB TO KEEP FROM BEING UTTERLY BORED.
BUT YOU AND I...?
WE ARE DONE. WE ARE A CONVENIENCE. THIS PLACE IS JUST ANOTHER SAFE HOUSE.
ARE YOU KIDDING? YOU'RE JUST BRUSHING ME ASIDE? FOR THE REST OF OUR LIVES?

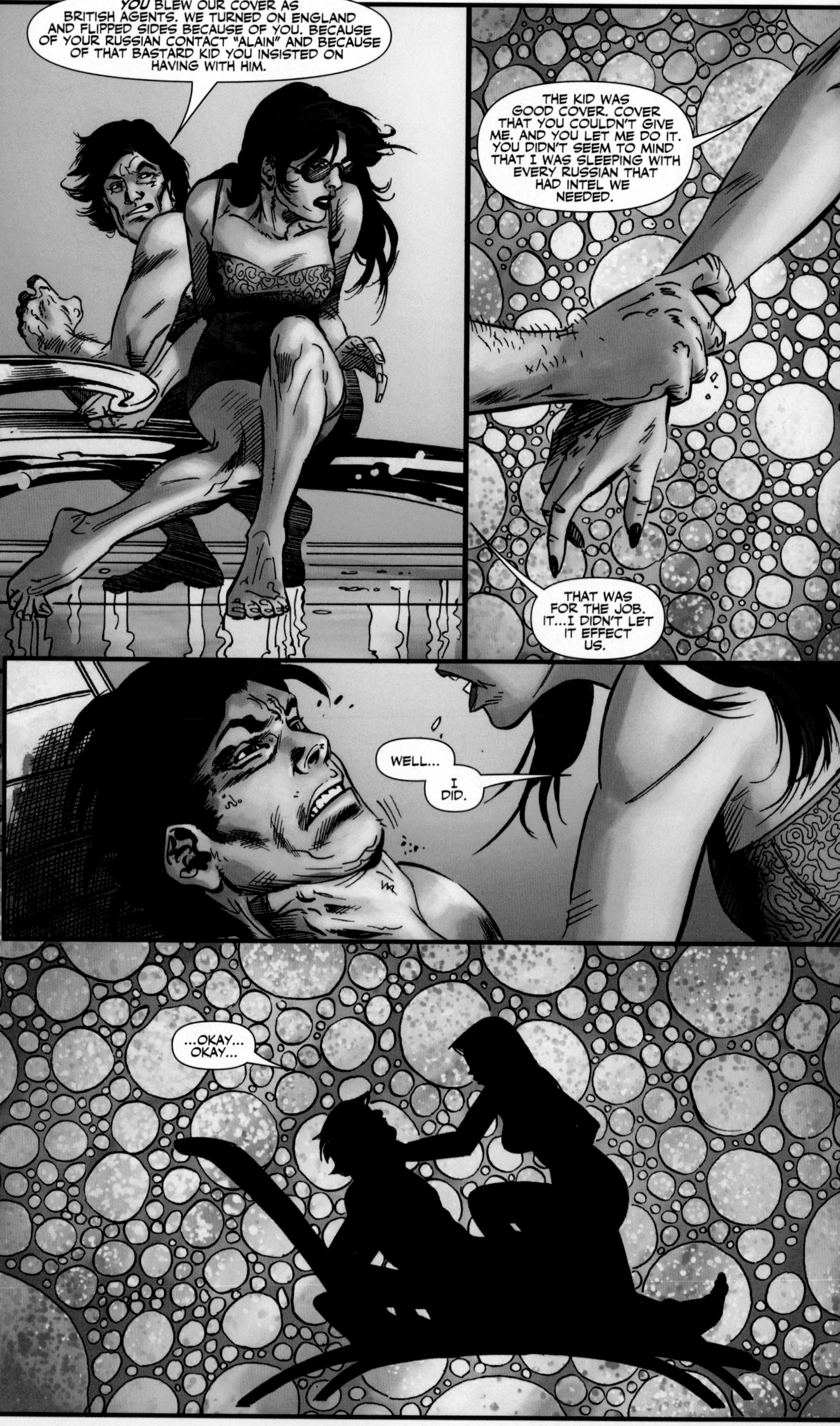
YOU BLEW OUR COVER AS BRITISH AGENTS. WE TURNED ON ENGLAND AND FLIPPED SIDES BECAUSE OF YOU. BECAUSE OF YOUR RUSSIAN CONTACT "ALAIN" AND BECAUSE OF THAT BASTARD KID YOU INSISTED ON HAVING WITH HIM.
THE KID WAS GOOD COVER. COVER THAT YOU COULDN'T GIVE ME. AND YOU LET ME DO IT. YOU DIDN'T SEEM TO MIND THAT I WAS SLEEPING WITH EVERY RUSSIAN THAT HAD INTEL WE NEEDED.
THAT WAS FOR THE JOB. IT...I DIDN'T LET IT EFFECT US.
WELL...
I DID.
...OKAY... OKAY...

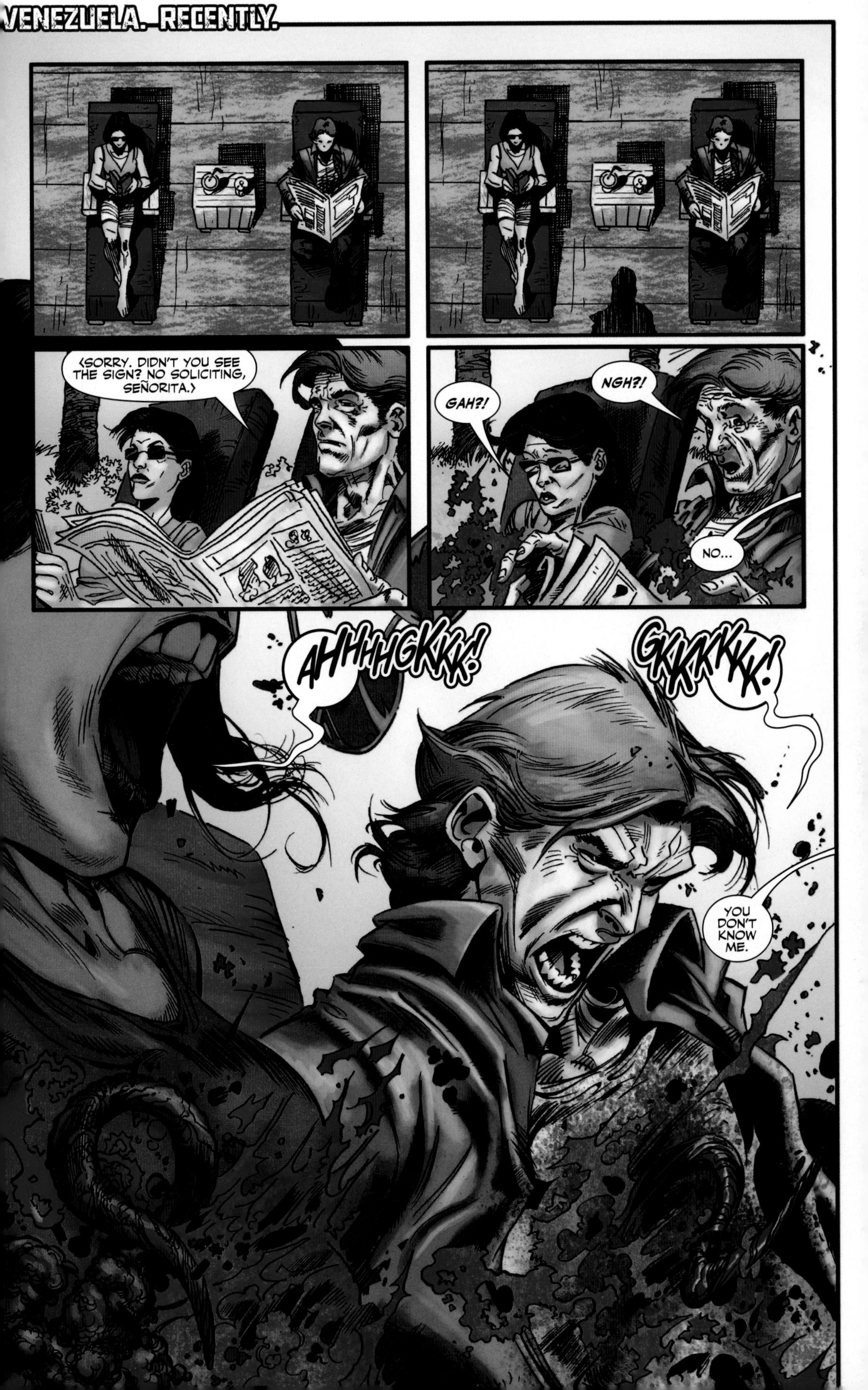
VENEZUELA. RECENTLY.
<SORRY. DIDN'T YOU SEE THE SIGN? NO SOLICITING, SEÑORITA.>
GAH?!
NGH?!
NO...
AHHHHGKKK!
GKKKKKKK!
YOU DON'T KNOW ME.

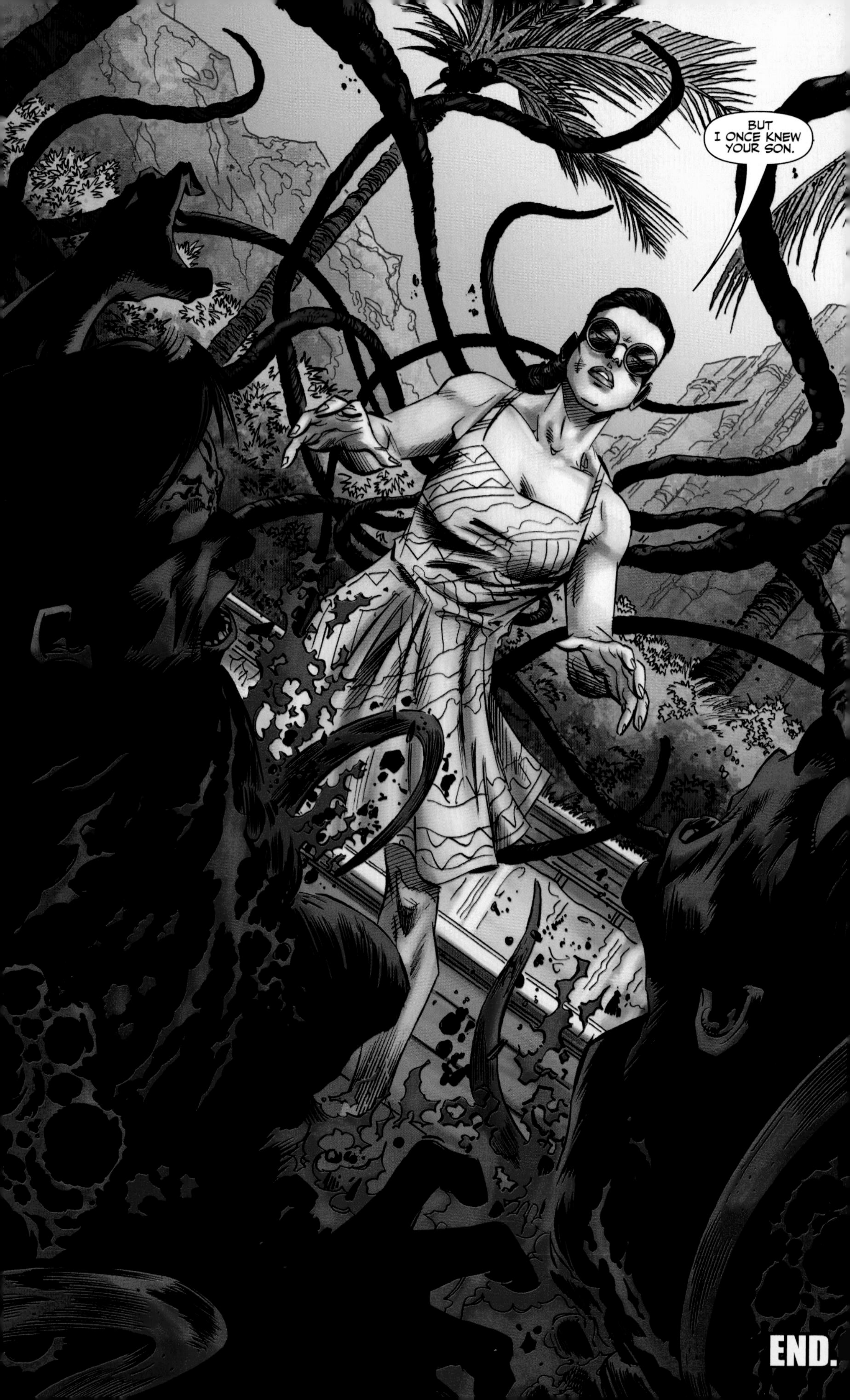
BUT I ONCE KNEW YOUR SON.
END.

GALLERY

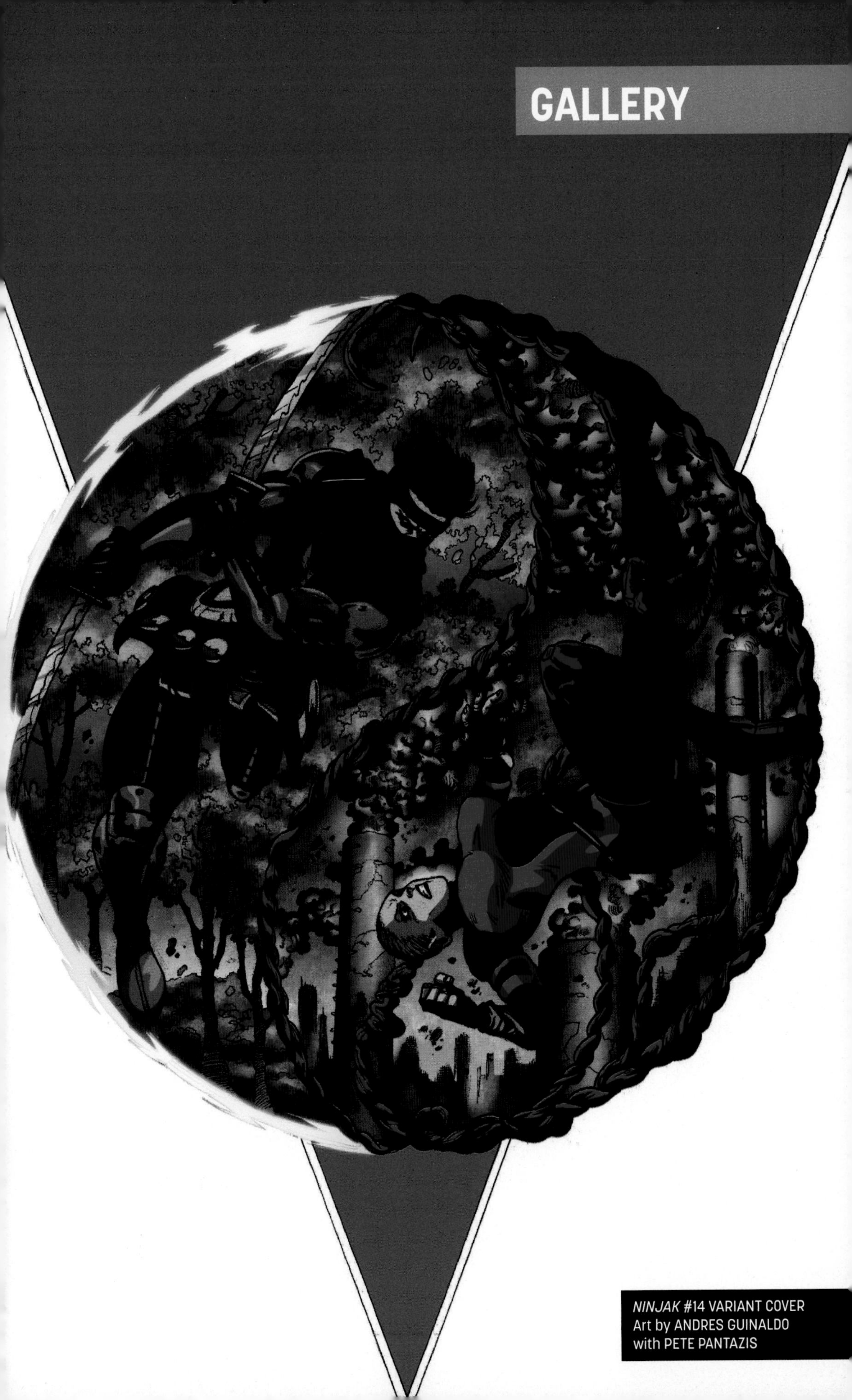

NINJAK #14 VARIANT COVER
Art by ANDRES GUINALDO
with PETE PANTAZIS

NINJAK #15 VARIANT COVER
Art by THONY SILAS

NINJAK #16 COVER B
Art by KHOI PHAM

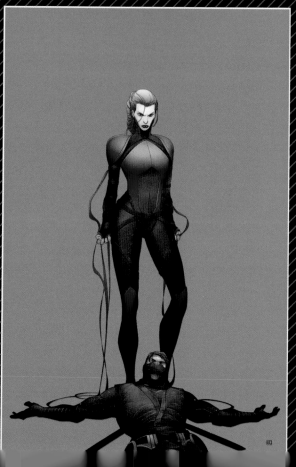

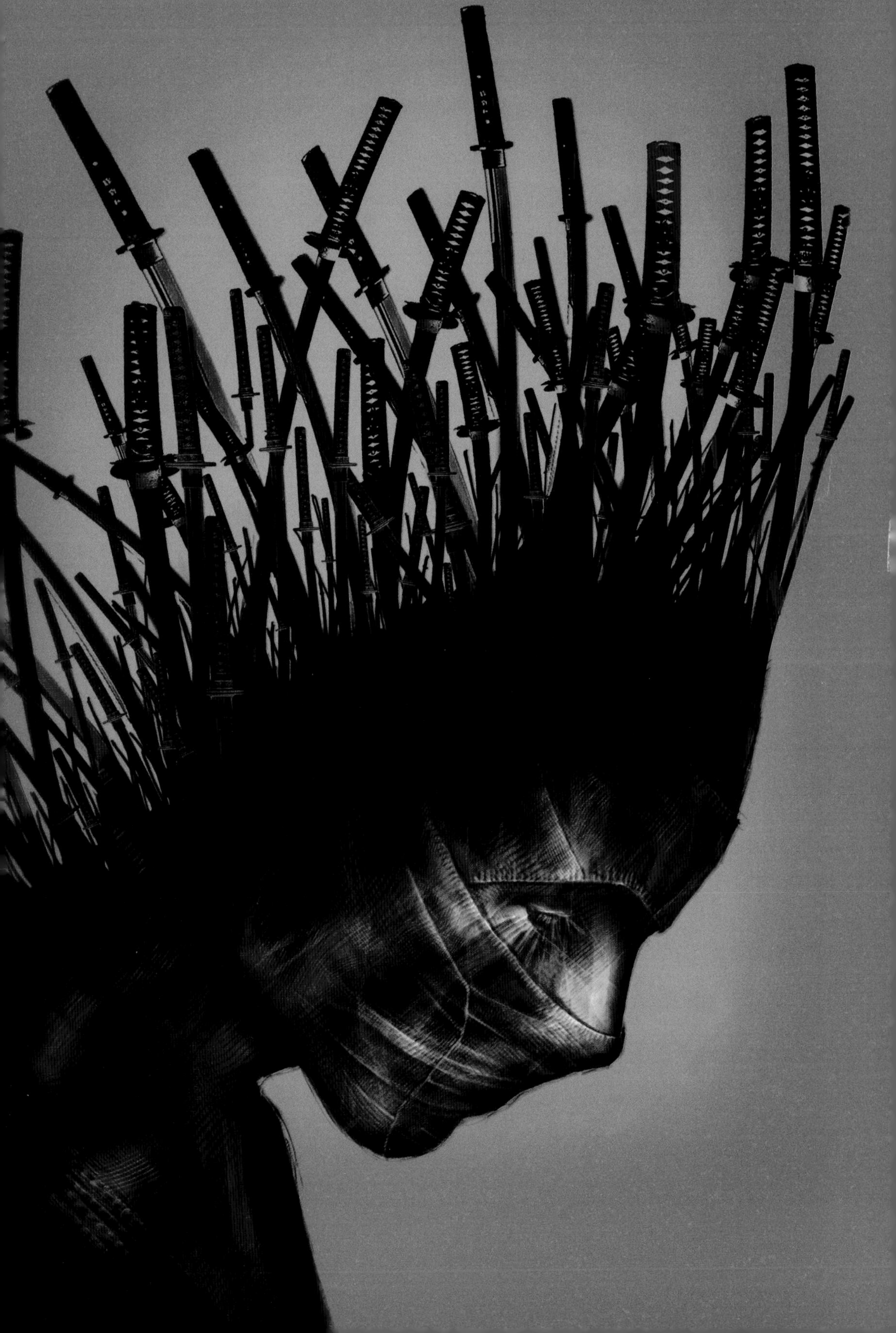

NINJAK #17 COVER B
Art by DIEGO LATORRE

NINJAK #16, p. 10
Art by DIEGO BERNARD
with ALISSON RODRIGUES

NINJAK #16, p. 13
Art by DIEGO BERNARD
with ALISSON RODRIGUES

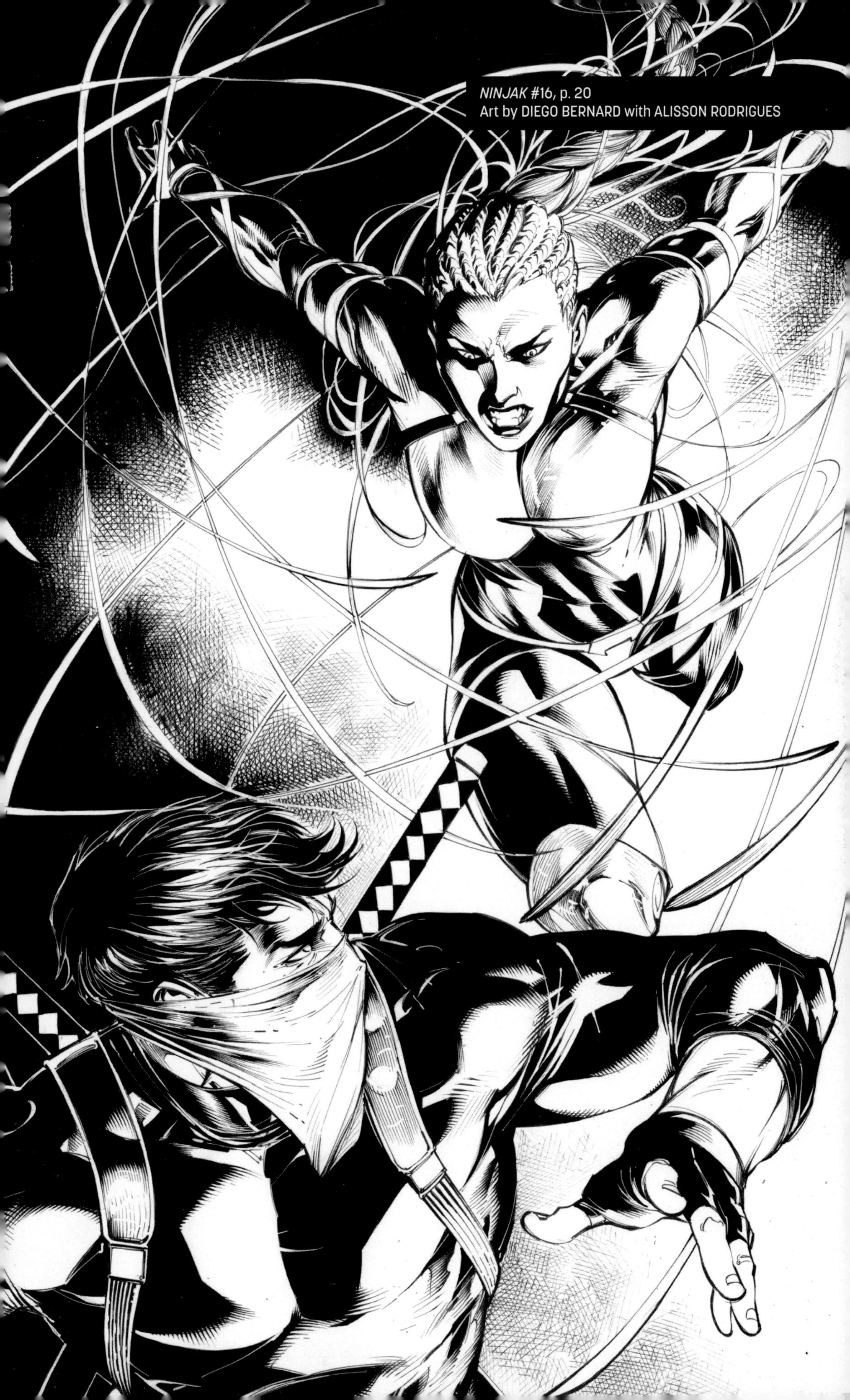

NINJAK #16, p. 20
Art by DIEGO BERNARD with ALISSON RODRIGUES

NINJAK #17, pages 10-11
Art by DIEGO BERNARD
with ALISSON RODRIGUES

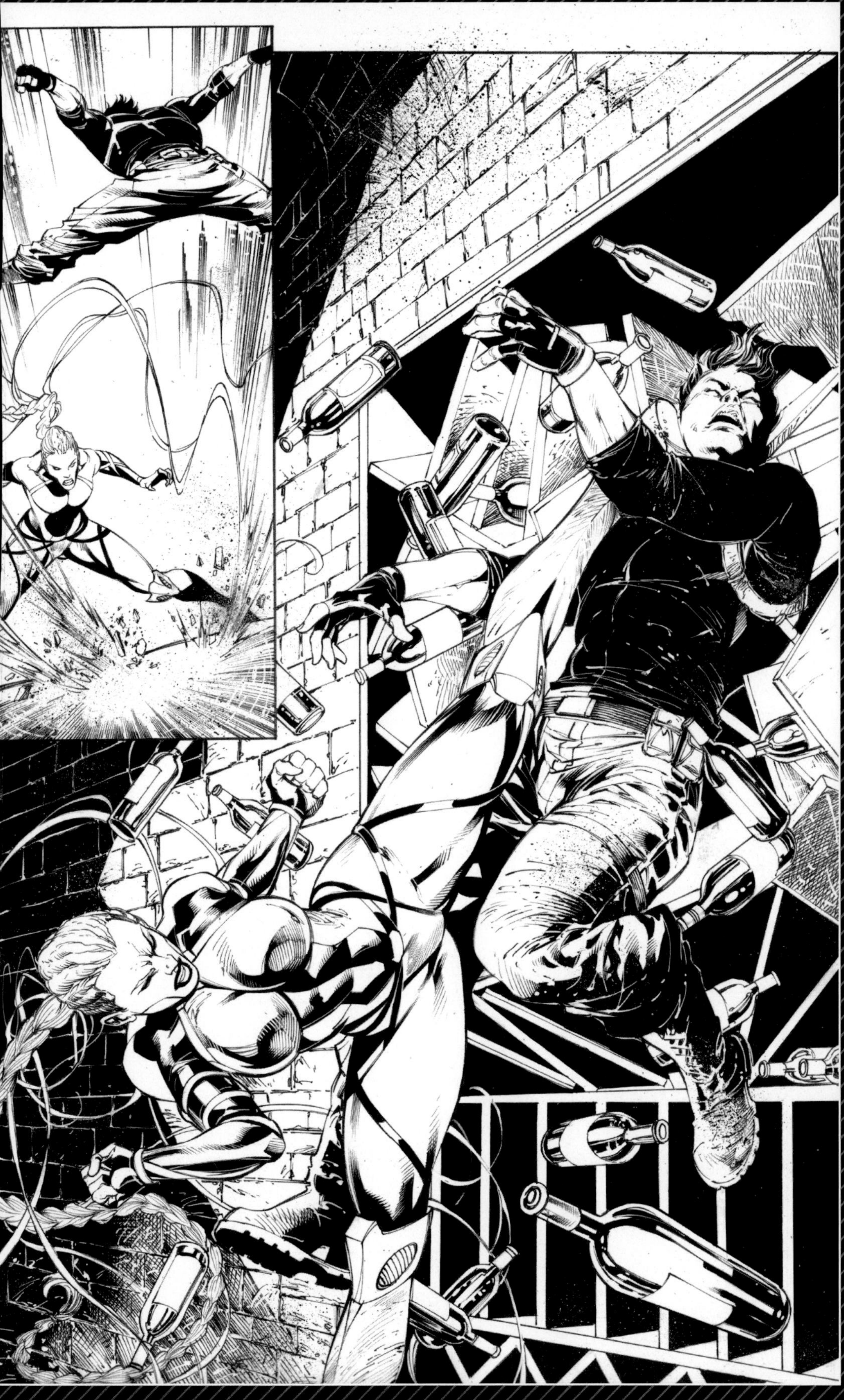

EXPLORE THE VALIANT UNIVERSE

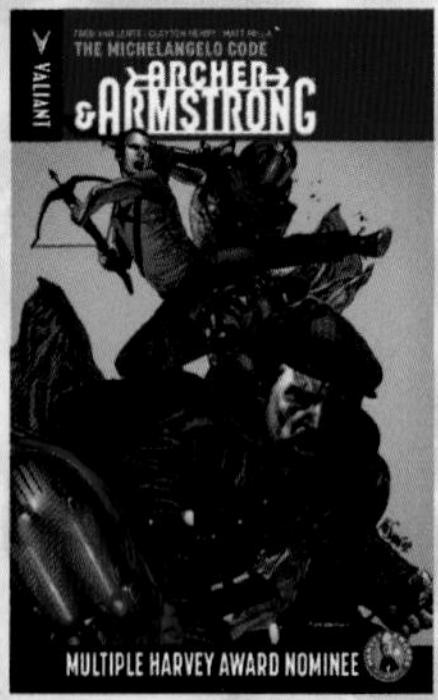
VALIANT
THE MICHELANGELO CODE
ARCHER & ARMSTRONG
MULTIPLE HARVEY AWARD NOMINEE

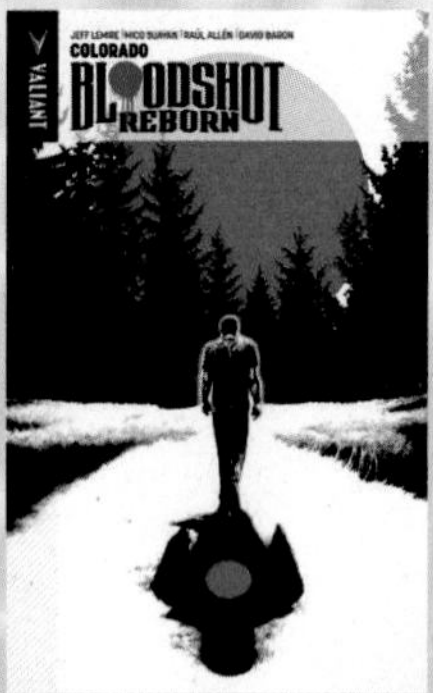
VALIANT
COLORADO
BLOODSHOT REBORN

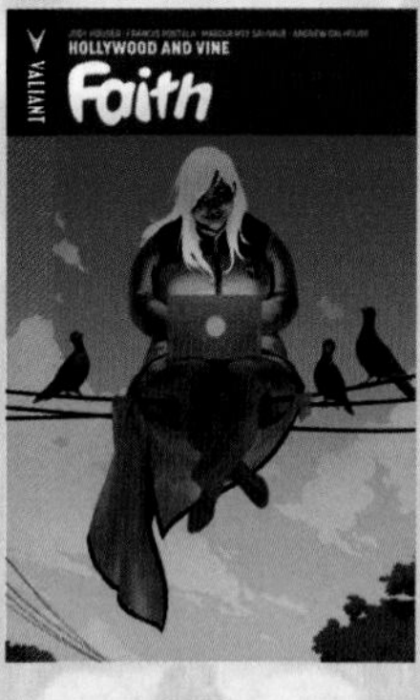
VALIANT
HOLLYWOOD AND VINE
Faith

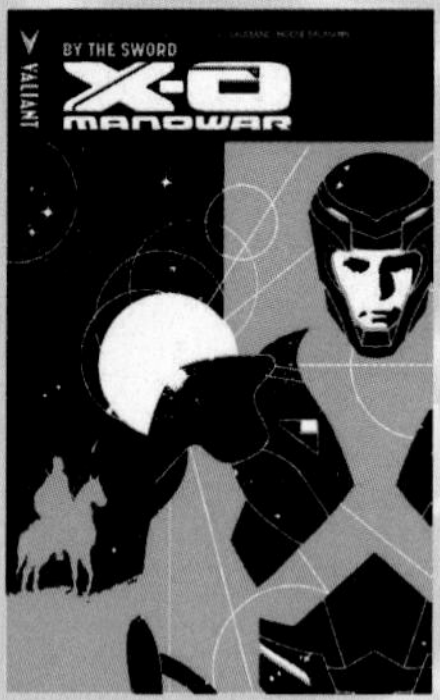
VALIANT
BY THE SWORD
X-O MANOWAR

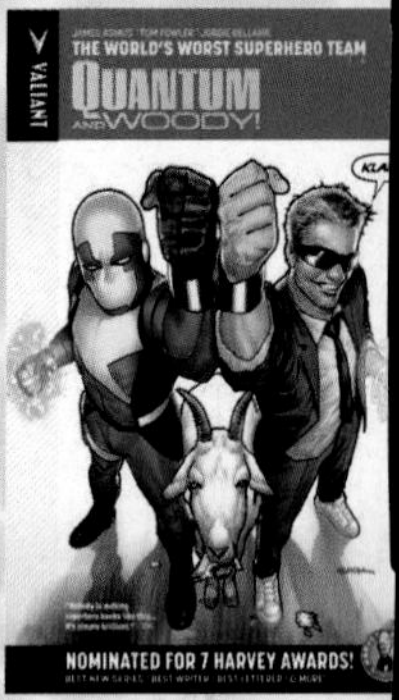
VALIANT
THE WORLD'S WORST SUPERHERO TEAM
QUANTUM AND WOODY!
NOMINATED FOR 7 HARVEY AWARDS!

A&A: THE ADVENTURES OF ARCHER AND ARMSTRONG

Volume 1: In the Bag
ISBN: 9781682151495

ARCHER & ARMSTRONG

Volume 1: The Michelangelo Code
ISBN: 9780979640988

Volume 2: Wrath of the Eternal Warrior
ISBN: 9781939346049

Volume 3: Far Faraway
ISBN: 9781939346148

Volume 4: Sect Civil War
ISBN: 9781939346254

Volume 5: Mission: Improbable
ISBN: 9781939346353

Volume 6: American Wasteland
ISBN: 9781939346421

Volume 7: The One Percent and Other Tales
ISBN: 9781939346537

ARMOR HUNTERS

Armor Hunters
ISBN: 9781939346452

Armor Hunters: Bloodshot
ISBN: 9781939346469

Armor Hunters: Harbinger
ISBN: 9781939346506

Unity Vol. 3: Armor Hunters
ISBN: 9781939346445

X-O Manowar Vol. 7: Armor Hunters
ISBN: 9781939346476

BLOODSHOT

Volume 1: Setting the World on Fire
ISBN: 9780979640964

Volume 2: The Rise and the Fall
ISBN: 9781939346032

Volume 3: Harbinger Wars
ISBN: 9781939346124

Volume 4: H.A.R.D. Corps
ISBN: 9781939346193

Volume 5: Get Some!
ISBN: 9781939346315

Volume 6: The Glitch and Other Tales
ISBN: 9781939346711

BLOODSHOT REBORN

Volume 1: Colorado
ISBN: 9781939346674

Volume 2: The Hunt
ISBN: 9781939346827

Volume 3: The Analog Man
ISBN: 9781682151334

BOOK OF DEATH

Book of Death
ISBN: 9781939346971

Book of Death: The Fall of the Valiant Universe
ISBN: 9781939346988

DEAD DROP

ISBN: 9781939346858

THE DEATH-DEFYING DOCTOR MIRAGE

Volume 1
ISBN: 9781939346490

Volume 2: Second Lives
ISBN: 9781682151297

THE DELINQUENTS

ISBN: 9781939346513

DIVINITY

Volume 1
ISBN: 9781939346766

Volume 2
ISBN: 9781682151518

ETERNAL WARRIOR

Volume 1: Sword of the Wild
ISBN: 9781939346209

Volume 2: Eternal Emperor
ISBN: 9781939346292

Volume 3: Days of Steel
ISBN: 9781939346742

WRATH OF THE ETERNAL WARRIOR

Volume 1: Risen
ISBN: 9781682151235

HARBINGER

Volume 1: Omega Rising
ISBN: 9780979640957

Volume 2: Renegades
ISBN: 9781939346025

Volume 3: Harbinger Wars
ISBN: 9781939346117

Volume 4: Perfect Day
ISBN: 9781939346155

Volume 5: Death of a Renegade
ISBN: 9781939346339

Volume 6: Omegas
ISBN: 9781939346384

HARBINGER WARS

Harbinger Wars
ISBN: 9781939346094

Bloodshot Vol. 3: Harbinger Wars
ISBN: 9781939346124

Harbinger Vol. 3: Harbinger Wars
ISBN: 9781939346117

EXPLORE THE VALIANT UNIVERSE

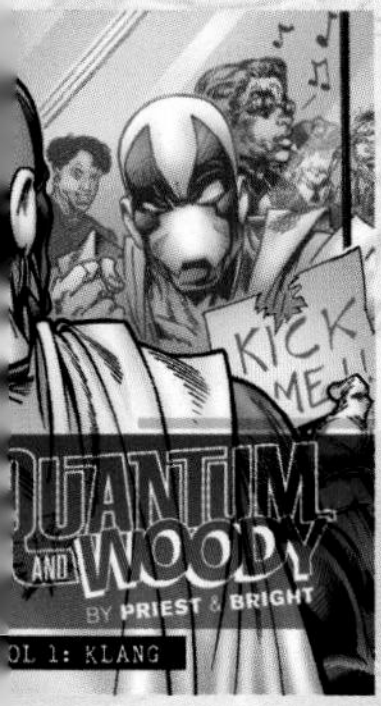

KICK ME
UANTUM AND WOODY
BY PRIEST & BRIGHT
OL 1: KLANG

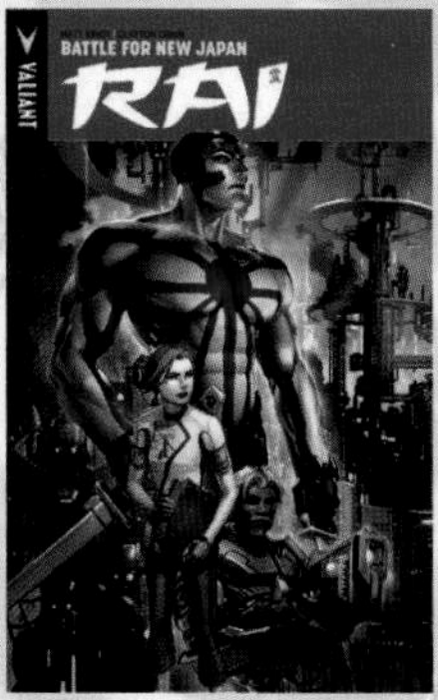

VALIANT
BATTLE FOR NEW JAPAN
RAI

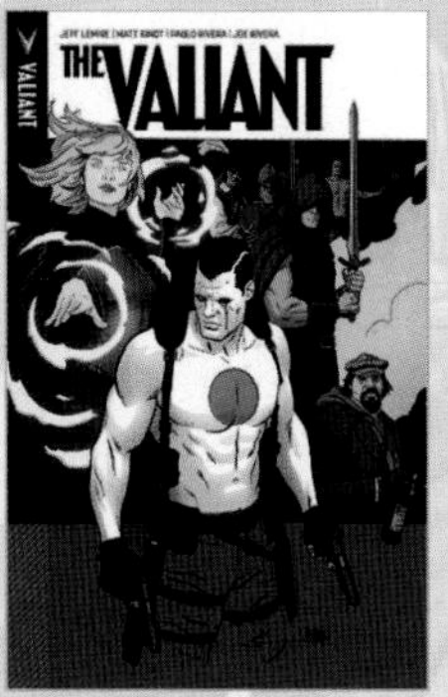

VALIANT
THE VALIANT

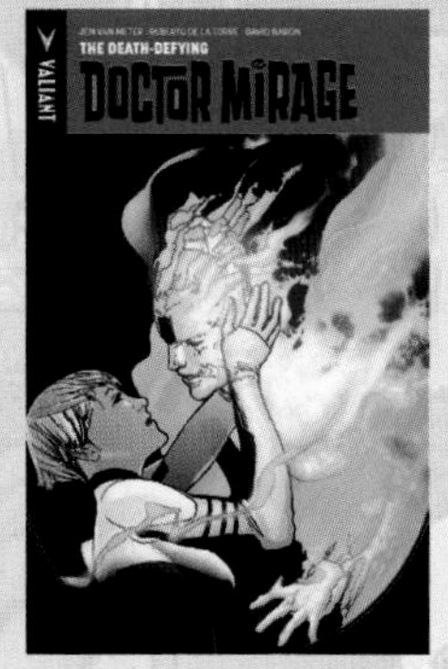

VALIANT
THE DEATH-DEFYING
DOCTOR MIRAGE

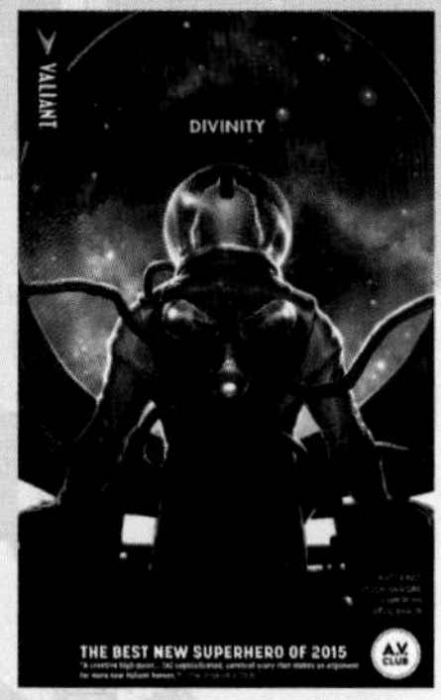

VALIANT
DIVINITY
THE BEST NEW SUPERHERO OF 2015

IPERIUM

ume 1: Collecting Monsters
N: 9781939346759

ume 2: Broken Angels
N: 9781939346896

ume 3: The Vine Imperative
N: 9781682151112

ume 4: Stormbreak
N: 9781682151372

INJAK

ume 1: Weaponeer
N: 9781939346667

ume 2: The Shadow Wars
N: 9781939346940

ume 3: Operation: Deadside
N: 9781682151259

ume 4: The Siege of King's Castle
N: 9781682151617

UANTUM ND WOODY

ume 1: The World's Worst Superhero Team
N: 9781939346186

ume 2: In Security
N: 9781939346230

ume 3: Crooked Pasts, Present Tense
N: 9781939346391

ume 4: Quantum and Woody Must Die!
N: 9781939346629

UANTUM AND WOODY Y PRIEST & BRIGHT

ume 1: Klang
N: 9781939346780

ume 2: Switch
N: 9781939346803

ume 3: And So...
N: 9781939346865

ume 4: Q2 - The Return
N: 9781682151099

RAI

Volume 1: Welcome to New Japan
ISBN: 9781939346414

Volume 2: Battle for New Japan
ISBN: 9781939346612

Volume 3: The Orphan
ISBN: 9781939346841

SHADOWMAN

Volume 1: Birth Rites
ISBN: 9781939346001

Volume 2: Darque Reckoning
ISBN: 9781939346056

Volume 3: Deadside Blues
ISBN: 9781939346162

Volume 4: Fear, Blood, And Shadows
ISBN: 9781939346278

Volume 5: End Times
ISBN: 9781939346377

SHADOWMAN BY ENNIS & WOOD

ISBN: 9781682151358

IVAR, TIMEWALKER

Volume 1: Making History
ISBN: 9781939346636

Volume 2: Breaking History
ISBN: 9781939346834

Volume 3: Ending History
ISBN: 9781939346995

UNITY

Volume 1: To Kill a King
ISBN: 9781939346261

Volume 2: Trapped by Webnet
ISBN: 9781939346346

Volume 3: Armor Hunters
ISBN: 9781939346445

Volume 4: The United
ISBN: 9781939346544

Volume 5: Homefront
ISBN: 9781939346797

Volume 6: The War-Monger
ISBN: 9781939346902

Volume 7: Revenge of the Armor Hunters
ISBN: 9781682151136

THE VALIANT

ISBN: 9781939346605

VALIANT ZEROES AND ORIGINS

ISBN: 9781939346582

X-O MANOWAR

Volume 1: By the Sword
ISBN: 9780979640940

Volume 2: Enter Ninjak
ISBN: 9780979640995

Volume 3: Planet Death
ISBN: 9781939346087

Volume 4: Homecoming
ISBN: 9781939346179

Volume 5: At War With Unity
ISBN: 9781939346247

Volume 6: Prelude to Armor Hunters
ISBN: 9781939346407

Volume 7: Armor Hunters
ISBN: 9781939346476

Volume 8: Enter: Armorines
ISBN: 9781939346551

Volume 9: Dead Hand
ISBN: 9781939346650

Volume 10: Exodus
ISBN: 9781939346933

Volume 11: The Kill List
ISBN: 9781682151273

EXPLORE THE VALIANT UNIVERSE

JOSHUA DYSART | BARRY KITSON | CLAYTON HENRY
KHARI EVANS | RAFA SANDOVAL
VALIANT
HARBINGER DELUXE EDITION 2

ROBERT VENDITTI MATT KINDT JOSHUA DYSART JOE HARRIS ROBERT GILL
DOUG BRAITHWAITE DIEGO BERNARD TREVOR HAIRSINE STEPHEN SEGOVIA
VALIANT
ARMOR HUNTERS DELUXE EDITION

JIM SHOOTER | DAVID LAPHAM
VALIANT
CHILDREN OF THE EIGHTH DAY
HARBINGER
VALIANT MASTERS

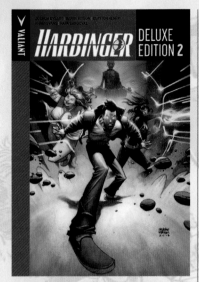

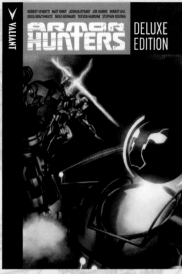

Omnibuses

Archer & Armstrong: The Complete Classic Omnibus
ISBN: 9781939346872
Collecting ARCHER & ARMSTRONG (1992) #0-26, ETERNAL WARRIOR (1992) #25 along with ARCHER & ARMSTRONG: THE FORMATION OF THE SECT.

Quantum and Woody: The Complete Classic Omnibus
ISBN: 9781939346360
Collecting QUANTUM AND WOODY (1997) #0, 1-21 and #32, THE GOAT: H.A.E.D.U.S. #1, and X-O MANOWAR (1996) #16

X-O Manowar Classic Omnibus Vol. 1
ISBN: 9781939346308
Collecting X-O MANOWAR (1992) #0-30, ARMORINES #0, X-O DATABASE #1, as well as material from SECRETS OF THE VALIANT UNIVERSE #1

Deluxe Editions

Archer & Armstrong Deluxe Edition Book 1
ISBN: 9781939346223
Collecting ARCHER & ARMSTRONG #0-13

Archer & Armstrong Deluxe Edition Book 2
ISBN: 9781939346957
Collecting ARCHER & ARMSTRONG #14-25, ARCHER & ARMSTRONG: ARCHER #0 and BLOODSHOT AND H.A.R.D. CORPS #20-21.

Armor Hunters Deluxe Edition
ISBN: 9781939346728
Collecting Armor Hunters #1-4, Armor Hunters: Aftermath #1, Armor Hunters: Bloodshot #1-3, Armor Hunters: Harbinger #1-3, Unity #8-11, and X-O MANOWAR #23-29

Bloodshot Deluxe Edition Book 1
ISBN: 9781939346216
Collecting BLOODSHOT #1-13

Bloodshot Deluxe Edition Book 2
ISBN: 9781939346810
Collecting BLOODSHOT AND H.A.R.D. CORPS #14-23, BLOODSHOT #24-25, BLOODSHOT #0, BLOODSHOT AND H.A.R.D. CORPS: H.A.R.D. CORPS #0, along with ARCHER & ARMSTRONG #18-19

Book of Death Deluxe Edition
ISBN: 9781682151150
Collecting BOOK OF DEATH #1-4, BOOK OF DEATH: THE FALL OF BLOODSHOT #1, BOOK OF DEATH: THE FALL OF NINJAK #1, BOOK OF DEATH: THE FALL OF HARBINGER #1, and BOOK OF DEATH: THE FALL OF X-O MANOWAR #1.

Divinity Deluxe Edition
ISBN: 97819393460993
Collecting DIVNITY #1-4

Harbinger Deluxe Edition Book 1
ISBN: 9781939346131
Collecting HARBINGER #0-14

Harbinger Deluxe Edition Book 2
ISBN: 9781939346773
Collecting HARBINGER #15-25, HARBINGER: OMEGAS #1-3, and HARBINGER: BLEEDING MONK #0

Harbinger Wars Deluxe Edition
ISBN: 9781939346322
Collecting HARBINGER WARS #1-4, HARBINGER #11-14, and BLOODSHOT #10-13

Ivar, Timewalker Deluxe Edition Book 1
ISBN: 9781682151198
Collecting IVAR, TIMEWALKER #1-12

Quantum and Woody Deluxe Edition Book 1
ISBN: 9781939346681
Collecting QUANTUM AND WOODY #1-12 and QUANTUM AND WOODY: THE GOAT #0

Q2: The Return of Quantum and Woody Deluxe Edition
ISBN: 9781939346568
Collecting Q2: THE RETURN OF QUANTUM AND WOODY #1-5

Rai Deluxe Edition Book 1
ISBN: 9781682151174
Collecting RAI #1-12, along with material from RAI #1 PLUS EDITION and RAI #5 PLUS EDITION

Shadowman Deluxe Edition Book 1
ISBN: 9781939346438
Collecting SHADOWMAN #0-10

Shadowman Deluxe Edition Book 2
ISBN: 9781682151075
Collecting SHADOWMAN #11-16, SHADOWMAN #13X, SHADOWMAN: END TIMES #1-3 and PUNK MAMBO #0

Unity Deluxe Edition Book 1
ISBN: 9781939346575
Collecting UNITY #0-14

The Valiant Deluxe Edition
ISBN: 97819393460986
Collecting THE VALIANT #1-4

X-O Manowar Deluxe Edition Book 1
ISBN: 9781939346100
Collecting X-O MANOWAR #1-14

X-O Manowar Deluxe Edition Book 2
ISBN: 9781939346520
Collecting X-O MANOWAR #15-22, and UNITY #1

X-O Manowar Deluxe Edition Book 3
ISBN: 9781682151310
Collecting X-O MANOWAR #23-29 and ARMOR HUNTERS #1-4.

Valiant Masters

Bloodshot Vol. 1 - Blood of the Machine
ISBN: 9780979640933

H.A.R.D. Corps Vol. 1 - Search and Destroy
ISBN: 9781939346285

Harbinger Vol. 1 - Children of the Eighth Day
ISBN: 9781939346483

Ninjak Vol. 1 - Black Water
ISBN: 9780979640971

Rai Vol. 1 - From Honor to Strength
ISBN: 9781939346070

Shadowman Vol. 1 - Spirits Within
ISBN: 9781939346018

NINJAK | READING ORDER

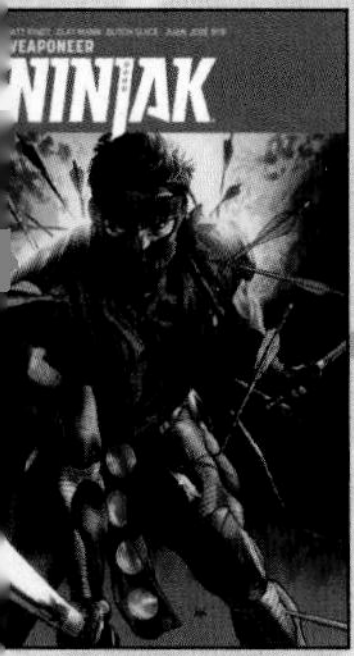
WEAPONEER
NINJAK

Ninjak Vol. 1:
Weaponeer

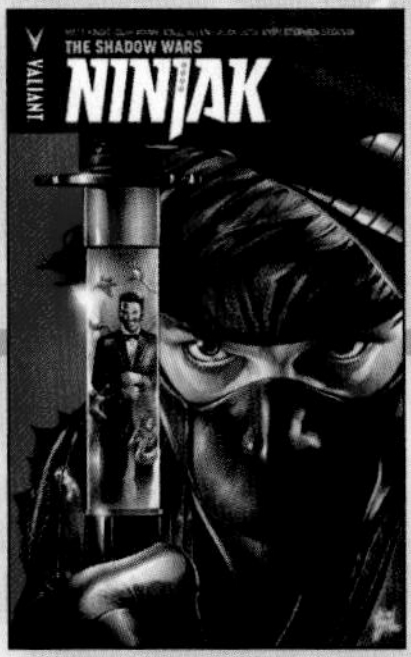
THE SHADOW WARS
NINJAK

Ninjak Vol. 2:
The Shadow Wars

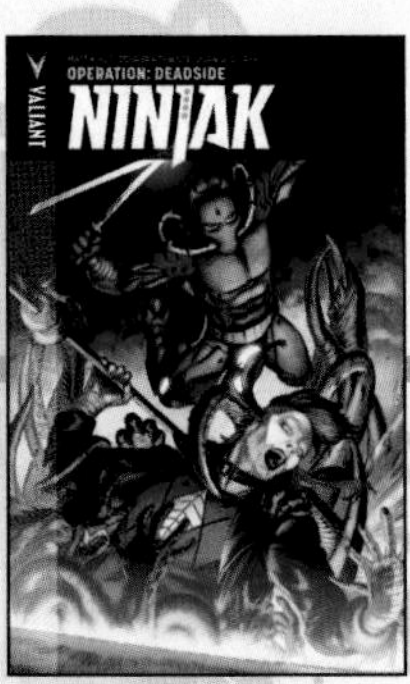
OPERATION: DEADSIDE
NINJAK

Ninjak Vol. 3:
Operation: Deadside

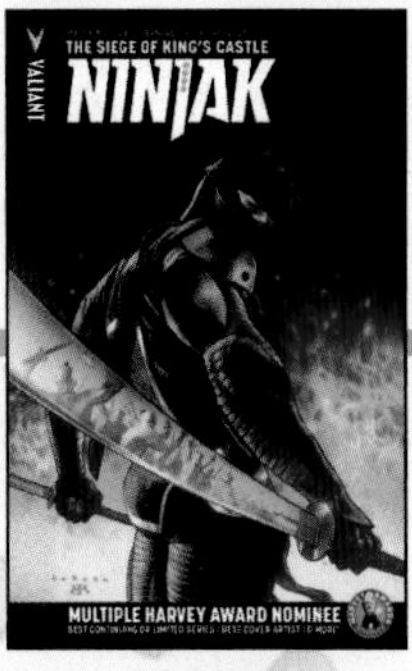
THE SIEGE OF KING'S CASTLE
NINJAK
MULTIPLE HARVEY AWARD NOMINEE

Ninjak Vol. 4:
The Siege of King's Castle

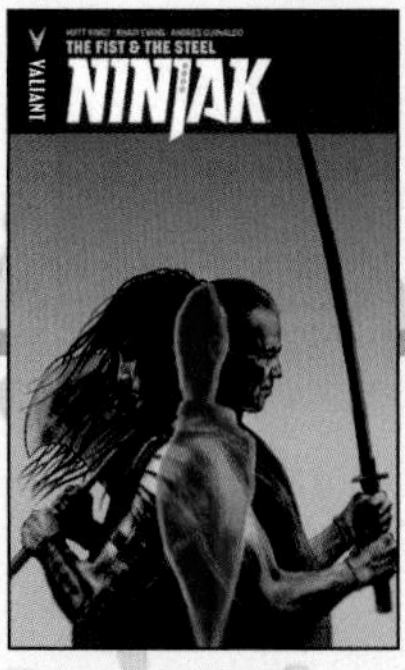
THE FIST & THE STEEL
NINJAK

Ninjak Vol. 5:
The Fist & The Steel

Read the smash-hit debut and earliest adventures of the Valiant Universe's deadliest master spy!

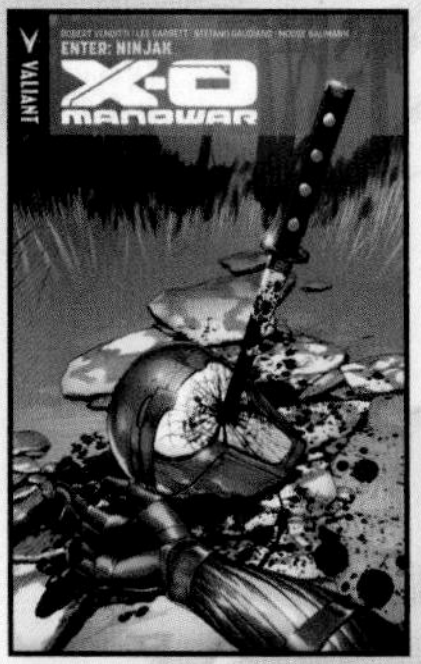
ENTER: NINJAK
X-O MANOWAR

X-O Manowar Vol. 2:
Enter Ninjak

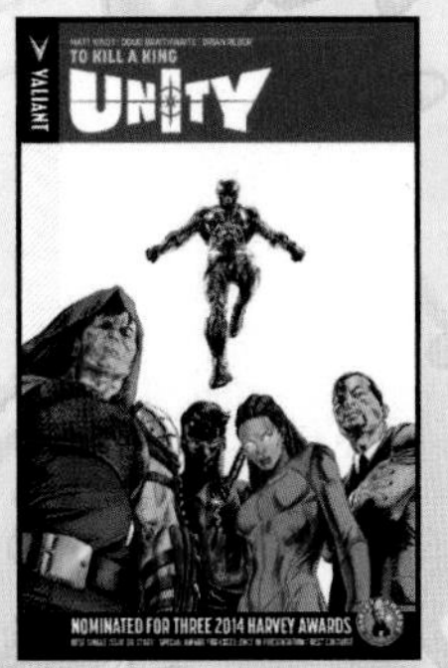
TO KILL A KING
UNITY
NOMINATED FOR THREE 2014 HARVEY AWARDS

Unity Vol. 1:
To Kill a King

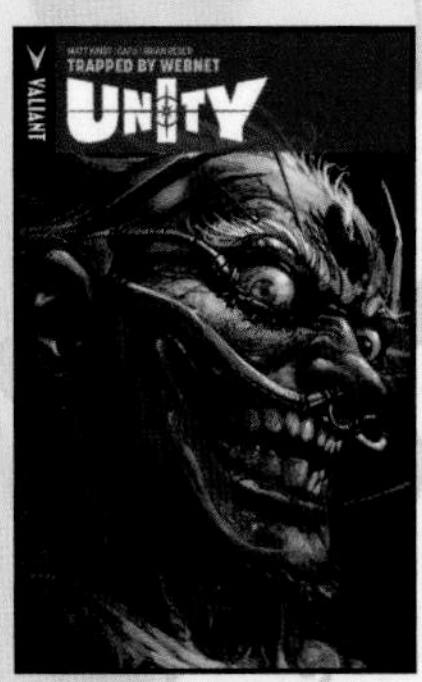
TRAPPED BY WEBNET
UNITY

Unity Vol. 2:
Trapped by Webnet

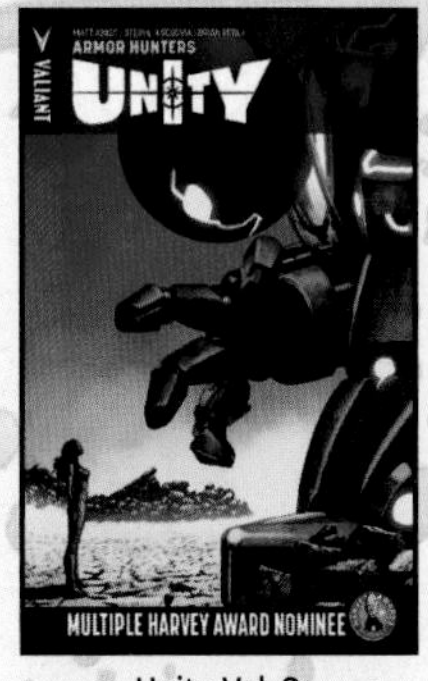
ARMOR HUNTERS
UNITY
MULTIPLE HARVEY AWARD NOMINEE

Unity Vol. 3:
Armor Hunters

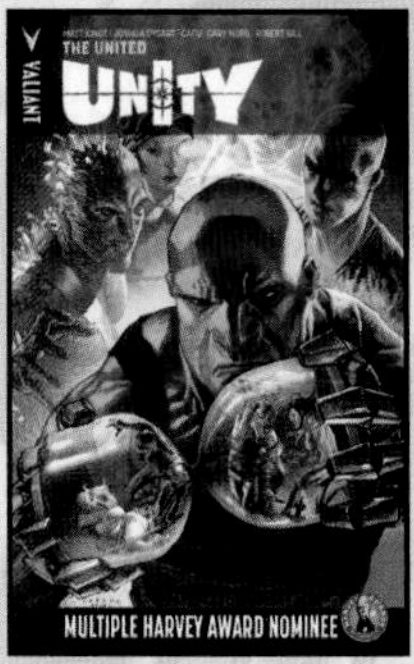
THE UNITED
UNITY
MULTIPLE HARVEY AWARD NOMINEE

Unity Vol. 4:
The United

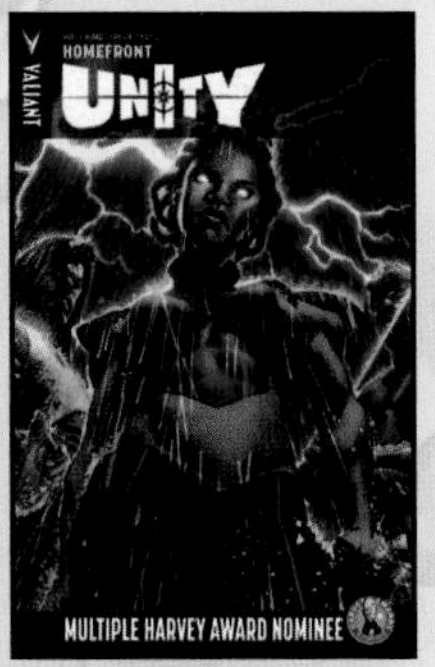
HOMEFRONT
UNITY
MULTIPLE HARVEY AWARD NOMINEE

Unity Vol. 5:
Homefront

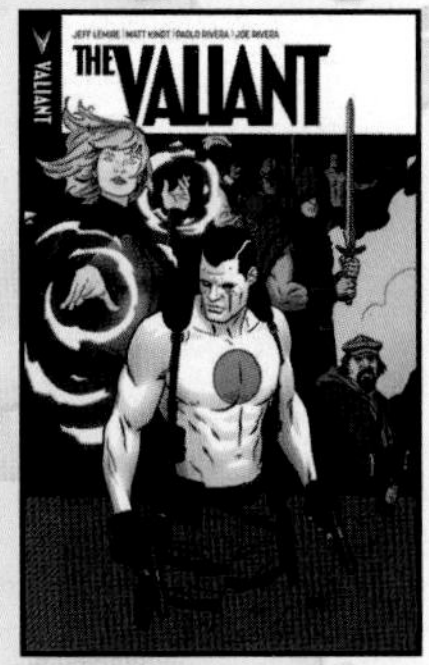
THE VALIANT

The Valiant

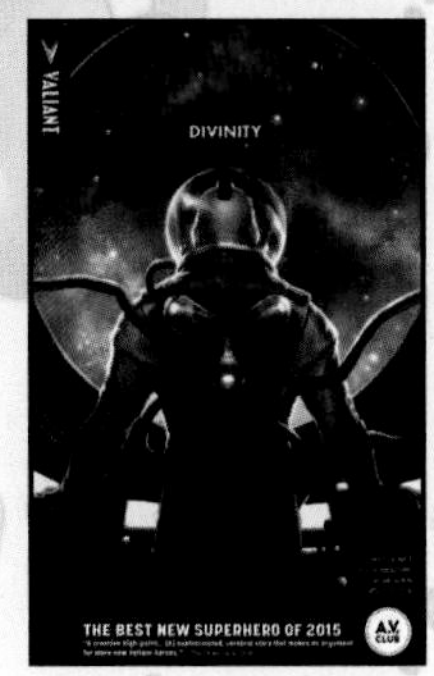
DIVINITY
THE BEST NEW SUPERHERO OF 2015

Divinity

VALIANT

NINJAK®

VOLUME FIVE: THE FIST & THE STEEL

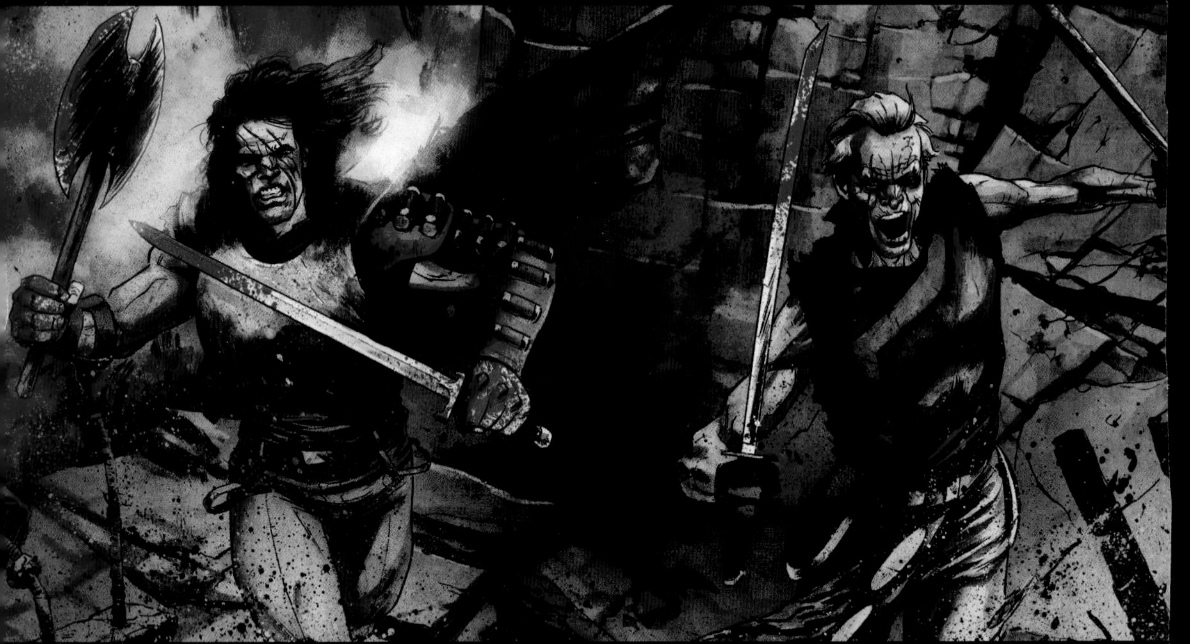

THE FIST & THE STEEL FIGHT ONWARD!

Many years from now, Earth's immortal master of war and the world's deadliest intelligence operative fight side-by-side. As was foretold in the BOOK OF DEATH, an aging Ninjak and Eternal Warrior are fated to spend their days as humanity's guardians, protecting it from the myriad threats that loom over the horizon of Earth's future. But when the ultimate menace rises to obliterate all traces of life, can Colin King and Gilad Anni-Padda - Ninjak and the Eternal Warrior - cement their status as the Valiant Universe's greatest heroic duo...or will their legacy go up in flames?

Plus: Back in the present, the unthinkable has happened to Ninjak and his fellow MI-6 agents that survived the horrors of the Deadside! Infected with an aggressive and lethal cancer from his exposure to a noxious parallel dimension, Ninjak must race against the clock for a cure before he makes a permanent trip to the realm of the dead!

New York Times best-selling writer Matt Kindt (4001 A.D.) and explosive artists Khari Evans (IMPERIUM) and Andres Guinaldo (*Justice League Dark*) read from the BOOK OF DEATH...and bring the full weight of the future crashing down on Ninjak and the Eternal Warrior!

Collecting NINJAK #18-21.

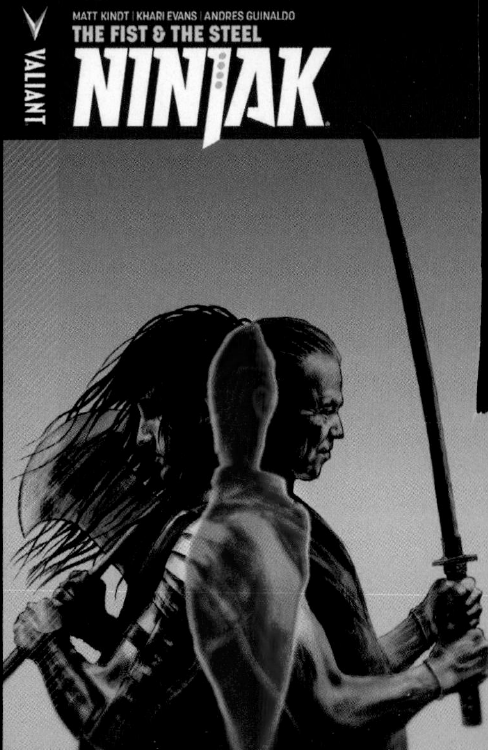
VALIANT
MATT KINDT | KHARI EVANS | ANDRES GUINALDO
THE FIST & THE STEEL
NINJAK

TRADE PAPERBACK
ISBN: 978-1-68215-179-2